Collins

Collins
Italian
Verbs

HarperCollins Publishers
Westerhill Road
Bishopbriggs
Glasgow
G64 2QT
Great Britain

First Edition 2006

Reprint 10 9 8 7 6 5 4 3 2 1

© HarperCollins Publishers 2006

ISBN-13   978-0-00-722110-3
ISBN-10   0-00-722110-X

Collins® and Bank of English® are registered
trademarks of HarperCollins Publishers
Limited

www.collins.co.uk

A catalogue record for this book is available
from the British Library

Typeset by Davidson's Prepress, Glasgow

Printed in Italy by Rotolito Lombarda SpA

PUBLISHING DIRECTOR
Lorna Knight

EDITORIAL DIRECTOR
Michela Clari

MANAGING EDITOR
Maree Airlie

PROJECT CO-ORDINATOR
Susie Beattie

CONTRIBUTORS
Daphne Day
Stefano Ondelli
Jeremy Butterfield
Loredana Riu

Acknowledgements
We would like to thank those authors and
publishers who kindly gave permission for
copyright material to be used in the Collins
Word Web. We would also like to thank
Times Newspapers Ltd for providing
valuable data.

William Collins' dream of knowledge for all began with the publication of his first book in 1819. A self-educated mill worker, he not only enriched millions of lives, but also founded a flourising publishing house. Today, staying true to this spirit, Collins books are packed with inspiration, innovation, and practical expertise. They place you at the centre of a world of possibility and give you exactly what you need to explore it.

Language is the key to this exploration, and at the heart of Collins Dictionaries is language as it is really used. New words, phrases, and meanings spring up every day, and all of them are captured and analysed by the Collins Word Web. Constantly updated, and with over 2.5 billion entries, this living language resource is unique to our dictionaries.

Words are tools for life. And a Collins Dictionary makes them work for you.

Collins. Do more.

Contents

Contents

Introduction

The *Easy Learning Italian Verbs* is designed for both young and adult learners. Whether you are starting to learn Italian for the very first time, brushing up your language skills or revising for exams, the *Easy Learning Italian Verbs* and its companion volume, the *Easy Learning Italian Grammar*, are here to help.

Newcomers can sometimes struggle with the technical terms they come across when they start to explore the grammar of a new language. The *Easy Learning Italian Verbs* contains a glossary which explains verb grammar terms using simple language and cutting out jargon.

The text is divided into sections to help you become confident in using and understanding Italian verbs. The first section looks at verb formation. Written in clear language, with numerous examples in real Italian, this section helps you to understand the rules which are used to form verb tenses.

The next section of text looks at certain common prepositions which are used with a number of verbs. Each combination of verb plus preposition is shown with a simple example of real Italian to show exactly how it is used.

The Verb Tables contain 120 important Italian verbs (both regular and irregular) which are given in full for various tenses. Examples show how to use these verbs in your own work. If you are unsure how a verb goes in Italian, you can look up the Verb Index at the back of the book to find either the conjugation of the verb itself, or a cross-reference to a model verb, which will show you the patterns that verb follows.

The *Easy Learning Italian Grammar* takes you a step further in your language learning. It supplements the information given in the *Easy Learning Italian Verbs* by offering even more guidance on the usage and meaning of verbs, as well as looking at the most important aspects of Italian grammar. Together, or individually, the *Easy Learning* titles offer you all the help you need when learning Italian.

Glossary of Verb Grammar Terms

ACTIVE a form of the verb that is used when the subject of the sentence does the action, for example, *A dog bit him* (subject: *a dog*; active verb: *bit*).Compare with passive.

ADVERB a word used with verbs to give information on where, when or how an action takes place, for example, *here*, *today*, *quickly*. An adverb can also add information to adjectives and other adverbs, for example, *extremely* quick, *very* quickly.

AGREEMENT the matching of words or word endings to the person or thing they refer to. For example, the verb *to be* has different forms for *I*, *you* and *he*: *I am*, *you are*, *he is*. In Italian you use verbs in the form appropriate to the person doing the action, and articles and adjectives have masculine, feminine and plural forms to match (or *agree* with) the noun they go with.

ARTICLE a word such as *the*, *a*, and *an* which goes with nouns: *the sun*, *a happy boy*, *an orange*. See also definite article, indefinite article.

AUXILIARY VERB a verb such as *be*, *have* and *do* that is used with a main verb to form tenses, negatives and questions.

BASE FORM the form of the verb that has no ending added to it, for example, *walk*, *have*, *be*, *go*. Compare with infinitive.

CLAUSE a group of words containing a verb.

CONDITIONAL a verb form used to talk about things that would happen or would be true under certain conditions, for example, *I would help you if I could*. It is also used in requests and offers, for example, *Could you lend me some money?*; *I could give you a lift*.

CONJUGATE (to) to give a verb different endings depending on whether its subject is *I*, *you*, *he* and so on, and depending on whether you are referring to the present, past or future, for example, *I have*, *she has*, *they listened*.

CONJUGATION a group of verbs that has a particular pattern of endings.

CONTINUOUS TENSE a verb form made up of *to be* and the *–ing* form, for example, *I'm thinking*; *They were quarrelling*. Italian continuous tenses are made with stare and the gerund.

DEFINITE ARTICLE the word *the*. Compare with indefinite article.

DEMONSTRATIVE PRONOUN a word used instead of a noun to point out people or things, for example, *That's my brother*. In English the demonstrative pronouns are *this*, *that*, *these* and *those*.

DIRECT OBJECT a noun or pronoun used to show who or what is affected by the verb. For example, in the sentence *He sent flowers*, the subject of the verb is *He* (the person who did the sending) and the direct object of the verb is *flowers* (what he sent). Compare with indirect object.

DIRECT OBJECT PRONOUN a word such as *me*, *him*, *us* and *them* used instead of a noun to show who or what is affected by the action of the verb, for example *His friends helped him*. Compare with indirect object pronoun.

ENDING something added to the end of a word. In English nouns have plural endings, for example boy → boys, child → children and verbs have the endings *–s*, *–ed* and –*ing*, for example *walk* → *walks, walked, walking*. In Italian there are plural endings for nouns, verb endings, and masculine, feminine and plural endings for adjectives and pronouns.

FEMININE a noun, pronoun, article or form of adjective used to refer to a living being, thing or idea that is not classed as masculine. For example, una (feminine indefinite article) bella (adjective with a feminine ending) casa (feminine noun).

FUTURE a tense used to talk about something that will happen, or be true in the future, for example *He'll be here soon; I'll give you a call; It will be sunny tomorrow.*

GERUND in English, a verb form ending in –*ing*, for example, *eating, sleeping*. In Italian the gerund ends in –ando or –endo.

IMPERATIVE a form of the verb used to give orders and instructions, for example, *Sit down!; Don't go!; Let's start!*

IMPERFECT a tense used to say what was happening, what used to happen and what things were like in the past, for example; *It was sunny at the weekend; They weren't listening; They used to live in Spain.*

IMPERSONAL VERB a verb with the subject *it*, where 'it' does not refer to any specific thing; for example, *It's going to rain; It's nine o'clock.*

INDEFINITE ARTICLE the word *a* or *an*. Compare with definite article.

INDEFINITE PRONOUN a word like *everything, nobody* and *something* which is used to refer to people or things in a non-specific way.

INDIRECT OBJECT a noun or pronoun used to show who benefits or suffers from an action. For example, in the sentence

He sent Claire flowers, the direct object (what was sent) is *flowers* and the indirect object is *Claire* (the person the flowers were sent to). An indirect object often has *to* in front of it: *He told lies to everyone; He told everyone lies.* In both these sentences the direct object is *lies* and the indirect object is *everyone*. Compare with direct object.

INDIRECT OBJECT PRONOUN a pronoun such as *to me* (or *me*), *to you* (or *you*) and *to her* (or *her*). In the sentence *He gave the chocolates to me and the flowers to her,* the direct objects are *the chocolates* and *the flowers* (what he gave), and the indirect object pronouns are *to me* and *to her* (who he gave them to). In the sentence *He gave me the chocolates and her the flowers,* the indirect object pronouns are *me* and *her*. Compare with direct object pronoun.

INDIRECT QUESTION a more roundabout way of asking a question, for example, instead of *Where are you going?* you can say *Tell me where you are going,* or *I'd like to know where you are going.*

INFINITIVE the base form of the verb, for example, *walk, see, hear*. It is used after other verbs such as *should, must* and *can*. The infinitive is often used with *to: to speak, to eat, to live*. Compare with base form.

INTRANSITIVE VERB a verb used without a direct object, for example, *The shop is closing; Nothing grows here*. Compare with transitive verb.

IRREGULAR VERB In Italian, a verb whose forms do not follow one of the three main patterns. Compare with regular verb.

MASCULINE a noun, pronoun, article or form of adjective used to refer to a living being, thing or idea that is not classed as feminine. For example, il (masculine definite article) primo (adjective with a masculine ending) treno (masculine noun).

NEGATIVE a question or statement which contains a word such as *not*, *never* or *nothing*: *Isn't he here?*; *I never eat meat*; *She's doing nothing about it*. Compare with positive.

NOUN a naming word for a living being, thing or idea, for example, *woman*, *Andrew*, *desk*, *happiness*.

NUMBER in grammar a verb agrees in number with its subject by being singular with a singular subject and plural with a plural subject, for example, *I am a teacher*; *They are teachers*.

OBJECT a noun or pronoun that, in English, usually comes after the verb and shows who or what is affected by it, for example, *I* (subject) *want* (verb) *a new car* (object), *They* (subject) *phoned* (verb) *him* (object). Compare with direct object, indirect object and subject.

OBJECT PRONOUN one of the following: *me, you, him, her, it, us, them*. They are used instead of nouns after prepositions, for example, *for me, with us* and as the object of verbs, for example, *The company sacked him*; *You'll enjoy it*. Compare with subject pronoun.

PART OF SPEECH a word with a particular grammatical function, for example, *noun, adjective, verb, preposition, pronoun*.

PASSIVE a verb form that is used when the subject of the verb is the person or thing the action is done to, for example, *Shaun was bitten by a dog*. *Shaun* is the subject of the sentence, but he did not do the action. Compare with active.

PAST PARTICIPLE a verb form usually ending *–ed*, for example *lived, worked*. Some past participles are irregular, for example, *gone, sat, broken*. Past participles are used to make the perfect, pluperfect

and passive, for example *They've gone*; *They hadn't noticed me*; *Nobody was hurt*. Past participles are also used as adjectives, for example, *a boiled egg*.

PAST PERFECT see pluperfect.

PERFECT a tense used in English to talk about what has or hasn't happened, for example *We've won*; *I haven't touched it*. Compare with simple past.

PERSON in grammar one of the following: the first person (*I, we*), the second person (*you*) or the third person (*he, she, it, they*).

PERSONAL PRONOUN a word such as *I, you, he, she, us, them*, which make it clear who you are talking about or talking to.

PLUPERFECT a tense used to talk about what had happened or had been true at a point in the past, for example, *I'd forgotten to send her a card*. Also called past perfect.

PLURAL the form of a word which is used to refer to more than one person or thing. In Italian, nouns, adjectives, articles, pronouns and verbs can be plural. Compare with singular.

POSITIVE a positive sentence does not contain a negative word such as *not*. Compare with negative.

PREPOSITION a word such as *at, for, with, into* or *from*, or a phrase such as *in front of* or *near to*. Prepositions are usually followed by a noun or a pronoun and show how people and things relate to the rest of the sentence, for example, *She's at home*; *It's for you*; *You'll get into trouble*; *It's in front of you*.

PRESENT a verb form used to talk about what is true at the moment, what generally happens and what is happening now; for example, *I'm a student*; *I travel to college by train*; *The phone's ringing*.

PRESENT PARTICIPLE a verb form ending in –ing, for example, *eating*, *sleeping*. Compare with gerund.

PRONOUN a word you use instead of a noun, when you do not need or want to name someone or something directly, for example, *it*, *you*, *somebody*.

PROPER NOUN the name of a person, place or organization. Proper nouns are always written with a capital letter, for example, *Kate*, *New York*, *the Forestry Commission*.

REFLEXIVE PRONOUN a word ending in –self or –selves, such as *myself* and *ourselves*, that is used as the object of a verb, for example *I surprised myself*; *We're going to treat ourselves*.

REFLEXIVE VERB a verb where the subject and object are the same, and which uses reflexive pronouns such as *myself, yourself* and *themselves*, for example *I've hurt myself*; *Look after yourself!*; *They're enjoying themselves*.

REGULAR VERB in Italian, a verb whose forms follow one of the three main patterns. Compare with irregular verb.

SIMPLE TENSE a verb form made up of one word, for example, *She lives here*; *They arrived late*. Compare with continuous tense and perfect tense.

SIMPLE PAST a tense used in English to say when exactly something happened, for example, *We met last summer*; *I ate it last night*; *It rained a lot yesterday*. In Italian the perfect tense is used in this kind of sentence.

SINGULAR the form of a word used to refer to one person or thing. Compare with plural.

STEM what is left of an Italian verb when you take away the –are, –ere or –ire ending of the infinitive.

STRESSED PRONOUN an object pronoun used in Italian after prepositions and when you want to stress the word for *me, him, them* and so on. Compare with unstressed pronoun.

SUBJECT a noun or pronoun that refers to the person or thing doing the action or being in the state described by the verb, for example *Pat likes climbing*; *The bus is late*. Compare with object.

SUBJECT PRONOUN a word such as *I, he, she* and *they* used for the person or thing carrying out the action described by the verb. Pronouns replace nouns when it is clear who is being talked about, for example, *My brother's not here at the moment. He'll be back in an hour*. Compare with object pronoun.

SUBJUNCTIVE a verb form often used in Italian to express wishes, thoughts and suppositions. In English the subjunctive is only used occasionally, for example, *If I were you…*; *So be it*; *He asked that they be removed*.

TENSE a particular form of the verb. It shows whether you are referring to the present, past or future.

TRANSITIVE VERB a verb used with a direct object, for example, *Close the door!*; *They grow wheat*. Compare with intransitive verb.

UNSTRESSED PRONOUN an object pronoun used in Italian when you don't want to put any special emphasis on the word for *me, him, them* and so on. Compare with stressed pronoun.

VERB a word that describes what somebody or something does, what they are, or what happens to them, for example, *play, be, disappear*.

Introduction to Verb Formation

Verbs are frequently used with a noun, with somebody's name, or, particularly in English, with a pronoun such as *I*, *you* or *she*. They can relate to the present, the past or the future; this is called their <u>tense</u>.

Verbs are either:

> <u>regular</u>; their forms follow the normal rules.
> <u>irregular</u>; their forms do not follow normal rules.

Almost all verbs have a form called the <u>infinitive</u> that isn't present, past or future, (for example, *walk*, *see*, *hear*). It is used after other verbs, for example, *You should walk*; *You can see*; *Kirsty wants to come*.

In English, the infinitive is usually shown with the word *to*, for example, *to speak*, *to eat*, *to live*.

In Italian the infinitive is always one word that in most cases ends in –are, –ere or –ire: for example, parl<u>are</u> (meaning *to speak*), cred<u>ere</u> (meaning *to believe*) and dorm<u>ire</u> (meaning *to sleep*).

Regular English verbs can add three endings to the infinitive: *–s* (*walks*), *–ing* (*walking*) and *–ed* (*walked*).

Italian verbs add many different endings to the verb <u>stem</u>, which is what is left of the verb when you take away the –are, –ere or –ire ending of the infinitive. This means the stem of parlare is parl-, the stem of credere is cred-, and the stem of dormire is dorm-.

Italian verb endings change according to who or what is doing the action. The person or thing that does the action is called the <u>subject</u> of the verb.

In English you nearly always put a noun or a pronoun in front of a verb to show who is doing the action, for example, *Jack speaks Italian; She's playing tennis*. In Italian, <u>nouns</u> are used as the subject of verbs just as they are in English, but <u>pronouns</u> are used much less often. This is because the ending of an Italian verb often shows you who the subject is.

> <u>Mia sorella</u> gioca a tennis.   My sister is playing tennis.
> <u>Gioca</u> bene.   She plays well.

Italian verb forms also change depending on whether you are talking about the present, past or future: cre<u>do</u> means *I believe*, cred<u>evo</u> means *I believed* and cred<u>erò</u> means *I will believe*.

In English some verbs are <u>irregular</u>: you do not add *-ed* to *speak*, *go*, or *see* to make the past tense. In the same way some Italian verbs do not follow the usual patterns. These irregular verbs include some very important and common verbs such as andare (meaning *to go*), essere (meaning *to be*), fare (meaning *to do* or *to make*).

The following sections give you all the help you need on how to make the different verb tenses used in Italian. If you would like even more information on how Italian verbs are used, the *Easy Learning Italian Grammar* shows you when and how numerous different verbs are used when writing and speaking modern Italian.

The present simple tense

Making the present simple tense of regular –are verbs

Verbs that have an infinitive ending in –are, such as parlare, abitare and studiare have a particular pattern of endings.

To make the present simple tense of regular –are verbs take off the –are ending to get the <u>stem</u> of the verb.

Infinitive	Meaning	Stem (without –are)
parlare	*to speak*	parl-
abitare	*to live*	abit-
studiare	*to study*	studi-

Then add the correct ending for the person you're talking about.

Here are the present simple endings for regular –are verbs:

Present simple endings	Present simple of parlare	Meaning: *to speak*
-o	(io) parl<u>o</u>	I speak/am speaking
-i	(tu) parl<u>i</u>	you speak/are speaking
-a	(lui/lei) parl<u>a</u>	he/she/it speaks/is speaking
	(lei/Lei) parl<u>a</u>	you speak/are speaking
-iamo	(noi) parl<u>iamo</u>	we speak/are speaking
-ate	(voi) parl<u>ate</u>	you speak/are speaking
-ano	(loro) parl<u>ano</u>	they speak/are speaking

For further explanation of grammatical terms, please see 8-11.

Note that lei means *she*, and is also the more formal equivalent of tu. The same form of the verb is used for both meanings.

> Parlo italiano. I speak Italian.
>
> Dove lavori? Where do you work?
>
> Carla studia medicina. Carla is studying medicine.
>
> Il cane mangia molto. The dog eats a lot.
>
> Parla italiano, signora? Do you speak Italian madam?
>
> Vedi l'autobus? – Sì, arriva. Can you see the bus? – Yes, it's coming.
>
> Parcheggiamo sempre lì. We always park there.
>
> Cercate qualcosa? Are you looking for something?
>
> Vuole queste? – No, costano troppo.
>
> Do you want these? – No, they cost too much.

Making the present simple tense of regular –ere verbs

Verbs that have an infinitive ending in –ere, such as credere, ricevere and ripetere have their own pattern of endings.

To make the present simple tense of regular –ere verbs, take off the –ere ending to get the <u>stem</u> and then add the correct ending for the person you're talking about.

Infinitive	Meaning	Stem (without –ere)
credere	*to believe*	cred-
ricevere	*to receive*	ricev-
ripetere	*to repeat*	ripet-

The io, tu and noi endings you add to the stem of –ere verbs are the same as –are verb endings. The other endings are different.

Here are the present simple endings for regular –ere verbs:

Present simple endings	Present simple of credere	Meaning: *to believe*
-o	(io) cred<u>o</u>	I believe
-i	(tu) cred<u>i</u>	you believe
-e	(lui/lei) cred<u>e</u>	he/she believes
	(lei/Lei) cred<u>e</u>	you believe
-iamo	(noi) cred<u>iamo</u>	we believe
-ete	(voi) cred<u>ete</u>	you believe
-ono	(loro) cred<u>ono</u>	they believe

Non ci credo. I don't believe it.

Cred<u>i</u> ai fantasmi? Do you believe in ghosts?

Lo credono tutti. They all believe it.

Dipend<u>e</u>. It depends.

Perd<u>ia</u>mo tempo. We're wasting time.

Making the present simple tense of regular –ire verbs

Most verbs that have an infinitive ending in –ire, such as finire (meaning *to finish*), pulire (meaning *to clean*) and capire (meaning *to understand*) follow one pattern of endings in the present. Some common verbs such as dormire and servire have a different pattern.

To make the present simple tense of <u>all</u> –ire verbs, take off the –ire ending to get the <u>stem</u> of the verb.

Infinitive	Meaning	Stem (without –ire)
finire	*to finish*	fin-
pulire	*to clean*	pul-
capire	*to understand*	cap-
dormire	*to sleep*	dorm-
servire	*to serve*	serv-

Here are the present simple endings for regular –ire verbs:

Present simple endings	Present simple of finire	Meaning: *to finish*
-isco	(io) fin<u>isco</u>	I finish/am finishing
-isci	(tu) fin<u>isci</u>	you finish/are finishing
-isce	(lui/lei) fin<u>isce</u>	he/she/it finishes/is finishing
	(lei/Lei) fin<u>isce</u>	you finish/are finishing
-iamo	(noi) fin<u>iamo</u>	we finish/are finishing
-ite	(voi) fin<u>ite</u>	you finish/are finishing
-iscono	(loro) fin<u>iscono</u>	they finish/are finishing

Il film fin*isce* alle dieci.   The film finishes at ten.

Fin*iscono* il lavoro.   They're finishing the work.

Non pul*isco* mai la macchina.   I never clean the car.

Prefer*isci* l'altro?   Do you prefer the other one?

Non cap*iscono*.   They don't understand.

Some common –ire verbs do not add –isc to the stem. The most important ones are dormire (meaning *to sleep*), servire (meaning *to serve*), aprire (meaning *to open*), partire (meaning *to leave*), sentire (meaning *to hear*) and soffrire (meaning *to suffer*).

The endings of these verbs are as follows:

Present simple endings	Present simple of dormire	Meaning: *to sleep*
-o	(io) dorm*o*	I sleep/am sleeping
-i	(tu) dorm*i*	you sleep/are sleeping
-e	(lui/lei) dorm*e*	he/she/it sleeps/is sleeping
	(lei/Lei) dorm*e*	you sleep/are sleeping
-iamo	(noi) dorm*iamo*	we sleep/are sleeping
-ite	(voi) dorm*ite*	you sleep/are sleeping
-ono	(loro) dorm*ono*	they sleep/are sleeping

Note that these endings are the same as –ere verb endings, except for the second person plural (voi).

Dorm*o* sempre bene.   I always sleep well.

A che cosa serv*e*?   What's it for?

Quando part*ite*?   When are you leaving?

Soffr*ono* molto.   They are suffering a lot.

Infinitives that end in –rre

All regular verbs have infinitives ending in –are, –ere, or –ire.

A few common irregular verbs have infinitives ending in –rre. For example:

comporre	to compose	condurre	to lead
porre	to put	produrre	to produce
proporre	to propose	ridurre	to reduce
supporre	to suppose	tradurre	to translate

Here are are the present simple forms of comporre:

	Present simple of comporre	Meaning: *to compose*
(io)	compongo	I compose/I am composing
(tu)	componi	you compose/you are composing
(lui/lei)	compone	he/she/it composes/is composing
(lei/Lei)	compone	you compose/are composing
(noi)	componiamo	we compose/are composing
(voi)	componete	you compose/are composing
(loro)	compongono	they compose/are composing

Here are the present simple forms of produrre:

	Present simple of produrre	Meaning: *to produce*
(io)	produco	I produce/I am producing
(tu)	produci	you produce/you are producing
(lui/lei)	produce	he/she/it produces/is producing
(lei/Lei)	produce	you produce/are producing
(noi)	produciamo	we produce/are producing
(voi)	producete	you produce/are producing
(loro)	producono	they produce/are producing

The present tense of all verbs ending in –porre follow the pattern of comporre, and all verbs ending in –durre follow the pattern of produrre.

All the most important irregular verbs are shown in full at the end of the book.

The present continuous tense

The Italian present continuous is made with the present tense of stare and the gerund of the verb. The gerund is a verb form that ends in –ando (for –are verbs), or –endo (for –ere and –ire verbs) and is the same as the *–ing* form of the verb in English, for example, *walking, swimming*.

> Sto cercando il mio passaporto.   I'm looking for my passport.
> Sta scrivendo.   He's writing.
> Stanno dormendo.   They're sleeping.
> Cosa stai facendo?   What are you doing?

To make the gerund of an –are verb, take off the –are ending of the infinitive and add –ando:

Infinitive	Meaning	Stem	Gerund	Meaning
parlare	to speak	parl-	parlando	speaking
mangiare	to eat	mangi-	mangiando	eating

> A chi stai pensando?   Who are you thinking about?
> Tutti stanno mangiando.   Everyone's eating.

To make the gerund of an –ere or –ire verb, take off the –ere or –ire ending of the infinitive and add –endo:

Infinitive	Meaning	Stem	Gerund	Meaning
scrivere	to write	scriv-	scrivendo	writing
partire	to leave	part-	partendo	leaving

> Sto scrivendo una lettera.   I'm writing a letter.
> Stanno partendo?   Are they leaving?

For further explanation of grammatical terms, please see 8-11.

The imperative

Making the imperative: instructions to do something

You make the imperative of regular verbs by adding endings to the verb <u>stem</u>.
There are different endings for –are, -ere and –ire verbs.

The endings for –are verb imperatives are –a (tu form), –i (lei/Lei form),
–iamo (let's), –ate (voi form) and –ino (polite plural).

Imperative of aspettare	Example	Meaning: *to wait*
aspett<u>a</u>!	Aspetta Marco!	Wait Marco!
aspett<u>i</u>!	Aspetti, signore!	Wait Sir!
aspett<u>iamo</u>	Aspettiamo qui.	Let's wait here.
aspett<u>ate</u>!	Aspettate ragazzi!	Wait children!
asp*e*tt<u>ino</u>!	Asp*e*ttino un *a*ttimo signori!	Wait a moment ladies and gentlemen!

The endings for –ere verb imperatives are –i (tu form), –a (lei/Lei form),
–iamo (let's), –ete (voi form) and –ano (polite plural).

Imperative of prendere	Example	Meaning: *to take*
prend<u>i</u>	Prendi quello, Marco!	Take that one Marco!
prend<u>a</u>	Prenda quello, signore!	Take that one, Sir!
prend<u>iamo</u>	Prendiamo quello.	Let's take that one.
prend<u>ete</u>	Prendete quelli, ragazzi!	Take those, children!
prend<u>ano</u>	Prendano quelli, signori!	Take those, ladies and gentlemen!

Italic letters in Italian words show where stress does not follow the usual rules.

The endings for most –ire verb imperatives are –isci (tu form), –isca (lei/Lei form), –iamo (let's), –ite (voi form) and –iscano (polite plural).

Note that sci is pronounced *she*; sca is pronounced *ska*.

Imperative of finire	Example	Meaning: *to finish*
fini**sci**	Finisci l'esercizio, Marco!	Finish the exercise, Marco!
fini**sca**	Finisca tutto, signore!	Finish it all, Sir!
fini**amo**	Finiamo tutto.	Let's finish it all.
fini**te**	Finite i compiti, ragazzi!	Finish your homework, children!
fini**scano**	Finíscano tutto signori!	Finish it all, ladies and gentlemen!

The endings for verbs that do not add –isc to the stem, such as partire (meaning *to leave*), dormire (meaning *to sleep*) aprire (meaning *to open*) and sentire (meaning *to listen*) are –i, –a, –iamo, –ite and –ano.

> Dormi Giulia! Go to sleep Giulia!
> Senta, signora. Listen, madam.
> Partiamo. Let's go.

Some of the commonest verbs in Italian have irregular imperative forms. Here are the forms for some important verbs:

	dare	dire	essere	fare	andare
(tu)	da'! *or* dai!	di'!	sii!	fa'! *or* fai!	va'! *or* vai!
(lei/Lei)	dia!	dica!	sia!	faccia!	vada!
(noi)	diamo	diciamo	siamo	facciamo	vadano!
(voi)	date!	dite!	siate!	fate!	andate!
(loro)	diano!	dicano!	siano!	facciano!	vadano!

Sii bravo, Paolo! Be good Paolo!
Faccia pure, signore! Carry on, sir!
Dite la verità, ragazzi! Tell the truth, children!

Where pronouns go

Pronouns come <u>after</u> the imperative in the tu and voi forms.

The pronoun joins with the imperative to make one word:

Guarda*mi*, mamma! Look at me, mum!
Aspett*ateli*! Wait for them!

When the imperative is only one syllable mi becomes mmi, ti becomes tti, lo becomes llo and so on.

Dim*mi*! Tell me!
Fa*llo* subito! Do it immediately!

When the pronouns mi, ti, ci and vi are followed by another pronoun they become me-, te-, ce- and ve-, and gli and le become glie-.

Mand*ameli*. Send me them.
Da*glielo*. Give it to him.

In Italian you <u>always</u> put the indirect object pronoun first.

Pronouns also come <u>after</u> the –iamo form of the imperative, joining onto it to make one word.

Provi*amolo*! Let's try it!
Mandi*amogliela*! Let's send it to them.

Pronouns come <u>before</u> the lei form of the imperative and the polite plural form.

Italic letters in Italian words show where stress does not follow the usual rules.

Mi dia un chilo d'uva, per favore. Give me a kilo of grapes please.
La prenda, signore. Take it, sir.
Ne assaggino un po', signori! Try a bit, ladies and gentlemen!
Si accomodi! Take a seat!

How to tell someone not to do something

When you are telling someone you call tu not to do something:

• use non with the infinitive of the verb

> Non dire bugie Andrea! Don't tell lies Andrea!
> Non dimenticare! Don't forget!

• join pronouns onto the infinitive, or put them in front

> Non toccar**lo**! OR
> Non **lo** toccare! Don't touch it!

> Non dir**glielo**! OR
> Non **glielo** dire! Don't tell him about it!

> Non far**mi** ridere! OR
> Non **mi** far ridere! Don't make me laugh!

> Non preoccupar**ti**! OR
> Non **ti** preoccupare! Don't worry!

> Non bagnar**ti**! OR
> Non **ti** bagnare! Don't get wet!

Note that the infinitive usually drops the final e when followed by a pronoun.

In all other cases, to tell someone not to do something:

- use non with the imperative

  <u>Non dimenticate</u> ragazzi.   Don't forget children.
  <u>Non *a*bbia</u> paura, signora.   Don't be afraid, madam.
  <u>Non esageriamo</u>!   Don't let's go too far!

- join pronouns onto the voi and –iamo forms of the imperative

  <u>Non guard*a*teli</u>!   Don't look at them.
  <u>Non dit*e*melo</u>!   Don't say it to me!

  <u>Non mangi*a*moli</u> tutti.   Don't let's eat them all.
  <u>Non diamogli*e*lo</u>.   Don't let's give it to them.

- put pronouns <u>in front of</u> the lei and polite plural forms of the imperative

  Non <u>li</u> guardi, signora.   Don't look at them, madam.
  Non si preoccupino, signori.   Don't worry ladies and gentlemen.

Reflexive verbs

Making the present tense of reflexive verbs

The present tense forms of a reflexive verb are just the same as those of an ordinary verb, except for the addition of the reflexive pronoun in front of the verb.

The following table shows the reflexive verb divertirsi (meaning *to enjoy oneself*) in full.

Subject pronoun	Reflexive pronoun	Present tense	Meaning
(io)	mi	diverto	I'm enjoying myself
(tu)	ti	diverti	you're enjoying yourself
(lui)	si	diverte	he is enjoying himself
(lei)	si	diverte	she is enjoying herself
(lei/Lei)	si	diverte	you are enjoying yourself
(noi)	ci	divertiamo	we're enjoying ourselves
(voi)	vi	divertite	you're enjoying yourselves
(loro)	si	divertono	they're enjoying themselves

Where to put reflexive pronouns

The reflexive pronoun usually goes in front of the verb, but there are some exceptions. The pronoun goes <u>in front</u> if the verb is:

- an ordinary tense, such as the present simple:

  <u>Si</u> diverte signora?   Are you enjoying yourself madam?
  <u>Mi</u> abituo al lavoro.   I'm getting used to the work.

- the polite imperative:

    <u>Si</u> avvicini, signore.   Come closer, sir.

- an imperative telling someone NOT to do something:

    Non <u>vi</u> avvicinate troppo ragazzi.   Don't come too close children.
    Non <u>si</u> lamenti, dottore.   Don't complain, doctor.

The pronoun comes <u>after</u> the verb if it is the tu or voi form of the imperative, used positively:

    Sveglia<u>ti</u>! Wake up!
    Divertite<u>vi</u>! Enjoy yourselves!

In the case of the infinitive, used with non to tell someone NOT to do something, the pronoun can either:

- go <u>in front of</u> the infinitive

    OR

- join onto the end of the infinitive

    Non <u>ti</u> bruciare! or Non bruciar<u>ti</u>!   Don't burn yourself!
    Non <u>ti</u> preoccupare! or Non preoccupar<u>ti</u>!   Don't worry!

Note that, when telling someone not to do something, you use non with the <u>infinitive</u> for people you call tu.

There are also two options when you use the infinitive of a reflexive verb after a verb such as *want*, *must*, *should* or *can't*. The pronoun can either:

- go in front of the main verb

    OR

- join onto the end of the infinitive

<u>Mi</u> voglio abbronzare. or Voglio abbronzar<u>mi</u>.   I want to get a tan.
<u>Ti</u> devi alzare. or Devi alzar<u>ti</u>.   You must get up.
<u>Vi</u> dovreste preparare. or Dovreste preparar<u>vi</u>.   You ought to get ready.
Non <u>mi</u> posso fermare molto. or Non posso fermar<u>mi</u> molto.
I can't stop for long.

In the same way, in <u>continuous tenses</u>, the reflexive pronoun can either:

• go in front of the verb stare

  OR

• join onto the gerund

  Ti stai annoiando? or Stai annoiandoti? **Are you getting bored?**
  Si stanno alzando? or Stanno alzandosi? **Are they getting up?**

Note that the pronoun is always joined onto the gerund when it is not used in a continuous tense.

Incontrand<u>oci</u> per caso, abbiamo parlato molto.
Meeting by chance, we had a long talk.
Pettinand<u>omi</u> ho trovato un capello bianco.
When I combed my hair I found a white hair.

The future tense

Making the future tense

To make the future of regular –are and –ere verbs take the <u>stem</u> and add the following endings:

- erò, erai, erà, eremo, erete, eranno

The following table shows the future tenses of parlare (meaning *to speak*) and credere (meaning *to believe*).

Pronoun	Future tense of parlare	Meaning: *to speak*
(io)	parl<u>erò</u>	I'll speak
(tu)	parl<u>erai</u>	you'll speak
(lui/lei) (lei/Lei)	parl<u>erà</u>	he/she'll speak you'll speak
(noi)	parl<u>eremo</u>	we'll speak
(voi)	parl<u>erete</u>	you'll speak
(loro)	parl<u>eranno</u>	they'll speak

Gli <u>parlerò</u> domani.   I'll speak to him tomorrow.

Pronoun	Future tense of credere	Meaning: *to speak*
(io)	cred<u>erò</u>	I'll believe
(tu)	cred<u>erai</u>	you'll believe
(lui/lei) (lei/Lei)	cred<u>erà</u>	he/she'll believe
(noi)	cred<u>eremo</u>	we'll believe
(voi)	cred<u>erete</u>	you'll believe
(loro)	cred<u>eranno</u>	they'll believe

Non ti <u>crederanno</u>.   They won't believe you.

Italic letters in Italian words show where stress does not follow the usual rules.

Note that there are accents on the first and third person singular forms, to show that you put the stress on the last syllable.

To make the future of regular –ire verbs take the <u>stem</u> and add the following endings:

- irò, irai, irà, iremo, irete, iranno

The following table shows the future tense of finire (meaning *to finish*).

Pronoun	Future tense of finire	Meaning: *to finish*
(io)	fin<u>irò</u>	I'll finish
(tu)	fin<u>irai</u>	you'll finish
(lui/lei) (lei/Lei)	fin<u>irà</u>	he/she'll finish you'll finish
(noi)	fin<u>iremo</u>	we'll finish
(voi)	fin<u>irete</u>	you'll finish
(loro)	fin<u>iranno</u>	they'll finish

Quando <u>finirai</u> il lavoro? When will you finish the work?

Irregular future forms

Some common verbs do not have a vowel before the r of the future ending.
These endings are: –ró, –rai, –rá, –remo, –rete, –ranno:

Verb	Meaning	io	tu	lui/lei	noi	voi	loro
andare	to go	andrò	andrai	andrà	andremo	andrete	andranno
cadere	to fall	cadrò	cadrai	cadrà	cadremo	cadrete	cadranno
dire	to say	dirò	dirai	dirà	diremo	direte	diranno
dovere	to have to	dovrò	dovrai	dovrà	dovremo	dovrete	dovranno
fare	to do/make	farò	farai	farà	faremo	farete	faranno
potere	to be able	potrò	potrai	potrà	potremo	potrete	potranno
sapere	to know	saprò	saprai	saprà	sapremo	saprete	sapranno
vedere	to see	vedrò	vedrai	vedrà	vedremo	vedrete	vedranno
vivere	to live	vivrò	vivrai	vivrà	vivremo	vivrete	vivranno

Andrò con loro.   I'll go with them.
Pensi che diranno la verità?   Do you think they'll tell the truth?
Non credo che farà bel tempo.   I don't think the weather will be nice.
Lo sapremo domani.   We'll know tomorrow.

Some verbs have no vowel before the future ending, and change their stem:

Verb	Meaning	io	tu	lui/lei	noi	voi	loro
rimanere	to remain	rimarrò	rimarrai	rimarrà	rimarremo	rimarrete	rimarranno
tenere	to hold	terrò	terrai	terrà	terremo	terrete	terranno
venire	to come	verrò	verrai	verrà	verremo	verrete	verranno
volere	to want	vorrò	vorrai	vorrà	vorremo	vorrete	vorranno

Verbs with infinitives that end in –ciare and –giare, for example, parcheggiare (meaning to park), cominciare (meaning to start), mangiare (meaning to eat) and viaggiare (meaning to travel) drop the i in the future.

> Comincerò domani.   I'll start tomorrow.
> Mangeranno alle otto.   They'll eat at eight o'clock.

Verbs with infinitives that end in –care and –gare, for example cercare (meaning to look for, to try), seccare (meaning to annoy), pagare (meaning to pay) and spiegare (meaning to explain) add an h in the future.

> Cercherò di aiutarvi.   I'll try to help you.
> Mi pagheranno sabato.   They'll pay me on Saturday.

The future tense of essere and avere

essere (meaning to be) and avere (meaning to have) have irregular future forms.

Pronoun	Future tense of essere	Meaning	Future tense of avere	Meaning
(io)	sarò	I'll be	avrò	I'll have
(tu)	sarai	you'll be	avrai	you'll have
(lui/lei) (lei/Lei)	sarà	he/she/it will be you'll be	avrà	he/she/it will have you'll have
(noi)	saremo	we'll be	avremo	we'll have
(voi)	sarete	you'll be	avrete	you'll have
(loro)	saranno	they'll be	avranno	they'll have

> Sarà difficile.   It'll be difficult.
> Non ne sarai deluso.   You won't be disappointed by it.
> Non avrò tempo.   I won't have time.
> Lo avrai domani.   You'll have it tomorrow.

The conditional

Making the conditional

To make the conditional of regular –are and –ere verbs take the <u>stem</u> and add the
following endings: –erei, –eresti, –erebbe, –eremmo, –ereste, –erebbero.

The following table shows the conditional of parlare (meaning *to speak*) and
credere (meaning *to believe*).

	Conditional of parlare	Meaning	Conditional of credere	Meaning
(io)	parlerei	I'd speak	crederei	I'd believe
(tu)	parleresti	you'd speak	crederesti	you'd believe
(lui/lei)	parlerebbe	he/she'd speak	crederebbe	he/she'd believe
(lei/Lei)	parlerebbe	you'd speak	crederebbe	you'd believe
(noi)	parleremmo	we'd speak	crederemmo	we'd believe
(voi)	parlereste	you'd speak	credereste	you'd believe
(loro)	parlerebbero	they'd speak	crederebbero	they'd believe

Con chi <u>parleresti</u>?   Who would you speak to?
Non ti <u>crederebbe</u>.   He wouldn't believe you.

To make the conditional of regular –ire verbs take the <u>stem</u> and add the
following endings: –irei, –iresti, –irebbe, –iremmo, –ireste, –irebbero.

The following table shows the conditional of finire (meaning *to finish*).

(io)	fin<u>irei</u>	I'd finish
(tu)	fin<u>iresti</u>	you'd finish
(lui/lei)	fin<u>irebbe</u>	he/she'd finish
(lei/Lei)	fin<u>irebbe</u>	you'd finish
(noi)	fin<u>iremmo</u>	we'd finish
(voi)	fin<u>ireste</u>	you'd finish
(loro)	fin<u>irebbero</u>	they'd finish

Non <u>finiremmo</u> in tempo.   We wouldn't finish in time.

The conditionals of volere, potere and dovere

The conditionals of volere (meaning *to want*), potere (meaning *to be able*) and dovere (meaning *to have to*) are as follows:

(io)	vorrei	I'd like
(tu)	vorresti	you'd like
(lui/lei) (lei/Lei)	vorrebbe	he/she'd like you'd like
(noi)	vorremmo	we'd like
(voi)	vorreste	you'd like
(loro)	vorrebbero	they'd like

<u>Vorrei</u> un'insalata.   I'd like a salad.

<u>Vorrei</u> vedere quel film.   I'd like to see that film.

<u>Vorremmo</u> venire con voi.   We'd like to come with you.

<u>Vorrebbero</u> rimanere qui.   They'd like to stay here.

For further explanation of grammatical terms, please see 8-11.

(io)	potrei	I could
(tu)	potresti	you could
(lui/lei) (lei/Lei)	potrebbe	he/she/it could you could
(noi)	potremmo	we could
(voi)	potreste	you could
(loro)	potrebbero	they could

<u>Potresti</u> avere ragione.   You could be right.
<u>Potrebbe</u> essere vero.   It could be true.
<u>Potrebbero</u> vendere la casa.   They could sell the house.
<u>Potresti</u> chiudere la finestra?   Could you close the window?

(io)	dovrei	I should
(tu)	dovresti	you should
(lui/lei) (lei/Lei)	dovrebbe	he/she/it should you should
(noi)	dovremmo	we should
(voi)	dovreste	you should
(loro)	dovrebbero	they should

<u>Dovrei</u> fare un po' di ginnastica.   I should do some exercise.
<u>Dovresti</u> telefonare ai tuoi.   You should phone your parents.
<u>Dovrebbe</u> arrivare verso le dieci.   He should arrive at around ten.
<u>Dovrebbe</u> essere bello.   It should be good.

Italic letters in Italian words show where stress does not follow the usual rules.

Irregular conditional forms

Some common verbs do not have a vowel before the r of the conditional ending, their endings are –rei, –resti, –rebbe, –remmo, –reste, –rebbero.

Verb	Meaning	io	tu	lui/lei	noi	voi	loro
andare	to go	andrei	andresti	andrebbe	andremmo	andreste	andrebbero
cadere	to fall	cadrei	cadresti	cadrebbe	cadremmo	cadreste	cadrebbero
dire	to say	direi	diresti	direbbe	diremmo	direste	direbbero
fare	to do/make	farei	faresti	farebbe	faremmo	fareste	farebbero
sapere	to know	saprei	sapresti	saprebbe	sapremmo	sapreste	saprebbero
vedere	to see	vedrei	vedresti	vedrebbe	vedremmo	vedreste	vedrebbero
vivere	to live	vivrei	vivresti	vivrebbe	vivremmo	vivreste	vivrebbero

> Non so se <u>andrebbe</u> bene.　I don't know if it would be okay.
> Non <u>direi</u>.　I wouldn't say that.
> Cosa <u>faresti</u>?　What would you do?

Some verbs have no vowel before the conditional ending, and change their stem:

Verb	Meaning	io	tu	lui/lei	noi	voi	loro
rimanere	to remain	rimarrei	rimarresti	rimarrebbe	rimarremmo	rimarreste	rimarrebbero
tenere	to hold	terrei	terresti	terrebbe	terremmo	terreste	terrebbero
venire	to come	verrei	verresti	verrebbe	verremmo	verreste	verrebbero

Verbs such as cominciare (meaning *to start*) and mangiare (meaning *to eat*), which end in –ciare or –giare, and which drop the i in the future also drop the i in the conditional.

> Quando <u>comincerebbe</u>? When would it start?
> <u>Mangeresti</u> quei funghi? Would you eat those mushrooms?

Verbs such as cercare (meaning *to look for*) and pagare (meaning *to pay*), which end in –care or –gare, and which add an h in the future also add an h in the conditional.

> Probabilmente <u>cercherebbe</u> una scusa. He'd probably look for an excuse.
> Quanto mi <u>pagheresti</u>? How much would you pay me?

Reflexive verbs in the conditional

The conditional of reflexive verbs is formed in just the same way as for ordinary verbs, except that you have to remember to give the reflexive pronoun (mi, ti, si, ci, vi, si).

> Ti divertiresti molto. You'd have a very good time.

The imperfect tense

Making the imperfect tense

You make the imperfect of regular –are, –ere, and –ire verbs by knocking off the –re from the infinitive and adding –vo, –vi, –va, –vamo, –vate, –vano.

The following tables show the imperfect of three regular verbs, parlare (meaning to speak), credere (meaning to believe) and finire (meaning to finish).

	Imperfect tense of parlare	Meaning	Imperfect tense of credere	Meaning
(io)	parlavo	I was speaking	credevo	I believed
(tu)	parlavi	you were speaking	credevi	you believed
(lui/lei) (lei/Lei)	parlava	he/she was speaking you were speaking	credeva	he/she believed you believed
(noi)	parlavamo	we were speaking	credevamo	we believed
(voi)	parlavate	you were speaking	credevate	you believed
(loro)	parlavano	they were speaking	credevano	they believed

	Imperfect tense of finire	Meaning
(io)	finivo	I was finishing
(tu)	finivi	you were finishing
(lui/lei) (lei/Lei)	finiva	he/she was finishing you were finishing
(noi)	finivamo	we were finishing
(voi)	finivate	you were finishing
(loro)	finivano	they were finishing

For further explanation of grammatical terms, please see 8-11.

Con chi <u>parlavi</u>? Who were you talking to?

Una volta <u>costava</u> di più. It used to cost more.

Mi <u>alzavo</u> sempre prima di lei. I always got up before she did.

<u>Credevamo</u> di aver vinto. We thought we'd won.

Loro si <u>divertivano</u> mentre io <u>lavoravo</u>. They had fun while I was working.

Verbs with an irregular imperfect tense

The imperfect of *essere* (meaning *to be*) is irregular:

(io)	ero	I was
(tu)	eri	you were
(lui/lei) (lei/Lei)	era	he/she/it was you were
(noi)	eravamo	we were
(voi)	eravate	you were
(loro)	erano	they were

<u>Era</u> un ragazzo molto simpatico. He was a very nice boy

<u>Eravamo</u> in Italia. We were in Italy.

<u>Erano</u> le quattro. It was four o'clock.

bere (meaning *to drink*), dire (meaning *to say*), fare (meaning *to do, to make*) and tradurre (meaning *to translate*) are common verbs which have the normal imperfect endings added onto an irregular stem.

Verb	(io)	(tu)	(lui/lei)	(noi)	(voi)	(loro)
bere	bevevo	bevevi	beveva	bevevamo	bevevate	bevevano
dire	dicevo	dicevi	diceva	dicevamo	dicevate	dicevano
fare	facevo	facevi	faceva	facevamo	facevate	facevano
tradurre	traducevo	traducevi	traduceva	traducevamo	traducevate	traducevano

Italic letters in Italian words show where stress does not follow the usual rules.

Di solito <u>bevevano</u> solo acqua.   They usually only drank water.

Cosa <u>dicevo</u>?   What was I saying?

<u>Faceva</u> molto freddo.   It was very cold.

<u>Traducevo</u> la lettera.   I was translating the letter.

The perfect tense

Making the perfect tense

In Italian there are two ways of making the perfect tense:

- the present tense of avere (meaning *to have*) followed by a past participle.
- the present tense of essere (meaning *to be*), followed by a past participle.

Making the past participle

To make the past participle of regular –are verbs, take off the –are ending of the infinitive and add –ato.

> parlare (*to speak*) → parlato (*spoken*)

To make the past participle of regular –ere verbs, take off the –ere ending of the infinitive and add –uto.

> credere (to *believe*) → creduto (*believed*)

To make the past participle of regular –ire verbs, take off the –ire ending of the infinitive and add –ito.

> finire (to *finish*) → finito (*finished*)

Making the perfect tense with avere

To make the perfect with avere:

- choose the present tense form of avere that matches the subject of the sentence.
- add the past participle. Do not change the ending of the participle to make it agree with the subject.

Italic letters in Italian words show where stress does not follow the usual rules.

The perfect tense of parlare (meaning *to speak*) is as follows:

	Present tense of avere	**Past participle**	**Meaning**
(io)	ho	parlato	I spoke *or* have spoken
(tu)	hai	parlato	you spoke *or* have spoken
(lui/lei) (lei/Lei)	ha	parlato	he/she spoke *or* has spoken you spoke *or* have spoken
(noi)	abbiamo	parlato	we spoke *or* have spoken
(voi)	avete	parlato	you spoke *or* have spoken
(loro)	hanno	parlato	they spoke *or* have spoken

Non gli <u>ho</u> mai <u>parlato</u>.   I've never spoken to him.

Roberta gli <u>ha parlato</u> ieri.   Roberta spoke to him yesterday.

Most verbs form their perfect tense with avere.

<u>Ho buttato</u> giù alcune idee.   <u>I've put down</u> some ideas.

<u>Abbiamo comprato</u> una macchina.   <u>We've bought</u> a car.

Dove <u>avete parcheggiato</u>?   Where <u>did you park</u>?

Non <u>hanno voluto</u> aiutarmi.   They <u>didn't want</u> to help me.

Verbs with irregular past participles

Some very common verbs have irregular past participles. These are some of the most important ones.

> aprire (*to open*) → aperto (*opened*)
> ALSO coprire (*to cover*) → coperto (*covered*)
> chiudere (*to close*) → chiuso (*closed*)
> decidere (*to decide*) → deciso (*decided*)
> dire (*to say*) → detto (*said*)
> fare (*to do, to make*) → fatto (*done, made*)
> friggere (*to fry*) → fritto (*fried*)
> leggere (*to read*) → letto (*read*)
> mettere (*to put*) → messo (*put*)
> ALSO promettere (*to promise*) → promesso (*promised*)
> morire (*to die*) → morto (*died*)
> offrire (*to offer*) → offerto (*offered*)
> prendere (*to take*) → preso (*taken*)
> ALSO sorprendere (*to surprise*) → sorpreso (*surprised*)
> rispondere (*to reply*) → risposto (*replied*)
> rompere (*to break*) → rotto (*broken*)
> scegliere (*to choose*) → scelto (*chosen*)
> scrivere (*to write*) → scritto (*written*)
> spendere (*to spend*) → speso (*spent*)
> vincere (*to win*) → vinto (*won*)
> ALSO convincere (*to convince*) → convinto (*convinced*)
> vedere (*to see*) → visto (*seen*)

<u>Ho preso</u> il treno delle dieci.   I <u>got</u> the ten o'clock train.
<u>L'hai messo</u> in frigo?   <u>Have you put</u> it in the fridge?
Perché <u>l'hai fatto</u>?   Why <u>did you do</u> it?
Carlo <u>ha speso</u> più di me.   Carlo <u>spent</u> more than me.
<u>Ha scelto</u>, signore?   <u>Have you chosen</u>, sir?

Italic letters in Italian words show where stress does not follow the usual rules.

Making the perfect tense with essere

The perfect tense of <u>some</u> verbs which do not take a direct object, and of <u>all</u> reflexive verbs is formed with essere.

To make the perfect with essere:

* choose the present tense form of essere that matches the subject of the sentence.

* add the past participle. Make the ending of the participle agree with the subject.

The perfect tense of andare (meaning *to go*) is as follows:

	Present tense of essere	**Past participle**	**Meaning**
(io)	sono	andato *or* andata	I went *or* have gone
(tu)	sei	andato *or* andata	you went *or* have gone
(lui)	è	andato	he/it went *or* has gone
(lei)	è	andata	she/it went *or* has gone
(lei/Lei)	è	andato *or* andata	you went *or* have gone
(noi)	siamo	andati *or* andate	we went *or* have gone
(voi)	siete	andati *or* andate	you went *or* have gone
(loro)	sono	andati *or* andate	they went *or* have gone

The most important verbs that form their perfect tense with essere are:

andare	to go	arrivare	to arrive
entrare	to come in	diventare	to become
partire	to leave	rimanere	to stay
riuscire	to succeed, manage	salire	to go up, get on
scendere	to go down	succedere	to happen
stare	to be	tornare	to come back
uscire	to go out	venire	to come

È rimasta a casa tutto il giorno.   She stayed at home all day.
Siamo riusciti a convincerla.   We managed to persuade her.
Sei mai stata a Bologna, Tina?   Have you ever been to Bologna, Tina?
Le tue amiche sono arrivate.   Your friends have arrived.
Cos'è successo?   What happened?

Note that essere is used to make the perfect of piacere (meaning literally to please). The past participle agrees with the subject of the Italian verb, and not with the subject of the English verb to like.

La musica ti è piaciuta, Roberto?   Did you like the music, Robert?
I cioccolatini mi sono piaciuti molto.   I liked the chocolates very much.
Le foto sono piaciute a tutti.   Everyone liked the photos.

Use essere to make the perfect tense of all reflexive verbs, putting the reflexive pronoun in front of sono, sei, è and so on.

I miei fratelli si sono alzati tardi.   My brothers got up late.
Le ragazze si sono alzate alle sei.   The girls got up at six.
Mi sono fatta tagliare i capelli.   I had my hair cut.
Ti sei fatto male?   Have you hurt yourself?

The pluperfect or past perfect tense

Making the pluperfect tense

In Italian there are two ways of making the pluperfect tense:

- the imperfect tense of avere (meaning *to have*) followed by a past participle.

- the imperfect tense of essere (meaning *to be*), followed by a past participle.

Making the pluperfect tense with avere

To make the pluperfect tense with avere:

- choose the <u>imperfect</u> form of avere that matches the subject of the sentence.

- add the past participle. <u>Do not</u> change the ending of the participle to make it agree with the subject.

Most verbs form their pluperfect tense with avere.

The pluperfect tense of parlare (meaning *to speak*) is as follows:

	Imperfect tense of avere	Past participle	Meaning
(io)	avevo	parlato	I had spoken
(tu)	avevi	parlato	you had spoken
(lui/lei) (lei/Lei)	aveva	parlato	he/she had spoken you had spoken
(noi)	avevamo	parlato	we had spoken
(voi)	avevate	parlato	you had spoken
(loro)	avevano	parlato	they had spoken

Non gli <u>avevo</u> mai <u>parlato</u> prima.   I'd never spoken to him before.

Sara gli <u>aveva parlato</u> il giorno prima.   Sara had spoken to him the day before.

Remember that some very common verbs have irregular past participles.

aprire (*to open*) → aperto (*opened*)

ALSO coprire (*to cover*) → coperto (*covered*)

chiudere (*to close*) → chiuso (*closed*)

decidere (*to decide*) → deciso (*decided*)

dire (*to say*) → detto (*said*)

fare (*to do, to make*) → fatto (*done, made*)

friggere (*to fry*) → fritto (*fried*)

leggere (*to read*) → letto (*read*)

mettere (*to put*) → messo (*put*)

ALSO promettere (*to promise*) → promesso (*promised*)

morire (*to die*) → morto (*died*)

offrire (*to offer*) → offerto (*offered*)

prendere (*to take*) → preso (*taken*)

ALSO sorprendere (*to surprise*) → sorpreso (*surprised*)

rispondere (*to reply*) → risposto (*replied*)

rompere (*to break*) → rotto (*broken*)

scegliere (*to choose*) → scelto (*chosen*)

scrivere (*to write*) → scritto (*written*)

spendere (*to spend*) → speso (*spent*)

vincere (*to win*) → vinto (*won*)

ALSO convincere (*to convince*) → convinto (*convinced*)

vedere (*to see*) → visto (*seen*)

Carlo <u>aveva speso</u> più di me.   Carlo had spent more than me.

Non gli <u>avevo detto</u> niente.   I hadn't said anything to him.

Making the pluperfect tense with *essere*

Verbs that make their perfect tense with *essere* also make their pluperfect tense with *essere*.

To make the pluperfect tense with *essere*:

- choose the <u>imperfect</u> form of *essere* that matches the subject of the sentence.
- add the past participle. Make the ending of the participle <u>agree</u> with the subject.

The pluperfect tense of *andare* (meaning *to go*) is as follows:

	Imperfect tense of *essere*	**Past participle**	**Meaning**
(io)	ero	andato *or* andata	I had gone
(tu)	eri	andato *or* andata	you had gone
(lui)	era	andato	he/it had gone
(lei)	era	andata	she/it had gone
(lei/Lei)	era	andato *or* andata	you had gone
(noi)	eravamo	andati *or* andate	we had gone
(voi)	eravate	andati *or* andate	you had gone
(loro)	erano	andati *or* andate	they had gone

Silvia era andata con loro.   Silvia had gone with them.

Tutti i miei amici erano andati alla festa.   All my friends had gone to the party.

Remember that *essere* is used to form the pluperfect of <u>all</u> reflexive verbs, and of <u>some</u> verbs that do not take a direct object, such as andare (meaning *to go*), venire (meaning *to come*), riuscire (meaning *to succeed*), diventare (meaning *to become*) and piacere (meaning *to like*).

For further explanation of grammatical terms, please see 8-11.

Ovviamente non gli <u>erano piaciuti</u> i quadri.
He obviously hadn't liked the pictures.
Sono arrivata alle cinque, ma <u>erano</u> già <u>partiti</u>.
I arrived at five, but they'd already gone.
Fortunatamente non <u>si era fatta</u> male.   Luckily she hadn't hurt herself.
Dopo che <u>si erano resi</u> conto del loro errore…
After they'd realized their mistake…

Note that the reflexive pronoun comes before ero, eri, era, eravamo, eravate
and erano in the pluperfect of reflexive verbs.

The passive

Making the passive

In English we use the verb *to be* with a <u>past participle</u> (*is done, was bitten*) to make the passive. In Italian the passive is formed in exactly the same way, using *essere* (meaning *to be*) and a <u>past participle</u>. When you say who or what is responsible for the action you use da (meaning *by*).

> <u>Siamo invitati</u> ad una festa a casa loro.
> We're invited to a party at their house.
> L'elettricità <u>è stata tagliata</u> ieri.   The electricity was cut off yesterday.
> La partita <u>è stata rinviata</u>.   The match has been postponed.
> <u>È stato costretto</u> a ritirarsi dalla gara.
> He was forced to withdraw from the competition
> I ladri <u>sono stati catturati</u> dalla polizia.
> The thieves were caught by the police.

Note that the past participle agrees with the subject of the verb *essere* in the same way an adjective would.

Here is the perfect tense of the –are verb *invitare* (meaning *to invite*) in its passive form.

(Subject pronoun)		Perfect tense of *essere*	Past Participle	Meaning
(io)	– masculine	sono stato	invitato	I was, have
	– feminine	sono stata	invitata	been invited
(tu)	– masculine	sei stato	invitato	you were, have
	– feminine	sei stata	invitata	been invited
(lui)		è stato	invitato	he was, has been invited
(lei)		è stata	invitata	she was, has been invited
(lei/Lei)	– masculine	è stato	invitato	you were, have been invited
	– feminine	è stata	invitata	you were, have been invited
(noi)	– masculine	siamo stati	invitati	we were, have been invited
	– feminine	siamo state	invitate	we were, have been invited
(voi)	– masculine	siete stati	invitati	you were, have been invited
	– feminine	siete state	invitate	you were, have been invited
(loro)	– masculine	sono stati	invitati	they were, have been invited
	– feminine	sono state	invitate	they were, have been invited

Change the tense of the verb *essere* to make whatever passive tense you want, for example:

Future: <u>Sarete</u> tutti <u>invitati</u>.   You'll all be invited.
Conditional: Non so se <u>sarebbe</u> <u>invitata</u>.   I don't know if she would be invited.

Irregular past participles are shown in the Verb Tables at the back of the book.

The gerund

Making the gerund

To make the gerund of –are verbs, take off the –are ending of the infinitive to get the stem, and add –ando.

Infinitive	Stem	Gerund
lavorare	lavor-	lavorando
andare	and-	andando
dare	d-	dando
stare	st-	stando

Note that the only –are verb that does not follow this rule is fare, and verbs made of fare with a prefix, such as rifare (meaning *to do again*) and disfare (meaning *to undo*). The gerund of fare is facendo.

To make the gerund of –ere and –ire verbs, take off the –ere or –ire ending of the infinitive to get the stem, and add –endo.

Infinitive	Stem	Gerund
credere	cred-	credendo
essere	ess-	essendo
dovere	dov-	dovendo
finire	fin-	finendo
dormire	dorm-	dormendo

Note that the only –ire verb that does not follow this rule is dire (and verbs made of dire with a prefix, such as disdire (meaning *to cancel*) and contraddire (meaning *to contradict*)). The gerund of dire is dicendo.

For further explanation of grammatical terms, please see 8-11.

Where to put pronouns used with the gerund

Pronouns are usually joined onto the end of the gerund.

> Vedendo<u>li</u> è scoppiata in lacrime.   When she saw them she burst into tears.
> Ascoltando<u>lo</u> mi sono addormentato.   Listening to him, I fell asleep.
> Incontrando<u>si</u> per caso sono andati al bar.
> Meeting each other by chance, they went to a café.

When the gerund is part of a continuous tense the pronoun can either come before stare or be joined onto the gerund.

> <u>Ti</u> sto parlando or Sto parlando<u>ti</u>.   I'm talking to you.
> <u>Si</u> sta vestendo or Sta vestendo<u>si</u>.   He's getting dressed.
> <u>Me lo</u> stavano mostrando or Stavano mostrando<u>melo</u>.
> They were showing me it.

The subjunctive

Making the present subjunctive

To make the present subjunctive of most verbs, take off the –o ending of the io form and add endings.

For –are verbs the endings are –i, –i, –i, –iamo, –iate, –ino.

For –ere and –ire verbs the endings are –a, –a, –a, –iamo, –iate, –ino.

Note that in the case of –ire verbs which add –isc in the io form, for example finisco (meaning *I finish*) and pulisco (meaning *I clean*), –isc is <u>not</u> added in the noi and voi forms.

The following table shows the present subjunctive of three regular verbs: parlare (meaning *to speak*), credere (meaning *to believe*) and finire (meaning *to finish*).

Infinitive	io, tu, lui, lei	noi	voi	loro
parlare	parli	parliamo	parliate	parlino
credere	creda	crediamo	crediate	credano
finire	finisca	finiamo	finiate	finiscano

Non voglio che mi <u>parlino</u>.   I don't want them to speak to me.
Può darsi che non ti <u>creda</u>.   Maybe she doesn't believe you.
È meglio che lo <u>finisca</u> io.   It'll be best if I finish it.

Some common verbs that are irregular in the ordinary present tense also have irregular present subjunctives:

Infinitive	io, tu, lui, lei	noi	voi	loro
andare *to go*	vada	andiamo	andiate	vadano
avere *to have*	abbia	abbiamo	abbiate	abbiano
dare *to give*	dia	diamo	diate	diano
dire *to say*	dica	diciamo	diciate	dicano
dovere *to have to*	debba	dobbiamo	dobbiate	debbano
essere *to be*	sia	siamo	siate	siano
fare *to do/make*	faccia	facciamo	facciate	facciano
potere *to be able*	possa	possiamo	possiate	possano
scegliere *to choose*	scelga	scegliamo	scegliate	scelgano
stare *to be*	stia	stiamo	stiate	stiano
tenere *to hold*	tenga	teniamo	teniate	tengano
tradurre *to translate*	traduca	traduciamo	traduciate	traducano
uscire *to go out*	esca	usciamo	usciate	escano
venire *to come*	venga	veniamo	veniate	vengano
volere *to want*	voglia	vogliamo	vogliate	vogliano

È meglio che tu te ne <u>vada</u>.   You'd better leave.
Vuoi che lo <u>traduca</u>?   Do you want me to translate it?
È facile che <u>scelgano</u> quelli rossi.   They'll probably choose those red ones.
Spero che tua madre <u>stia</u> meglio ora.   I hope your mother is better now.
Credi che <u>possa</u> essere vero?   Do you think it can be true?

Making the perfect subjunctive

To make the perfect subjunctive you use the subjunctive of avere (meaning *to have*) or essere (meaning *to be*) with the past participle.

For example, fare (meaning *to make* or *to do*) makes its ordinary perfect tense and its perfect subjunctive with avere, while essere makes its ordinary perfect tense and its perfect subjunctive with essere.

		ordinary perfect	perfect subjunctive
fare *to do/make*	io, tu, lui, lei	ho fatto, hai fatto, ha fatto	abbia fatto
	noi	abbiamo fatto	abbiamo fatto
	voi	avete fatto	abbiate fatto
	loro	hanno fatto	*a*bbiano fatto
essere *to be*	io	sono stato, sono stata	sia stato, sia stata
	tu	sei stato, sei stata	sia stato, sia stata
	lui	è stato	sia stato
	lei	è stata	sia stata
	lei/Lei	è stato, è stata	sia stato, sia stata
	noi	siamo stati, siamo state	siamo stati, siamo state
	voi	siete stati, siete state	siate stati, siate state
	loro	sono stati, sono state	siano stati, siano state

Non credo che l'abbiano fatto loro.   I don't think they did it.

È possibile che sia stato un errore.   It might have been a mistake.

Making the imperfect subjunctive

The imperfect subjunctive is made by adding endings to the verb <u>stem</u>.

The endings for –are verbs are –assi, –assi, –asse, –assimo, –aste, and –assero;
the endings for –ere verbs are –essi, –essi, –esse, –essimo, –este, and –essero;
the endings for –ire verbs are –issi, –issi, –isse, –issimo, –iste and –issero.

The following table shows the imperfect subjunctive of three regular verbs:
parlare (meaning to speak), credere (meaning to believe) and finire (meaning
to finish).

	parlare	**credere**	**finire**
(io)	parlassi	credessi	finissi
(tu)	parlassi	credessi	finissi
(lui/lei)	parlasse	credesse	finisse
(lei/Lei)	parlasse	credesse	finisse
(noi)	parlassimo	credessimo	finissimo
(voi)	parlaste	credeste	finiste
(loro)	parlassero	credessero	finissero

Volevano che <u>parlassi</u> con l'inquilino.
They wanted me to speak to the tenant.
Anche se mi credesse, non farebbe niente.
Even if he believed me he wouldn't do anything.
Se solo <u>finisse</u> prima delle otto!   If only it finished before eight o'clock!

The imperfect subjunctive of *essere* is as follows:

(io)	fossi
(tu)	fossi
(lui/lei)	fosse
(lei/Lei)	fosse
(noi)	fossimo
(voi)	foste
(loro)	fossero

Se <u>fossi</u> in te non lo pagherei.   If I were you I wouldn't pay it.

Se <u>fosse</u> più furba verrebbe.   If she had more sense she'd come.

The imperfect subjunctive of other important irregular verbs – bere (meaning *to drink*), dare (meaning *to give*), dire (meaning *to say*), fare (meaning *to make* or *to do*) and stare (meaning *to be*) – is as follows:

	(io)	(tu)	(lui/lei)	(noi)	(voi)	(loro)
bere	bevessi	bevessi	bevesse	bevessimo	beveste	bevessimo
dare	dessi	dessi	desse	dessimo	deste	dessero
dire	dicessi	dicessi	dicesse	dicessimo	diceste	dicessero
fare	facessi	facessi	facesse	facessimo	faceste	facessero
stare	stessi	stessi	stesse	stessimo	steste	stessero

Se solo be<u>vesse</u> meno!   If only he drank less!

Voleva che gli <u>dessero</u> il permesso.

He wanted them to give him permission.

Verb combinations

Many Italian verbs can be followed by the infinitive. In some cases the infinitive follows directly, in others a linking preposition is used.

Verbs followed by an infinitive with no preposition

The following important Italian verbs are followed directly by the infinitive:

- dovere   (to have to, must)

    È dovuto partire.   He had to leave.

    Dev'essere tardi.   It must be late.

- potere   (can, may)

    Non posso aiutarti.   I can't help you.

    Potresti aprire la finestra?   Could you open the window?

    Potrebbe essere vero.   It might be true.

- sapere   (to know how to, can)

    Sai farlo?   Do you know how to do it?

    Non sapeva nuotare.   He couldn't swim.

- volere   (to want)

    Voglio comprare una macchina nuova.   I want to buy a new car.

Note that voler dire is the Italian for to mean.

    Cosa vuol dire?   What does it mean?

- verbs such as piacere (meaning to like), dispiacere (meaning to be sorry) and convenire (meaning to be advisable)

    Mi piace andare in bici.   I like cycling.

    Ci dispiace andar via.   We're sorry to be leaving.

    Ti conviene partire presto.   You'd best set off early.

- vedere (meaning *to see*), ascoltare (meaning *to listen to*) and sentire (meaning *to hear*)

    Ci <u>ha visto arrivare</u>.   He saw us arriving.
    Ti <u>ho sentito cantare</u>.   I heard you singing.
    <u>L'abbiamo ascoltato parlare</u>.   We listened to him talking.

- fare (meaning *to make*) and lasciare (meaning *to let*)

    Non mi <u>far ridere</u>!   Don't make me laugh!
    <u>Lascia fare</u> a me.   Let me do it.

Note that far fare qualcosa and farsi fare qualcosa both mean *to have something done*:

    Ho <u>fatto riparare</u> la macchina.   I had the car repaired.
    Mi <u>sono fatta tagliare</u> i capelli.   I had my hair cut.

The following common verbs are also followed directly by the infinitive:

- bisognare   (to be necessary)

    <u>Bisogna prenotare</u>.   You have to book.

- desiderare   (to want)

    <u>Desiderava migliorare</u> il suo inglese.   He wanted to improve his English.

- odiare   (to hate)

    <u>Odio alzar</u>mi presto al mattino.   I hate getting up early in the morning.

- preferire   (to prefer)

    <u>Preferisco</u> non <u>parlar</u>ne.   I prefer not to talk about it.

Verbs followed by the preposition a and the infinitive

The following are the most common verbs that can be followed by a and the infinitive:

andare a fare qualcosa   to go to do something
È andato _a_ chiudere la porta.   He went to shut the door.

venire a fare qualcosa   to come to do something
Sono venuti _a_ trovarci.   They came to see us.

imparare a fare qualcosa   to learn to do something
Sto imparando _a_ suonare la chitarra.   I'm learning to play the guitar.

cominciare a fare qualcosa   to start to do _or_ doing something
Hanno cominciato _a_ ridere.   They started laughing.

continuare a fare qualcosa   to go on doing something
Ha continuato _a_ dormire.   He went on sleeping.

abituarsi a fare qualcosa   to get used to doing something
Dovrò abituarmi _ad_ alzarmi presto.
I'll have to get used to getting up early.

riuscire a fare qualcosa   to manage to do something
Siamo riusciti _a_ convincerla   We managed to persuade her.

Italic letters in Italian words show where stress does not follow the usual rules.

Verbs followed by the preposition di and the infinitive

The following are the most common verbs that can be followed by di and the infinitive:

cercare di fare qualcosa to try to do something
Cerca _di_ smettere di fumare. He's trying to stop smoking.

decidere di fare qualcosa to decide to do something
Ho deciso _di_ non andarci. I decided not to go.

dimenticare di fare qualcosa to forget to do something
Ho dimenticato _di_ prendere la chiave. I forgot to take my key.

smettere di fare qualcosa to stop doing something
Quando sono entrato hanno smesso _di_ parlare.
When I came in they stopped talking.

ricordarsi di aver fatto qualcosa to remember doing something
Non mi ricordo _di_ aver detto una cosa del genere.
I don't remember saying anything like that.

negare di aver fatto qualcosa to deny doing something
Ha negato di aver preso i soldi. He denied taking the money.

stufarsi di fare qualcosa to get fed up of doing something
Mi sono stufato _di_ aspettarlo. I got fed up of waiting for him.

Verbs followed by a and an object

a is used with the indirect object of verbs such as dire (meaning *to say*) and dare (meaning *to give*).

dare qualcosa a qualcuno   to give something to someone
Ho dato un libro a mia madre.   I gave my mother a book.

dire qualcosa a qualcuno   to say something to someone
Ha detto la veritá a Paolo.   He told Paolo the truth

mandare qualcosa a qualcuno   to send something to someone
Manderó una cartolina a Loredana.   I'll send Loredana a postcard.

mostrare qualcosa a qualcuno   to show something to someone
Ho mostrato le foto a Daphne.   I showed Daphne the photos.

scrivere qualcosa a qualcuno   to write something to someone
Ho scritto una lettera a Luca.   I wrote Luca a letter.

Here are some verbs taking a in Italian when you might not expect it, since the English equivalent either does not have the preposition *to* or has no preposition at all:

arrivare a (una città)   to arrive at (*a town*)
Quandi arrivi a Londra?   When do you arrive in London?

avvicinarsi a qualcuno   to approach someone
Matteo, non avvicinarti troppa a Chiara.
Matteo, don't go too close to Chiara.

chiedere qualcosa a qualcuno   to ask someone for something
Chiedi a Lidia come si chiama il suo cane.   Ask Lidia what her dog's called.

far male a qualcuno   to hurt someone
Marcello ha fatto male a Paolo.   Marcello hurt Paolo.
giocare a qualcosa   to play something (*game/sport*)
Giochi a calcio?   Do you play football?

insegnare qualcosa a qualcuno   to teach somebody something
Ha insegnato ai bambini i nomi delle piante.
She taught the children the names of plants.

partecipare a qualcosa   to take part in something
Parteciperai alla gara?   Are you going to take part in the competition?

permettere a qualcuno di fare qualcosa   to allow someone to do something
Non permette a Luca di uscire.   She doesn't allow Luca to go out.

proibire a qualcuno di fare qualcosa   to forbid someone to do something
Hai proibito ai bambini di uscire.   She's forbidden the children to go out.

rispondere a qualcuno   to answer someone
A me non ha risposto nessuno.   Nobody answered me.

rivolgersi a qualcuno   to ask someone
Dovrebbe rivolgersi all'impiegato laggiù.
You should go and ask the man over there.

rubare qualcosa a qualcuno   to steal something from someone
Ha rubato i soldi alla madre.   He stole the money from his mother.

somigliare a qualcuno   to look like someone
Somiglio moltissimo a mia madre.   I look very like my mother.

Verbs followed by di and an object

Here are some verbs taking di in Italian when the English verb is not followed by *of*:

accorgersi di qualcosa   to realize something
Si è accorto del furto solo il giorno dopo.
He only realized it had been stolen the next day.

aver bisogno di qualcosa   to need something
Ho bisogno di soldi.   I need money.

aver voglia di qualcosa   to want something
Adesso non ho voglia di mangiare.   I don't want to eat just now.

discutere di qualcosa   to discuss something
Discutono spesso di politica.   They often discuss politics.

fidarsi di qualcosa/qualcuno   to trust something/someone
Non mi fido di lui.   I don't trust him.

intendersi di qualcosa   to know about something
Si intende di fotografia.   She knows about photography.

interessarsi di qualcosa   to be interested in something
Non mi interessa di politica.   I'm not interested in politics.

lamentarsi di qualcosa   to complain about something
Si sono lamentati del cibo.   They complained about the food.

ricordarsi di qualcosa/qualcuno   to remember something/someone
Ti ricordi di Laura?   Do you remember Laura?

ridere di qualcosa/qualcuno   to laugh at something/someone
Hanno riso della sua proposta.   They laughed at his suggestion.
stufarsi di qualcosa/qualcuno   to get fed up with something/someone
Mi sono stufato di loro.   I got fed up with them.

stupirsi di qualcosa   to be amazed by something
Mi sono stupito del suo coraggio.   I was amazed at his courage.

trattare di qualcosa   to be about something
Di cosa tratta il libro?   What's the book about?

vantarsi di qualcosa   to boast about something
Si vanta sempre del proprio successo.
He's always boasting about his success.

Verbs followed by da and an object

Here are some verbs taking da in Italian when the English verb is not followed by *from*:

dipendere <u>da</u> qualcosa/qualcuno   to depend on something/someone
Dipende <u>dal</u> tempo.   It depends on the weather.

giudicare <u>da</u> qualcosa   to judge by something
A giudicare <u>da</u> quello che dice.   Judging by what he says.

scendere <u>da</u> qualcosa   to get off something (*bus, train, plane*)
Siamo tutti scesi dall'autobus.   We all got off the bus.

sporgersi <u>da</u> qualcosa   to lean out of something
Non sporgerti <u>dal</u> finestrino.   Don't lean out of the window.

Verbs that are followed by a preposition in English but not in Italian

Although the English verb is followed by a preposition, you <u>don't</u> use a preposition with the following Italian verbs:

ascoltare qualcosa/qualcuno   to listen to something/someone
Mi stai ascoltando?   Are you listening to me?

aspettare qualcosa/qualcuno   to wait for something/someone
Aspettami!   Wait for me!

cercare qualcosa/qualcuno   to look for something/someone
Sto cercando la chiave.   I'm looking for my key.

chiedere qualcosa   to ask for something
Ha chiesto qualcosa da mangiare.   He asked for something to eat.

guardare qualcosa/qualcuno   to look at something/someone
Guarda la sua faccia.   Look at his face.

pagare qualcosa   to pay for something
Ho già pagato il biglietto.   I've already paid for my ticket.

VERB TABLES

Introduction

The Verb Tables in the following section contain 120 tables of Italian verbs (some regular and some irregular) in alphabetical order. Each table shows you the following forms: Present, Present Subjunctive, Perfect, Imperfect, Future, Conditional, Past Historic, Pluperfect, Imperative and the Past Participle and Gerund. For more information on these tenses, how they are formed, when they are used and so on, you should look at the section on Verb Formation on pages ... to ... If you want to find out in more detail how verbs are used in different contexts, the Easy Learning Italian Grammar will give you additional information.

In order to help you use the verbs shown in Verb Tables correctly, there are also a number of example phrases at the bottom of each page to show the verb as it is used in context.

In Italian there are regular verbs (their forms follow the regular patterns of -are, -ere or -ire verbs), and irregular verbs (their forms do not follow the normal rules). Examples of regular verbs in these tables are:

      parlare (regular -are verb, Verb Table 134)
      credere (regular -ere verb, Verb Table 52)
      capire (regular -ire verb, Verb Table 28)

Some irregular verbs are irregular in most of their forms, while others may only have a couple of irregular forms.

The Verb Index at the end of this section contains over 1000 verbs, each of which is cross-referred to one of the verbs given in the Verb Tables. The table shows the patterns that the verb listed in the index follows.

accadere (to happen)

PRESENT

io	–
tu	–
lui/lei/Lei	**accade**
noi	–
voi	–
loro	**accadono**

PRESENT SUBJUNCTIVE

io	–
tu	–
lui/lei/Lei	**accada**
noi	–
voi	–
loro	**accadano**

PERFECT

io	–
tu	–
lui/lei/Lei	**è accaduto/a**
noi	–
voi	–
loro	**sono accaduti/e**

IMPERFECT

io	–
tu	–
lui/lei/Lei	**accadeva**
noi	–
voi	–
loro	**accadevano**

GERUND
accadendo

PAST PARTICIPLE
accaduto

EXAMPLE PHRASES

All'epoca questo **accadeva** spesso. At that time this often happened.

Stanno **accadendo** molte cose strane. A lot of strange things are happening.

Remember that subject pronouns are not used very often in Italian.

accadere

FUTURE

io	–
tu	–
lui/lei/Lei	**accadrà**
noi	–
voi	–
loro	**accadranno**

CONDITIONAL

io	–
tu	–
lui/lei/Lei	**accadrebbe**
noi	–
voi	–
loro	**accadrebbero**

PAST HISTORIC

io	–
tu	–
lui/lei/Lei	**accadde**
noi	–
voi	–
loro	–

PLUPERFECT

io	–
tu	–
lui/lei/Lei	**era accaduto/a**
noi	–
voi	–
loro	**erano accaduti/e**

IMPERATIVE

–

EXAMPLE PHRASES

Che cosa ti **accadrà**? What will happen to you?

Non sappiamo cosa ci **accadrebbe**. We don't know what would happen to us.

Accadde un fatto meraviglioso. A wonderful thing happened.

Non capivamo ciò che **era accaduto**. We couldn't understand what had happened.

accendere (to light)

PRESENT

io	**accendo**
tu	**accendi**
lui/lei/Lei	**accende**
noi	**accendiamo**
voi	**accendete**
loro	**accendono**

PRESENT SUBJUNCTIVE

io	**accenda**
tu	**accenda**
lui/lei/Lei	**accenda**
noi	**accendiamo**
voi	**accendiate**
loro	**accendano**

PERFECT

io	**ho acceso**
tu	**hai acceso**
lui/lei/Lei	**ha acceso**
noi	**abbiamo acceso**
voi	**avete acceso**
loro	**hanno acceso**

IMPERFECT

io	**accendevo**
tu	**accendevi**
lui/lei/Lei	**accendeva**
noi	**accendevamo**
voi	**accendevate**
loro	**accendevano**

GERUND

accendendo

PAST PARTICIPLE

acceso

EXAMPLE PHRASES

Abbiamo acceso le candeline. We lit the candles.

Appena entrava in casa **accendeva** sempre la radio. He always switched on the radio as soon as he came into the house.

Mi stavo **accendendo** una sigaretta quando è arrivato il bus. I was lighting a cigarette when the bus arrived.

Mi fai **accendere**? Have you got a light?

Remember that subject pronouns are not used very often in Italian.

accendere

(to realize)

FUTURE

io	**accenderò**
tu	**accenderai**
lui/lei/Lei	**accenderà**
noi	**accenderemo**
voi	**accenderete**
loro	**accenderanno**

CONDITIONAL

io	**accenderei**
tu	**accenderesti**
lui/lei/Lei	**accenderebbe**
noi	**accenderemmo**
voi	**accendereste**
loro	**accenderebbero**

PAST HISTORIC

io	**accesi**
tu	**accendesti**
lui/lei/Lei	**accese**
noi	**accendemmo**
voi	**accendeste**
loro	**accesero**

PLUPERFECT

io	**avevo acceso**
tu	**avevi acceso**
lui/lei/Lei	**aveva acceso**
noi	**avevamo acceso**
voi	**avevate acceso**
loro	**avevano acceso**

IMPERATIVE

accendi
accendiamo
accendete

EXAMPLE PHRASES

Appena arrivati **accenderemo** un fuoco. We'll light a fire as soon as we arrive.
Accendi la TV. Turn on the TV.
Avevamo acceso il riscaldamento perché era freddo.
Accese una candela in chiesa. She lit a candle in church.

Italic letters in Italian words show where stress does not follow the usual rules.

accorgersi (to realize)

PRESENT		PRESENT SUBJUNCTIVE	
io	**mi accorgo**	io	**mi accorga**
tu	**ti accorgi**	tu	**ti accorga**
lui/lei/Lei	**si accorge**	lui/lei/Lei	**si accorga**
noi	**ci accorgiamo**	noi	**ci accorgiamo**
voi	**vi accorgete**	voi	**vi accorgiate**
loro	**si accorgono**	loro	**si accorgano**

PERFECT		IMPERFECT	
io	**mi sono accorto/a**	io	**mi accorgevo**
tu	**ti sei accorto/a**	tu	**ti accorgevi**
lui/lei/Lei	**si è accorto/a**	lui/lei/Lei	**si accorgeva**
noi	**ci siamo accorti/e**	noi	**ci accorgevamo**
voi	**vi siete accorti/e**	voi	**vi accorgevate**
loro	**si sono accorti/e**	loro	**si accorgevano**

GERUND	PAST PARTICIPLE
accorgendosi	accorto

EXAMPLE PHRASES

Avvisami se non **mi accorgo** che è tardi. **Warn me if I don't notice it's getting late.**

Mi sono accorto subito che qualcosa non andava. **I immediately realized something was wrong.**

Si è accorto del furto solo il giorno dopo. **He only noticed it had been stolen the next day.**

accorgersi

FUTURE

io	**mi accorgerò**
tu	**ti accorgerai**
lui/lei/Lei	**si accorgerà**
noi	**ci accorgeremo**
voi	**vi accorgerete**
loro	**si accorgeranno**

CONDITIONAL

io	**mi accorgerei**
tu	**ti accorgeresti**
lui/lei/Lei	**si accorgerebbe**
noi	**ci accorgeremmo**
voi	**vi accorgereste**
loro	**si accorgerebbero**

PAST HISTORIC

io	**mi accorsi**
tu	**ti accorgesti**
lui/lei/Lei	**si accorse**
noi	**ci accorgemmo**
voi	**vi accorgeste**
loro	**si accorsero**

PLUPERFECT

io	**mi ero accorto/a**
tu	**ti eri accorto/a**
lui/lei/Lei	**si era accorto/a**
noi	**ci eravamo accorti/e**
voi	**vi eravate accorti/e**
loro	**si erano accorti/e**

IMPERATIVE
accorgiti
accorgiamoci
accorgetevi

EXAMPLE PHRASES

Un giorno si **accorgerà** di te. Some day he'll notice you.

Se tu mi ingannassi, **me ne accorgerei**. If you were tricking me I'd notice.

Era malato ma nessuno se ne **accorse**. He was ill, but nobody noticed.

Non si **erano accorti** che ero nella stanza. They hadn't noticed that I was in the room.

È difficile **accorgersi** degli errori di battitura. It's difficult to notice typing errors.

Italic letters in Italian words show where stress does not follow the usual rules.

addormentarsi (to go to sleep)

PRESENT

io	**mi addormento**
tu	**ti addormenti**
lui/lei/Lei	**si addormenta**
noi	**ci addormentiamo**
voi	**vi addormentate**
loro	**si addormentano**

PRESENT SUBJUNCTIVE

io	**mi addormenti**
tu	**ti addormenti**
lui/lei/Lei	**si addormenti**
noi	**ci addormentiamo**
voi	**vi addormentiate**
loro	**si addormentino**

PERFECT

io	**mi sono addormentato/a**
tu	**ti sei addormentato/a**
lui/lei/Lei	**si è addormentato/a**
noi	**ci siamo addormentati/e**
voi	**vi siete addormentati/e**
loro	**si sono addormentati/e**

IMPERFECT

io	**mi addormentavo**
tu	**ti addormentavi**
lui/lei/Lei	**si addormentava**
noi	**ci addormentavamo**
voi	**vi addormentavate**
loro	**si addormentavano**

GERUND
addormentando

PAST PARTICIPLE
addormentato

EXAMPLE PHRASES

Mio padre **si addormenta** sempre davanti alla TV. My father always goes to sleep in front of the TV.

Mi **si è addormentato** un piede. My foot has gone to sleep.

Non riesco ad **addormentarmi**. I can't get to sleep.

Non voleva **addormentarsi**. He didn't want to go to sleep.

addormentarsi

FUTURE

io	**mi addormenterò**
tu	**ti addormenterai**
lui/lei/Lei	**si addormenterà**
noi	**ci addormenteremo**
voi	**vi addormenterete**
loro	**si addormenteranno**

CONDITIONAL

io	**mi addormenterei**
tu	**ti addormenteresti**
lui/lei/Lei	**si addormenterebbe**
noi	**ci addormenteremmo**
voi	**vi addormentereste**
loro	**si addormenterebbero**

PAST HISTORIC

io	**mi addormentai**
tu	**ti addormentasti**
lui/lei/Lei	**si addormentò**
noi	**ci addormentammo**
voi	**vi addormentaste**
loro	**si addormentarono**

PLUPERFECT

io	**mi ero addormentato/a**
tu	**ti eri addormentato/a**
lui/lei/Lei	**si era addormentato/a**
noi	**ci eravamo addormentati/e**
voi	**vi eravate addormentati/e**
loro	**si erano addormentati/e**

IMPERATIVE

addormentati
addormentiamoci
addormentatevi

EXAMPLE PHRASES

Leggo sempre prima di **addormentarmi**. I always read before I go to sleep.
Sono stanco: stasera **mi addormenterò** subito. I'm tired: I'll go to sleep
immediately tonight.
Non mi accorsi che **si era addormentata**. I didn't realize she'd gone to sleep.

Italic letters in Italian words show where stress does not follow the usual rules.

andare (to go)

PRESENT		PRESENT SUBJUNCTIVE	
io	**vado**	io	**vada**
tu	**vai**	tu	**vada**
lui/lei/Lei	**va**	lui/lei/Lei	**vada**
noi	**andiamo**	noi	**andiamo**
voi	**andate**	voi	**andiate**
loro	**vanno**	loro	**vadano**

PERFECT		IMPERFECT	
io	**sono andato/a**	io	**andavo**
tu	**sei andato/a**	tu	**andavi**
lui/lei/Lei	**è andato/a**	lui/lei/Lei	**andava**
noi	**siamo andati/e**	noi	**andavamo**
voi	**siete andati/e**	voi	**andavate**
loro	**sono andati/e**	loro	**andavano**

GERUND

andando

PAST PARTICIPLE

andato

EXAMPLE PHRASES

Su, **andiamo**! Come on, let's go!

Come **va**? – bene, grazie! How are you? – fine thanks!

La mamma vuole che tu **vada** a fare la spesa. Mum wants you to go and do the shopping.

Questo mese non **sono** ancora **andata** al cinema. I haven't been to the cinema yet this month.

Com'**è andata**? How did it go?

L'anno scorso **andavo** sempre a dormire tardi. Last year I always went to bed late.

Remember that subject pronouns are not used very often in Italian.

andare

FUTURE

io	andrò
tu	andrai
lui/lei/Lei	andrà
noi	andremo
voi	andrete
loro	andranno

CONDITIONAL

io	andrei
tu	andresti
lui/lei/Lei	andrebbe
noi	andremmo
voi	andreste
loro	andrebbero

PAST HISTORIC

io	andai
tu	andasti
lui/lei/Lei	andò
noi	andammo
voi	andaste
loro	andarono

PLUPERFECT

io	ero andato/a
tu	eri andato/a
lui/lei/Lei	era andato/a
noi	eravamo andati/e
voi	eravate andati/e
loro	erano andati/e

IMPERATIVE

vai
andiamo
andate

EXAMPLE PHRASES

Andremo in Grecia quest'estate. We're going *to* Greece this summer.

Stasera **andrei** volentieri al ristorante. I'd like to go to a restaurant this evening.

Andarono a trovare la nonna. They went to see their grandmother.

Era **andato** all'estero, ma è tornato quasi subito. He'd gone abroad, and returned almost immediately.

Italic letters in Italian words show where stress does not follow the usual rules.

apparire (to appear)

PRESENT	
io	appaio
tu	appari
lui/lei/Lei	appare
noi	appariamo
voi	apparite
loro	appaiono

PRESENT SUBJUNCTIVE	
io	appaia
tu	appaia
lui/lei/Lei	appaia
noi	appaiamo
voi	appaiate
loro	appaiano

PERFECT	
io	sono apparso/a
tu	sei apparso/a
lui/lei/Lei	è apparso/a
noi	siamo apparsi/e
voi	siete apparsi/e
loro	sono apparsi/e

IMPERFECT	
io	apparivo
tu	apparivi
lui/lei/Lei	appariva
noi	apparivamo
voi	apparivate
loro	apparivano

GERUND

apparendo

PAST PARTICIPLE

apparso

EXAMPLE PHRASES

Oggi Mario **appare** turbato. Mario seems upset today.

Aspettiamo che **appaia** la luce del faro. Let's wait until we see the beam of the lighthouse.

Il fantasma **appariva** ogni sera a mezzanotte. The ghost appeared every night at twelve o'clock.

Finalmente una nave **apparve** all'orizzonte. At last a ship appeared on the horizon.

Remember that subject pronouns are not used very often in Italian.

apparire

FUTURE		**CONDITIONAL**	
io	apparirò	io	apparirei
tu	apparirai	tu	appariresti
lui/lei/Lei	apparirà	lui/lei/Lei	apparirebbe
noi	appariremo	noi	appariremmo
voi	apparirete	voi	apparireste
loro	appariranno	loro	apparirebbero

PAST HISTORIC		**PLUPERFECT**	
io	apparvi	io	ero apparso/a
tu	apparisti	tu	eri apparso/a
lui/lei/Lei	apparve	lui/lei/Lei	era apparso/a
noi	apparimmo	noi	eravamo apparsi/e
voi	appariste	voi	eravate apparsi/e
loro	apparvero	loro	erano apparsi/e

IMPERATIVE

appari
appariamo
apparite

EXAMPLE PHRASES

Tra poco il sole **apparirà** in cielo. The sun will soon appear in the sky.

Con quel vestito **appariresti** ridicolo. You'd look silly in that suit.

I soldati si fermarono: i banditi **erano apparsi** tra le rocce. The soldiers halted: the bandits had appeared from among the rocks.

Non vorrei **apparire** maleducato. I wouldn't want to seem rude.

---

aprire (to open)

PRESENT

io	**apro**
tu	**apri**
lui/lei/Lei	**apre**
noi	**apriamo**
voi	**aprite**
loro	**aprono**

PRESENT SUBJUNCTIVE

io	**apra**
tu	**apra**
lui/lei/Lei	**apra**
noi	**apriamo**
voi	**apriate**
loro	**aprano**

PERFECT

io	**ho aperto**
tu	**hai aperto**
lui/lei/Lei	**ha aperto**
noi	**abbiamo aperto**
voi	**avete aperto**
loro	**hanno aperto**

IMPERFECT

io	**aprivo**
tu	**aprivi**
lui/lei/Lei	**apriva**
noi	**aprivamo**
voi	**aprivate**
loro	**aprivano**

GERUND

aprendo

PAST PARTICIPLE

aperto

EXAMPLE PHRASES

Posso **aprire** la finestra? Can I open the window?

Dai, non **apri** i regali? Come on, aren't you going to open your presents?

Non **ha aperto** bocca. She didn't say a word.

Non voglio che **apriate** i regali prima di Natale. I don't want you to open your presents before Christmas.

Si è tagliato **aprendo** una scatola di tonno. He cut himself opening a tin of tuna.

Remember that subject pronouns are not used very often in Italian.

aprire

FUTURE

io	**aprirò**
tu	**aprirai**
lui/lei/Lei	**aprirà**
noi	**apriremo**
voi	**aprirete**
loro	**apriranno**

CONDITIONAL

io	**aprirei**
tu	**apriresti**
lui/lei/Lei	**aprirebbe**
noi	**apriremmo**
voi	**aprireste**
loro	**aprirebbero**

PAST HISTORIC

io	**aprii**
tu	**apristi**
lui/lei/Lei	**aprì**
noi	**aprimmo**
voi	**apriste**
loro	**aprirono**

PLUPERFECT

io	**avevo aperto**
tu	**avevi aperto**
lui/lei/Lei	**aveva aperto**
noi	**avevamo aperto**
voi	**avevate aperto**
loro	**avevano aperto**

IMPERATIVE

apri
apriamo
aprite

EXAMPLE PHRASES

Aprirono lo champagne e festeggiarono. **They opened the champagne and celebrated.**

Aveva aperto la busta per leggere la lettera. **She'd opened the envelope to read the letter.**

Apri il rubinetto e innaffia il giardino. **Turn on the tap and water the garden.**

Polizia! **Aprite** questa porta! **Police! Open the door!**

Italic letters in Italian words show where stress does not follow the usual rules.

arrivare (to arrive)

PRESENT		**PRESENT SUBJUNCTIVE**	
io	**arrivo**	io	**arrivi**
tu	**arrivi**	tu	**arrivi**
lui/lei/Lei	**arriva**	lui/lei/Lei	**arrivi**
noi	**arriviamo**	noi	**arriviamo**
voi	**arrivate**	voi	**arriviate**
loro	**arrivano**	loro	**arrivino**

PERFECT		**IMPERFECT**	
io	**sono arrivato/a**	io	**arrivavo**
tu	**sei arrivato/a**	tu	**arrivavi**
lui/lei/Lei	**è arrivato/a**	lui/lei/Lei	**arrivava**
noi	**siamo arrivati/e**	noi	**arrivavamo**
voi	**siete arrivati/e**	voi	**arrivavate**
loro	**sono arrivati/e**	loro	**arrivavano**

GERUND	**PAST PARTICIPLE**
arrivando	arrivato

EXAMPLE PHRASES

Come si **arriva** al castello? How do you get to the castle?
A che ora **arrivi** a scuola? What time do you get to school?
Sono arrivato a Londra alle sette. I arrived in London at seven.
È troppo in alto, non ci **arrivo**. It's too high, I can't reach it.
Non **arrivava** mai in orario. He never arrived on time.
Aspettami, sto **arrivando**! Wait, I'm coming!

Remember that subject pronouns are not used very often in Italian.

arrivare

FUTURE

io	**arriverò**
tu	**arriverai**
lui/lei/Lei	**arriverà**
noi	**arriveremo**
voi	**arriverete**
loro	**arriveranno**

CONDITIONAL

io	**arriverei**
tu	**arriveresti**
lui/lei/Lei	**arriverebbe**
noi	**arriveremmo**
voi	**arrivereste**
loro	**arriverebbero**

PAST HISTORIC

io	**arrivai**
tu	**arrivasti**
lui/lei/Lei	**arrivò**
noi	**arrivammo**
voi	**arrivaste**
loro	**arrivarono**

PLUPERFECT

io	**ero arrivato/a**
tu	**eri arrivato/a**
lui/lei/Lei	**era arrivato/a**
noi	**eravamo arrivati/e**
voi	**eravate arrivati/e**
loro	**erano arrivati/e**

IMPERATIVE

arriva
arriviamo
arrivate

EXAMPLE PHRASES

Arriveremo in ritardo per colpa del traffico. We'll get there late because of the traffic.

Arrivammo al rifugio molto stanchi. We were very tired when we got to the mountain refuge.

Dopo due giorni di viaggio **era** finalmente **arrivata**. After two days' travelling he'd at last arrived.

Italic letters in Italian words show where stress does not follow the usual rules.

assumere (to take on, to employ)

PRESENT

io	**assumo**
tu	**assumi**
lui/lei/Lei	**assume**
noi	**assumiamo**
voi	**assumete**
loro	**assumono**

PRESENT SUBJUNCTIVE

io	**assuma**
tu	**assuma**
lui/lei/Lei	**assuma**
noi	**assumiamo**
voi	**assumiate**
loro	**assumano**

PERFECT

io	**ho assunto**
tu	**hai assunto**
lui/lei/Lei	**ha assunto**
noi	**abbiamo assunto**
voi	**avete assunto**
loro	**hanno assunto**

IMPERFECT

io	**assumevo**
tu	**assumevi**
lui/lei/Lei	**assumeva**
noi	**assumevamo**
voi	**assumevate**
loro	**assumevano**

GERUND

assumendo

PAST PARTICIPLE

assunto

EXAMPLE PHRASES

La ditta **assumeva** e ho presentato il curriculum. The company was taking on staff and I sent in my CV.

Sua moglie vuole **assumere** una colf. His wife wants to employ someone to help in the house.

C'è troppo lavoro: **assumiamo** del personale. There's too much work: let's take on some more staff.

È stata **assunta** come programmatrice. She's got a job as a programmer.

Remember that subject pronouns are not used very often in Italian.

assumere

FUTURE

io	**assumerò**
tu	**assumerai**
lui/lei/Lei	**assumerà**
noi	**assumeremo**
voi	**assumerete**
loro	**assumeranno**

CONDITIONAL

io	**assumerei**
tu	**assumeresti**
lui/lei/Lei	**assumerebbe**
noi	**assumeremmo**
voi	**assumereste**
loro	**assumerebbero**

PAST HISTORIC

io	**assunsi**
tu	**assumesti**
lui/lei/Lei	**assunse**
noi	**assumemmo**
voi	**assumeste**
loro	**assunsero**

PLUPERFECT

io	**avevo assunto**
tu	**avevi assunto**
lui/lei/Lei	**aveva assunto**
noi	**avevamo assunto**
voi	**avevate assunto**
loro	**avevano assunto**

IMPERATIVE

assumi
assumiamo
assumete

EXAMPLE PHRASES

L'azienda **assumerà** due operai. The company is going to take on two workers.

Sei bravo: ti **assumerei** come assistente. You're good: I'd give you a job as an assistant.

avere (to have)

PRESENT		PRESENT SUBJUNCTIVE	
io	**ho**	io	**abbia**
tu	**hai**	tu	**abbia**
lui/lei/Lei	**ha**	lui/lei/Lei	**abbia**
noi	**abbiamo**	noi	**abbiamo**
voi	**avete**	voi	**abbiate**
loro	**hanno**	loro	**abbiano**

PERFECT		IMPERFECT	
io	**ho avuto**	io	**avevo**
tu	**hai avuto**	tu	**avevi**
lui/lei/Lei	**ha avuto**	lui/lei/Lei	**aveva**
noi	**abbiamo avuto**	noi	**avevamo**
voi	**avete avuto**	voi	**avevate**
loro	**hanno avuto**	loro	**avevano**

GERUND	PAST PARTICIPLE
avendo	avuto

EXAMPLE PHRASES

All'inizio **ha avuto** un sacco di problemi. **He had a lot of problems at first.**

Ho già mangiato. **I've already eaten.**

Ha la macchina nuova. **She's got a new car.**

Non penso che tu **abbia** il coraggio necessario per farlo. **I don't think you're brave enough to do it.**

Quanti ne **abbiamo** oggi? **What's the date today?**

Aveva la mia età. **He was the same age as me.**

Remember that subject pronouns are not used very often in Italian.

avere

FUTURE		**CONDITIONAL**	
io	avrò	io	avrei
tu	avrai	tu	avresti
lui/lei/Lei	avrà	lui/lei/Lei	avrebbe
noi	avremo	noi	avremmo
voi	avrete	voi	avreste
loro	avranno	loro	avrebbero

PAST HISTORIC		**PLUPERFECT**	
io	ebbi	io	avevo avuto
tu	avesti	tu	avevi avuto
lui/lei/Lei	ebbe	lui/lei/Lei	aveva avuto
noi	avemmo	noi	avevamo avuto
voi	aveste	voi	avevate avuto
loro	ebbero	loro	avevano avuto

IMPERATIVE

abbi
abbiamo
abbiate

EXAMPLE PHRASES

Quanti anni **avrà**? How old do you think she is?

Quando **ebbe** fame, mangiò. When he was hungry he had something to eat.

Prima di atterrare **avevano avuto** veramente paura. Before the plane landed they'd been really frightened.

Abbi pazienza, non ho ancora finito! Be patient, I've not finished yet!

Italic letters in Italian words show where stress does not follow the usual rules.

bere (to drink)

PRESENT		**PRESENT SUBJUNCTIVE**	
io	**bevo**	io	**beva**
tu	**bevi**	tu	**beva**
lui/lei/Lei	**beve**	lui/lei/Lei	**beva**
noi	**beviamo**	noi	**beviamo**
voi	**bevete**	voi	**beviate**
loro	**bevono**	loro	**bevano**

PERFECT		**IMPERFECT**	
io	**ho bevuto**	io	**bevevo**
tu	**hai bevuto**	tu	**bevevi**
lui/lei/Lei	**ha bevuto**	lui/lei/Lei	**beveva**
noi	**abbiamo bevuto**	noi	**bevevamo**
voi	**avete bevuto**	voi	**bevevate**
loro	**hanno bevuto**	loro	**bevevano**

GERUND	**PAST PARTICIPLE**
bevendo	bevuto

EXAMPLE PHRASES

Vuoi **bere** qualcosa? Would you like something to drink?

Chi porta da **bere**? Who's going to bring the drinks?

Ho l'impressione che tu **beva** troppo. I've a feeling you drink too much.

Mai **bevuto** un vino così! I've never tasted a wine like this!

Beveva sei caffè al giorno, ma ora ha smesso. He used to drink six cups of coffee a day, but he's stopped now.

Bevendo così si ubriacherà di sicuro. If he drinks like that he'll be bound to get drunk.

Remember that subject pronouns are not used very often in Italian.

bere

FUTURE

io	**berrò**
tu	**berrai**
lui/lei/Lei	**berrà**
noi	**berremo**
voi	**berrete**
loro	**berranno**

CONDITIONAL

io	**berrei**
tu	**berresti**
lui/lei/Lei	**berrebbe**
noi	**berremmo**
voi	**berreste**
loro	**berrebbero**

PAST HISTORIC

io	**bevvi**
tu	**bevesti**
lui/lei/Lei	**bevve**
noi	**bevemmo**
voi	**beveste**
loro	**bevvero**

PLUPERFECT

io	**avevo bevuto**
tu	**avevi bevuto**
lui/lei/Lei	**aveva bevuto**
noi	**avevamo bevuto**
voi	**avevate bevuto**
loro	**avevano bevuto**

IMPERATIVE

bevi
beviamo
bevete

EXAMPLE PHRASES

Berrei volentieri un bicchiere di vino bianco. I'd love a glass of white wine.

Non sono potuti tornare in auto perché **avevano bevuto**. They couldn't drive back because they'd been drinking.

Beviamo alla salute degli sposi! Let's drink to the health of the bride and groom!

Italic letters in Italian words show where stress does not follow the usual rules.

cadere (to fall)

PRESENT

io	**cado**
tu	**cadi**
lui/lei/Lei	**cade**
noi	**cadiamo**
voi	**cadete**
loro	**cadono**

PRESENT SUBJUNCTIVE

io	**cada**
tu	**cada**
lui/lei/Lei	**cada**
noi	**cadiamo**
voi	**cadiate**
loro	**cadano**

PERFECT

io	**sono caduto/a**
tu	**sei caduto/a**
lui/lei/Lei	**è caduto/a**
noi	**siamo caduti/e**
voi	**siete caduti/e**
loro	**sono caduti/e**

IMPERFECT

io	**cadevo**
tu	**cadevi**
lui/lei/Lei	**cadeva**
noi	**cadevamo**
voi	**cadevate**
loro	**cadevano**

GERUND
cadendo

PAST PARTICIPLE
caduto

EXAMPLE PHRASES

Il mio compleanno **cade** di lunedì. My birthday is on a Monday.

Ti **è caduta** la sciarpa. You've dropped your scarf.

Ho inciampato e **sono caduta**. I tripped and fell.

È caduta la linea. We were cut off.

Attento che fai **cadere** il bicchiere. Mind you don't knock over your glass.

Ha fatto **cadere** il vassoio. She dropped the tray.

Si è fatta male **cadendo** con i pattini. She fell and hurt herself when she was skating.

Remember that subject pronouns are not used very often in Italian.

cadere

FUTURE

io	cadrò
tu	cadrai
lui/lei/Lei	cadrà
noi	cadremo
voi	cadrete
loro	cadranno

CONDITIONAL

io	cadrei
tu	cadresti
lui/lei/Lei	cadrebbe
noi	cadremmo
voi	cadreste
loro	cadrebbero

PAST HISTORIC

io	caddi
tu	cadesti
lui/lei/Lei	cadde
noi	cademmo
voi	cadeste
loro	caddero

PLUPERFECT

io	ero caduto/a
tu	eri caduto/a
lui/lei/Lei	era caduto/a
noi	eravamo caduti/e
voi	eravate caduti/e
loro	erano caduti/e

IMPERATIVE

cadi
cadiamo
cadete

EXAMPLE PHRASES

Quando glielo diremo **cadranno** dalle nuvole. When we tell them they'll be amazed.
Cadde dalla bicicletta. She fell off her bike.

---

cambiare (to change)

PRESENT		**PRESENT SUBJUNCTIVE**	
io	cambio	io	cambi
tu	cambi	tu	cambi
lui/lei/Lei	cambia	lui/lei/Lei	cambi
noi	cambiamo	noi	cambiamo
voi	cambiate	voi	cambiate
loro	cambiano	loro	cambino

PERFECT		**IMPERFECT**	
io	ho cambiato	io	cambiavo
tu	hai cambiato	tu	cambiavi
lui/lei/Lei	ha cambiato	lui/lei/Lei	cambiava
noi	abbiamo cambiato	noi	cambiavamo
voi	avete cambiato	voi	cambiavate
loro	hanno cambiato	loro	cambiavano

GERUND

cambiando

PAST PARTICIPLE

cambiato

EXAMPLE PHRASES

È necessario che **cambiate** atteggiamento. You need to change your attitude.

Era confuso e **cambiava** opinione in continuazione. He was confused and kept changing his mind.

Ultimamente è molto **cambiato**. He's changed a lot recently.

Vorrei **cambiare** questi euro in sterline. I'd like to change these euros into pounds.

Remember that subject pronouns are not used very often in Italian.

cambiare

FUTURE

io	**cambierò**
tu	**cambierai**
lui/lei/Lei	**cambierà**
noi	**cambieremo**
voi	**cambierete**
loro	**cambieranno**

CONDITIONAL

io	**cambierei**
tu	**cambieresti**
lui/lei/Lei	**cambierebbe**
noi	**cambieremmo**
voi	**cambiereste**
loro	**cambierebbero**

PAST HISTORIC

io	**cambiai**
tu	**cambiasti**
lui/lei/Lei	**cambiò**
noi	**cambiammo**
voi	**cambiaste**
loro	**cambiarono**

PLUPERFECT

io	**avevo cambiato**
tu	**avevi cambiato**
lui/lei/Lei	**aveva cambiato**
noi	**avevamo cambiato**
voi	**avevate cambiato**
loro	**avevano cambiato**

IMPERATIVE

cambia
cambiamo
cambiate

EXAMPLE PHRASES

Cambieremo casa il mese prossimo. We're moving house next month.

Cambiammo idea e prendemmo quell'altro. We changed our mind and took the other one.

Ci **cambiammo** prima di uscire. We got changed before we went out.

Aveva cambiato l'auto poco prima del furto. She'd changed the car shortly before it was stolen.

Cambiamo argomento. Let's change the subject.

Italic letters in Italian words show where stress does not follow the usual rules.

capire (to understand)

PRESENT		PRESENT SUBJUNCTIVE	
io	**capisco**	io	**capisca**
tu	**capisci**	tu	**capisca**
lui/lei/Lei	**capisce**	lui/lei/Lei	**capisca**
noi	**capiamo**	noi	**capiamo**
voi	**capite**	voi	**capiate**
loro	**capiscono**	loro	**capiscano**

PERFECT		IMPERFECT	
io	**ho capito**	io	**capivo**
tu	**hai capito**	tu	**capivi**
lui/lei/Lei	**ha capito**	lui/lei/Lei	**capiva**
noi	**abbiamo capito**	noi	**capivamo**
voi	**avete capito**	voi	**capivate**
loro	**hanno capito**	loro	**capivano**

GERUND	PAST PARTICIPLE
capendo	capito

EXAMPLE PHRASES

Va bene, **capisco**. OK, I understand.

È necessario che **capiate** bene le istruzioni. You've got to understand the
instructions properly.

Non **ho capito** una parola. I didn't understand a word.

Non **ho capito**, puoi ripetere? I *don't* understand, could you say it again?

Fammi **capire**... Let me get this straight...

Capivamo le sue ragioni, ma aveva torto. We understood his motives,
but he was wrong.

Remember that subject pronouns are not used very often in Italian.

capire

FUTURE

io	capirò
tu	capirai
lui/lei/Lei	capirà
noi	capiremo
voi	capirete
loro	capiranno

CONDITIONAL

io	capirei
tu	capiresti
lui/lei/Lei	capirebbe
noi	capiremmo
voi	capireste
loro	capirebbero

PAST HISTORIC

io	capii
tu	capisti
lui/lei/Lei	capì
noi	capimmo
voi	capiste
loro	capirono

PLUPERFECT

io	avevo capito
tu	avevi capito
lui/lei/Lei	aveva capito
noi	avevamo capito
voi	avevate capito
loro	avevano capito

IMPERATIVE

capisci
capiamo
capite

EXAMPLE PHRASES

Non ti **capirò** mai. I'll never understand you.

Se mi volessi bene, mi **capiresti**. If you loved me, you'd understand me.

Capirono che era ora di andarsene. They realized it was time to go.

Avevamo capito male le sue intenzioni. We'd misunderstood his intentions.

Italic letters in Italian words show where stress does not follow the usual rules.

cercare (to look for)

PRESENT

io	**cerco**
tu	**cerchi**
lui/lei/Lei	**cerca**
noi	**cerchiamo**
voi	**cercate**
loro	**cercano**

PRESENT SUBJUNCTIVE

io	**cerchi**
tu	**cerchi**
lui/lei/Lei	**cerchi**
noi	**cerchiamo**
voi	**cerchiate**
loro	**cerchino**

PERFECT

io	**ho cercato**
tu	**hai cercato**
lui/lei/Lei	**ha cercato**
noi	**abbiamo cercato**
voi	**avete cercato**
loro	**hanno cercato**

IMPERFECT

io	**cercavo**
tu	**cercavi**
lui/lei/Lei	**cercava**
noi	**cercavamo**
voi	**cercavate**
loro	**cercavano**

GERUND

cercando

PAST PARTICIPLE

cercato

EXAMPLE PHRASES

Io non **cerco** guai. I'm not looking for trouble.

È bene che **cerchiate** di essere puntuali. You'd do well to try to be punctual.

Le **ho cercate** dappertutto. I've looked for them everywhere.

Stai **cercando** lavoro? Are you looking for a job?

Sta **cercando** di imparare l'inglese. He's trying to learn English.

Remember that subject pronouns are not used very often in Italian.

cercare

FUTURE

io	cercherò
tu	cercherai
lui/lei/Lei	cercherà
noi	cercheremo
voi	cercherete
loro	cercheranno

CONDITIONAL

io	cercherei
tu	cercheresti
lui/lei/Lei	cercherebbe
noi	cercheremmo
voi	cerchereste
loro	cercherebbero

PAST HISTORIC

io	cercai
tu	cercasti
lui/lei/Lei	cercò
noi	cercammo
voi	cercaste
loro	cercarono

PLUPERFECT

io	avevo cercato
tu	avevi cercato
lui/lei/Lei	aveva cercato
noi	avevamo cercato
voi	avevate cercato
loro	avevano cercato

IMPERATIVE

cerca
cerchiamo
cercate

EXAMPLE PHRASES

Mi **cercheresti** il suo numero nell'agenda? Would you look for his number in your diary?

Cercammo di spiegargli il motivo. We tried to explain the reason to him.

Cerca di non fare tardi. Try not to be late.

chiedere (to ask)

PRESENT

io	**chiedo**
tu	**chiedi**
lui/lei/Lei	**chiede**
noi	**chiediamo**
voi	**chiedete**
loro	**chiedono**

PRESENT SUBJUNCTIVE

io	**chieda**
tu	**chieda**
lui/lei/Lei	**chieda**
noi	**chiediamo**
voi	**chiediate**
loro	**chiedano**

PERFECT

io	**ho chiesto**
tu	**hai chiesto**
lui/lei/Lei	**ha chiesto**
noi	**abbiamo chiesto**
voi	**avete chiesto**
loro	**hanno chiesto**

IMPERFECT

io	**chiedevo**
tu	**chiedevi**
lui/lei/Lei	**chiedeva**
noi	**chiedevamo**
voi	**chiedevate**
loro	**chiedevano**

GERUND

chiedendo

PAST PARTICIPLE

chiesto

EXAMPLE PHRASES

Non **chiedo** mai favori a nessuno. I never ask anyone for favours.

Mi **ha chiesto** l'ora. He asked me the time.

Se non lo sai, basta **chiedere**. If you don't know, just ask.

chiedere

FUTURE

io	**chiederò**
tu	**chiederai**
lui/lei/Lei	**chiederà**
noi	**chiederemo**
voi	**chiederete**
loro	**chiederanno**

CONDITIONAL

io	**chiederei**
tu	**chiederesti**
lui/lei/Lei	**chiederebbe**
noi	**chiederemmo**
voi	**chiedereste**
loro	**chiederebbero**

PAST HISTORIC

io	**chiesi**
tu	**chiedesti**
lui/lei/Lei	**chiese**
noi	**chiedemmo**
voi	**chiedeste**
loro	**chiesero**

PLUPERFECT

io	**avevo chiesto**
tu	**avevi chiesto**
lui/lei/Lei	**aveva chiesto**
noi	**avevamo chiesto**
voi	**avevate chiesto**
loro	**avevano chiesto**

IMPERATIVE

chiedi
chiediamo
chiedete

EXAMPLE PHRASES

Chiederemo agli amici di ospitarci. We'll ask our friends to put us up.

Chiederesti a Giulia di spostarsi un po'? Would you ask Giulia to move a bit?

Chiedemmo la strada per la stazione. We asked the way to the station.

Avevo chiesto il conto al cameriere, ma è sparito. I'd asked the waiter for the bill, but he disappeared.

Chiedi a Lidia come si chiama il suo cane. Ask Lidia what her dog's called.

Italic letters in Italian words show where stress does not follow the usual rules.

chiudere (to close)

PRESENT

io	chiudo
tu	chiudi
lui/lei/Lei	chiude
noi	chiudiamo
voi	chiudete
loro	chiudono

PRESENT SUBJUNCTIVE

io	chiuda
tu	chiuda
lui/lei/Lei	chiuda
noi	chiudiamo
voi	chiudiate
loro	chiudano

PERFECT

io	ho chiuso
tu	hai chiuso
lui/lei/Lei	ha chiuso
noi	abbiamo chiuso
voi	avete chiuso
loro	hanno chiuso

IMPERFECT

io	chiudevo
tu	chiudevi
lui/lei/Lei	chiudeva
noi	chiudevamo
voi	chiudevate
loro	chiudevano

GERUND

chiudendo

PAST PARTICIPLE

chiuso

EXAMPLE PHRASES

Un momento! **Chiudo** casa e scendo. I'll just be a minute. I'll lock the door and come down.

È meglio che tu **chiuda** a chiave. You'd better lock the door.

La fabbrica **ha chiuso** due anni fa. The factory closed two years ago.

Con lui **ho chiuso**. I've finished with him.

Remember that subject pronouns are not used very often in Italian.

chiudere

FUTURE

io	**chiuderò**
tu	**chiuderai**
lui/lei/Lei	**chiuderà**
noi	**chiuderemo**
voi	**chiuderete**
loro	**chiuderanno**

CONDITIONAL

io	**chiuderei**
tu	**chiuderesti**
lui/lei/Lei	**chiuderebbe**
noi	**chiuderemmo**
voi	**chiudereste**
loro	**chiuderebbero**

PAST HISTORIC

io	**chiusi**
tu	**chiudesti**
lui/lei/Lei	**chiuse**
noi	**chiudemmo**
voi	**chiudeste**
loro	**chiusero**

PLUPERFECT

io	**avevo chiuso**
tu	**avevi chiuso**
lui/lei/Lei	**aveva chiuso**
noi	**avevamo chiuso**
voi	**avevate chiuso**
loro	**avevano chiuso**

IMPERATIVE

chiudi
chiudiamo
chiudete

EXAMPLE PHRASES

A che ora **chiuderà** il negozio? What time will the shop shut?

La porta si **chiuse**. The door closed.

L'ho sgridato perché non **aveva chiuso** il gas. I told him off because he'd not turned the gas off.

Chiudi bene il rubinetto. Turn the tap off properly.

Italic letters in Italian words show where stress does not follow the usual rules.

cogliere (to pick)

PRESENT

io	colgo
tu	cogli
lui/lei/Lei	coglie
noi	cogliamo
voi	cogliete
loro	colgono

PRESENT SUBJUNCTIVE

io	colga
tu	colga
lui/lei/Lei	colga
noi	cogliamo
voi	cogliate
loro	colgano

PERFECT

io	ho colto
tu	hai colto
lui/lei/Lei	ha colto
noi	abbiamo colto
voi	avete colto
loro	hanno colto

IMPERFECT

io	coglievo
tu	coglievi
lui/lei/Lei	coglieva
noi	coglievamo
voi	coglievate
loro	coglievano

GERUND

cogliendo

PAST PARTICIPLE

colto

EXAMPLE PHRASES

Colgo l'occasione per augurarvi buon Natale. May I take this opportunity to wish you a happy Christmas.

L'**ho colto** sul fatto. I caught him red-handed.

Stavamo **cogliendo** dei fiori quando arrivò il temporale. We were picking flowers when the storm started.

Remember that subject pronouns are not used very often in Italian.

cogliere

FUTURE

io	**coglierò**
tu	**coglierai**
lui/lei/Lei	**coglierà**
noi	**coglieremo**
voi	**coglierete**
loro	**coglieranno**

CONDITIONAL

io	**coglierei**
tu	**coglieresti**
lui/lei/Lei	**coglierebbe**
noi	**coglieremmo**
voi	**cogliereste**
loro	**coglierebbero**

PAST HISTORIC

io	**colsi**
tu	**cogliesti**
lui/lei/Lei	**colse**
noi	**cogliemmo**
voi	**coglieste**
loro	**colsero**

PLUPERFECT

io	**avevo colto**
tu	**avevi colto**
lui/lei/Lei	**aveva colto**
noi	**avevamo colto**
voi	**avevate colto**
loro	**avevano colto**

IMPERATIVE

cogli
cogliamo
cogliete

EXAMPLE PHRASES

Tra qualche giorno **coglieranno** le fragole. In a few days' time they'll be picking the strawberries.

Colsi una mela dall'albero. I picked an apple off the tree.

Andiamo in campagna a **cogliere** la frutta. Let's go into the countryside and pick some fruit.

Italic letters in Italian words show where stress does not follow the usual rules.

cominciare (to start)

PRESENT		**PRESENT SUBJUNCTIVE**	
io	comincio	io	cominci
tu	cominci	tu	cominci
lui/lei/Lei	comincia	lui/lei/Lei	cominci
noi	cominciamo	noi	cominciamo
voi	cominciate	voi	cominciate
loro	cominciano	loro	comincino

PERFECT		**IMPERFECT**	
io	ho cominciato	io	cominciavo
tu	hai cominciato	tu	cominciavi
lui/lei/Lei	ha cominciato	lui/lei/Lei	cominciava
noi	abbiamo cominciato	noi	cominciavamo
voi	avete cominciato	voi	cominciavate
loro	hanno cominciato	loro	cominciavano

GERUND

cominciando

PAST PARTICIPLE

cominciato

EXAMPLE PHRASES

Il film **comincia** con un'esplosione. The film starts with an explosion.

Hai **cominciato** il libro che ti ho prestato? Have you started the book
 I lent you?

Faceva freddo e **cominciava** a nevicare. It was cold and starting to snow.

Cominciando oggi, dovrei finire lunedì. If I start today I should finish
 on Monday.

cominciare

FUTURE		**CONDITIONAL**	
io	comincerò	io	comincerei
tu	comincerai	tu	cominceresti
lui/lei/Lei	comincerà	lui/lei/Lei	comincerebbe
noi	cominceremo	noi	cominceremmo
voi	comincerete	voi	comincereste
loro	cominceranno	loro	comincerebbero

PAST HISTORIC		**PLUPERFECT**	
io	cominciai	io	avevo cominciato
tu	cominciasti	tu	avevi cominciato
lui/lei/Lei	cominciò	lui/lei/Lei	aveva cominciato
noi	cominciammo	noi	avevamo cominciato
voi	cominciaste	voi	avevate cominciato
loro	cominciarono	loro	avevano cominciato

IMPERATIVE

comincia
cominciamo
cominciate

EXAMPLE PHRASES

Adesso **cominceranno** di sicuro a lamentarsi. Now they're sure to start complaining.

Cominciarono tutti a ridere. They all started to laugh.

Non **avevo** ancora **cominciato** che lui mi interruppe. I hadn't even started and he interrupted me.

Cominciamo bene! This is a fine start!

Italic letters in Italian words show where stress does not follow the usual rules.

compiere (to complete)

PRESENT		PRESENT SUBJUNCTIVE	
io	compio	io	compia
tu	compi	tu	compia
lui/lei/Lei	compie	lui/lei/Lei	compia
noi	compiamo	noi	compiamo
voi	compite	voi	compiate
loro	compiono	loro	compiano

PERFECT		IMPERFECT	
io	ho compiuto	io	compivo
tu	hai compiuto	tu	compivi
lui/lei/Lei	ha compiuto	lui/lei/Lei	compiva
noi	abbiamo compiuto	noi	compivamo
voi	avete compiuto	voi	compivate
loro	hanno compiuto	loro	compivano

GERUND

compiendo

PAST PARTICIPLE

compiuto

EXAMPLE PHRASES

Quando **compi** gli anni? When is your birthday?

Quanti anni **compi**? How old will you be?

Ho compiuto sedici anni il mese scorso. I was sixteen last month.

Per essere maggiorenne devi **compiere** 18 anni. To be of age you have to be 18.

compiere

FUTURE

io	**compirò**
tu	**compirai**
lui/lei/Lei	**compirà**
noi	**compiremo**
voi	**compirete**
loro	**compiranno**

CONDITIONAL

io	**compirei**
tu	**compiresti**
lui/lei/Lei	**compirebbe**
noi	**compiremmo**
voi	**compireste**
loro	**compirebbero**

PAST HISTORIC

io	**compii**
tu	**compisti**
lui/lei/Lei	**compì**
noi	**compimmo**
voi	**compiste**
loro	**compirono**

PLUPERFECT

io	**avevo compiuto**
tu	**avevi compiuto**
lui/lei/Lei	**aveva compiuto**
noi	**avevamo compiuto**
voi	**avevate compiuto**
loro	**avevano compiuto**

IMPERATIVE

compi
compiamo
compite

EXAMPLE PHRASES

Quando **compirai** gli anni faremo una bella festa. When it's your birthday we'll have a great party.

Aveva compiuto 18 anni e gli regalarono l'auto. He was 18 and they gave him a car.

Italic letters in Italian words show where stress does not follow the usual rules.

confondere (to mix up)

PRESENT		**PRESENT SUBJUNCTIVE**	
io	confondo	io	confonda
tu	confondi	tu	confonda
lui/lei/Lei	confonde	lui/lei/Lei	confonda
noi	confondiamo	noi	confondiamo
voi	confondete	voi	confondiate
loro	confondono	loro	confondano

PERFECT		**IMPERFECT**	
io	ho confuso	io	confondevo
tu	hai confuso	tu	confondevi
lui/lei/Lei	ha confuso	lui/lei/Lei	confondeva
noi	abbiamo confuso	noi	confondevamo
voi	avete confuso	voi	confondevate
loro	hanno confuso	loro	confondevano

GERUND	**PAST PARTICIPLE**
confondendo	confuso

EXAMPLE PHRASES

Ho confuso le date. I mixed up the dates.

No, scusa, mi **sono confuso**: era ieri. No, sorry, I've got mixed up: it was yesterday.

Maria **confondeva** sempre i sogni e la realtà. Maria always mixed up dreams and reality.

Tutti questi discorsi mi **confondono** le idee. All this talk is getting me confused.

Non starai **confondendo** i nomi? You're not mixing up the names, are you?

Remember that subject pronouns are not used very often in Italian.

confondere

FUTURE

io	**confonderò**
tu	**confonderai**
lui/lei/Lei	**confonderà**
noi	**confonderemo**
voi	**confonderete**
loro	**confonderanno**

CONDITIONAL

io	**confonderei**
tu	**confonderesti**
lui/lei/Lei	**confonderebbe**
noi	**confonderemmo**
voi	**confondereste**
loro	**confonderebbero**

PAST HISTORIC

io	**confusi**
tu	**confondesti**
lui/lei/Lei	**confuse**
noi	**confondemmo**
voi	**confondeste**
loro	**confusero**

PLUPERFECT

io	**avevo confuso**
tu	**avevi confuso**
lui/lei/Lei	**aveva confuso**
noi	**avevamo confuso**
voi	**avevate confuso**
loro	**avevano confuso**

IMPERATIVE

confondi
confondiamo
confondete

EXAMPLE PHRASES

All'esame di storia **confonderò** di certo le date. In the history exam I'm sure to mix up the dates.

Se fossi stanca come me, ti **confonderesti** anche tu. If you were as tired as I am, you'd get mixed up too.

Avevate confuso i dati e l'esperimento è fallito. You had got the data mixed up and the experiment was a failure.

Italic letters in Italian words show where stress does not follow the usual rules.

connettere (to connect)

PRESENT

io	**connetto**
tu	**connetti**
lui/lei/Lei	**connette**
noi	**connettiamo**
voi	**connettete**
loro	**connettono**

PRESENT SUBJUNCTIVE

io	**connetta**
tu	**connetta**
lui/lei/Lei	**connetta**
noi	**connettiamo**
voi	**connettiate**
loro	**connettano**

PERFECT

io	**ho connesso**
tu	**hai connesso**
lui/lei/Lei	**ha connesso**
noi	**abbiamo connesso**
voi	**avete connesso**
loro	**hanno connesso**

IMPERFECT

io	**connettevo**
tu	**connettevi**
lui/lei/Lei	**connetteva**
noi	**connettevamo**
voi	**connettevate**
loro	**connettevano**

GERUND

connettendo

PAST PARTICIPLE

connesso

EXAMPLE PHRASES

Non **connetti** più: hai bisogno di un caffè. **You're not thinking straight:
you need a coffee.**

Non **hanno connesso** il suo buon umore con l'arrivo di Carla. **They didn't
make the connection between his good mood and Carla's arrival.**

Sta **connettendo** il computer alla presa elettrica. **She's plugging the computer
into the socket.**

La mattina non riesco a **connettere**. **I can't think straight in the morning.**

Remember that subject pronouns are not used very often in Italian.

connettere

FUTURE

io	connetter**ò**
tu	connetterai
lui/lei/Lei	connetter**à**
noi	connetteremo
voi	connetterete
loro	connetteranno

CONDITIONAL

io	connetterei
tu	connetteresti
lui/lei/Lei	connetterebbe
noi	connetteremmo
voi	connettereste
loro	connetter**e**bbero

PAST HISTORIC

io	connettei
tu	connettesti
lui/lei/Lei	connett**é**
noi	connettemmo
voi	connetteste
loro	connett**e**rono

PLUPERFECT

io	avevo connesso
tu	avevi connesso
lui/lei/Lei	aveva connesso
noi	avevamo connesso
voi	avevate connesso
loro	av**e**vano connesso

IMPERATIVE
connetti
connettiamo
connettete

EXAMPLE PHRASES

Attento ai cortocircuiti quando **connetterai** la batteria. Mind you don't get a short-circuit when you connect the battery.

Non **avevo connesso** i due fatti. I hadn't connected the two facts.

conoscere (to know)

PRESENT

io	conosco
tu	conosci
lui/lei/Lei	conosce
noi	conosciamo
voi	conoscete
loro	conoscono

PRESENT SUBJUNCTIVE

io	conosca
tu	conosca
lui/lei/Lei	conosca
noi	conosciamo
voi	conosciate
loro	conoscano

PERFECT

io	ho conosciuto
tu	hai conosciuto
lui/lei/Lei	ha conosciuto
noi	abbiamo conosciuto
voi	avete conosciuto
loro	hanno conosciuto

IMPERFECT

io	conoscevo
tu	conoscevi
lui/lei/Lei	conosceva
noi	conoscevamo
voi	conoscevate
loro	conoscevano

GERUND

conoscendo

PAST PARTICIPLE

conosciuto

EXAMPLE PHRASES

Non **conosco** bene la città. I don't know the town well.

Ci **conosciamo** da poco tempo. We haven't known each other long.

Voglio che tu **conosca** i miei. I'd like you to meet my parents.

Ci siamo **conosciuti** a Firenze. We first met in Florence.

Lo **conoscevamo** solo di vista. We only knew him by sight.

conoscere

FUTURE

io	conoscerò
tu	conoscerai
lui/lei/Lei	conoscerà
noi	conosceremo
voi	conoscerete
loro	conosceranno

CONDITIONAL

io	conoscerei
tu	conosceresti
lui/lei/Lei	conoscerebbe
noi	conosceremmo
voi	conoscereste
loro	conoscerebbero

PAST HISTORIC

io	conobbi
tu	conoscesti
lui/lei/Lei	conobbe
noi	conoscemmo
voi	conosceste
loro	conobbero

PLUPERFECT

io	avevo conosciuto
tu	avevi conosciuto
lui/lei/Lei	aveva conosciuto
noi	avevamo conosciuto
voi	avevate conosciuto
loro	avevano conosciuto

IMPERATIVE

conosci
conosciamo
conoscete

EXAMPLE PHRASES

Viaggeremo e **conosceremo** posti nuovi. We'll travel and get to know
   new places.
Ci **conoscemmo** in vacanza. We met on holiday.
Conoscendoti, credo che farai la scelta giusta. Knowing you, I think you'll
   make the right choice.

Italic letters in Italian words show where stress does not follow the usual rules.

correggere (to correct)

PRESENT

io	correggo
tu	correggi
lui/lei/Lei	corregge
noi	correggiamo
voi	correggete
loro	correggono

PRESENT SUBJUNCTIVE

io	corregga
tu	corregga
lui/lei/Lei	corregga
noi	correggiamo
voi	correggiate
loro	correggano

PERFECT

io	ho corretto
tu	hai corretto
lui/lei/Lei	ha corretto
noi	abbiamo corretto
voi	avete corretto
loro	hanno corretto

IMPERFECT

io	correggevo
tu	correggevi
lui/lei/Lei	correggeva
noi	correggevamo
voi	correggevate
loro	correggevano

GERUND

correggendo

PAST PARTICIPLE

corretto

EXAMPLE PHRASES

Correggimi se faccio un errore. Correct me if I make a mistake.

Non **ha** ancora **corretto** i compiti di ieri. She hasn't corrected yesterday's homework yet.

Non **correggevano** mai gli errori del figlio. They never corrected their son's mistakes.

Si migliora **correggendo** i propri errori. You improve by correcting your own mistakes.

Remember that subject pronouns are not used very often in Italian.

correggere

FUTURE		CONDITIONAL	
io	**correggerò**	io	**correggerei**
tu	**correggerai**	tu	**correggeresti**
lui/lei/Lei	**correggerà**	lui/lei/Lei	**correggerebbe**
noi	**correggeremo**	noi	**correggeremmo**
voi	**correggerete**	voi	**correggereste**
loro	**correggeranno**	loro	**correggerebbero**

PAST HISTORIC		PLUPERFECT	
io	**corressi**	io	**avevo corretto**
tu	**correggesti**	tu	**avevi corretto**
lui/lei/Lei	**corresse**	lui/lei/Lei	**aveva corretto**
noi	**correggemmo**	noi	**avevamo corretto**
voi	**correggeste**	voi	**avevate corretto**
loro	**corressero**	loro	**avevano corretto**

IMPERATIVE
correggi
correggiamo
correggete

EXAMPLE PHRASES

Se non ti sforzi, non **correggerai** mai la tua pronuncia. If you don't make
an effort you'll never get your pronunciation right.

Si è offeso perché lo **avevo corretto**. He took offence because I'd corrected him.

Se sbaglia, lo **correggiamo**. If he makes a mistake we correct him.

Italic letters in Italian words show where stress does not follow the usual rules.

correre (to run)

PRESENT

io	**corro**
tu	**corri**
lui/lei/Lei	**corre**
noi	**corriamo**
voi	**correte**
loro	**corrono**

PRESENT SUBJUNCTIVE

io	**corra**
tu	**corra**
lui/lei/Lei	**corra**
noi	**corriamo**
voi	**corriate**
loro	**corrano**

PERFECT

io	**ho corso**
tu	**hai corso**
lui/lei/Lei	**ha corso**
noi	**abbiamo corso**
voi	**avete corso**
loro	**hanno corso**

IMPERFECT

io	**correvo**
tu	**correvi**
lui/lei/Lei	**correva**
noi	**correvamo**
voi	**correvate**
loro	**correvano**

GERUND

correndo

PAST PARTICIPLE

corso

EXAMPLE PHRASES

Corre troppo in macchina. He drives too fast.

Non voglio che **corriate** dei rischi. I don't want you to take risks.

Abbiamo corso come pazzi per non perdere il treno. We ran like mad to catch the train.

Sono inciampato mentre **correvo**. I tripped when I was running.

Sono corso subito fuori. I immediately rushed outside.

Remember that subject pronouns are not used very often in Italian.

correre

FUTURE

io	**correrò**
tu	**correrai**
lui/lei/Lei	**correrà**
noi	**correremo**
voi	**correrete**
loro	**correranno**

CONDITIONAL

io	**correrei**
tu	**correresti**
lui/lei/Lei	**correrebbe**
noi	**correremmo**
voi	**correreste**
loro	**correrebbero**

PAST HISTORIC

io	**corsi**
tu	**corresti**
lui/lei/Lei	**corse**
noi	**corremmo**
voi	**correste**
loro	**corsero**

PLUPERFECT

io	**avevo corso**
tu	**avevi corso**
lui/lei/Lei	**aveva corso**
noi	**avevamo corso**
voi	**avevate corso**
loro	**avevano corso**

IMPERATIVE

corri
corriamo
correte

EXAMPLE PHRASES

Paola **correrà** i cento metri. Paola is going to run the hundred metres.

È prudente: non **correrebbe** mai rischi inutili. She's sensible: she'd never take unnecessary risks.

Aveva corso e ansimava ancora. He'd been running and was still out of breath.

Corri o perdiamo l'*au*tobus! Run or we'll miss the bus!

Italic letters in Italian words show where stress does not follow the usual rules.

credere (to believe)

PRESENT

io	**credo**
tu	**credi**
lui/lei/Lei	**crede**
noi	**crediamo**
voi	**credete**
loro	**credono**

PRESENT SUBJUNCTIVE

io	**creda**
tu	**creda**
lui/lei/Lei	**creda**
noi	**crediamo**
voi	**crediate**
loro	**credano**

PERFECT

io	**ho creduto**
tu	**hai creduto**
lui/lei/Lei	**ha creduto**
noi	**abbiamo creduto**
voi	**avete creduto**
loro	**hanno creduto**

IMPERFECT

io	**credevo**
tu	**credevi**
lui/lei/Lei	**credeva**
noi	**credevamo**
voi	**credevate**
loro	**credevano**

GERUND

credendo

PAST PARTICIPLE

creduto

EXAMPLE PHRASES

Non ci **credo**! I don't believe it!

Non dirmi che **credi** ai fantasmi! Don't tell me you believe in ghosts!

Non voglio che lei **creda** che sono un bugiardo. I don't want her to think
I'm a liar.

Non **ha** mai **creduto** nell'astrologia. She's never believed in astrology.

Non **credeva** ai suoi occhi. She couldn't believe her eyes.

Remember that subject pronouns are not used very often in Italian.

credere

FUTURE

io	**crederò**
tu	**crederai**
lui/lei/Lei	**crederà**
noi	**crederemo**
voi	**crederete**
loro	**crederanno**

CONDITIONAL

io	**crederei**
tu	**crederesti**
lui/lei/Lei	**crederebbe**
noi	**crederemmo**
voi	**credereste**
loro	**crederebbero**

PAST HISTORIC

io	**credetti** or **credei**
tu	**credesti**
lui/lei/Lei	**credette**
noi	**credemmo**
voi	**credeste**
loro	**credettero**

PLUPERFECT

io	**avevo creduto**
tu	**avevi creduto**
lui/lei/Lei	**aveva creduto**
noi	**avevamo creduto**
voi	**avevate creduto**
loro	**avevano creduto**

IMPERATIVE

credi
crediamo
credete

EXAMPLE PHRASES

Non ti **crederò** mai più. I'll never believe you again.
Ci **credereste**? Ho comprato casa. Would you believe it! I've bought a house.
Stento a **crederci**! I can hardly believe it!
Credemmo di aver perso le chiavi. We thought we'd lost our keys.

Italic letters in Italian words show where stress does not follow the usual rules.

crescere (to grow)

PRESENT		**PRESENT SUBJUNCTIVE**	
io	cresco	io	cresca
tu	cresci	tu	cresca
lui/lei/Lei	cresce	lui/lei/Lei	cresca
noi	cresciamo	noi	cresciamo
voi	crescete	voi	cresciate
loro	crescono	loro	crescano

PERFECT		**IMPERFECT**	
io	sono cresciuto/a	io	crescevo
tu	sei cresciuto/a	tu	crescevi
lui/lei/Lei	è cresciuto/a	lui/lei/Lei	cresceva
noi	siamo cresciuti/e	noi	crescevamo
voi	siete cresciuti/e	voi	crescevate
loro	sono cresciuti/e	loro	crescevano

GERUND	**PAST PARTICIPLE**
crescendo	cresciuto

EXAMPLE PHRASES

Tuo figlio **cresce** a vista d'occhio. Your son is growing very fast.

Più lavora e più **cresce** la sua insoddisfazione. The harder she works the more dissatisfied she becomes.

Com'**è cresciuto** tuo fratello! Hasn't your brother grown!

È cresciuto in campagna. He grew up in the country.

Si sta facendo **crescere** i capelli. She's growing her hair.

Le tue piante stanno **crescendo** molto bene. Your plants are growing very well.

Remember that subject pronouns are not used very often in Italian.

crescere

FUTURE

io	**crescerò**
tu	**crescerai**
lui/lei/Lei	**crescerà**
noi	**cresceremo**
voi	**crescerete**
loro	**cresceranno**

CONDITIONAL

io	**crescerei**
tu	**cresceresti**
lui/lei/Lei	**crescerebbe**
noi	**cresceremmo**
voi	**crescereste**
loro	**crescerebbero**

PAST HISTORIC

io	**crebbi**
tu	**crescesti**
lui/lei/Lei	**crebbe**
noi	**crescemmo**
voi	**cresceste**
loro	**crebbero**

PLUPERFECT

io	**ero cresciuto/a**
tu	**eri cresciuto/a**
lui/lei/Lei	**era cresciuto/a**
noi	**eravamo cresciuti/e**
voi	**eravate cresciuti/e**
loro	**erano cresciuti/e**

IMPERATIVE

cresci
cresciamo
crescete

EXAMPLE PHRASES

I prezzi **cresceranno** durante le feste. Prices will go up during the holiday season.

Era molto **cresciuta** e non la riconoscevo. She'd grown a lot and I didn't recognize her.

Italic letters in Italian words show where stress does not follow the usual rules.

cucire (to sew)

PRESENT

io	**cucio**
tu	**cuci**
lui/lei/Lei	**cuce**
noi	**cuciamo**
voi	**cucite**
loro	**cuciono**

PRESENT SUBJUNCTIVE

io	**cucia**
tu	**cucia**
lui/lei/Lei	**cucia**
noi	**cuciamo**
voi	**cuciate**
loro	**cuciano**

PERFECT

io	**ho cucito**
tu	**hai cucito**
lui/lei/Lei	**ha cucito**
noi	**abbiamo cucito**
voi	**avete cucito**
loro	**hanno cucito**

IMPERFECT

io	**cucivo**
tu	**cucivi**
lui/lei/Lei	**cuciva**
noi	**cucivamo**
voi	**cucivate**
loro	**cucivano**

GERUND

cucendo

PAST PARTICIPLE

cucito

EXAMPLE PHRASES

Bisogna che entro domani **cucia** il vestito. **She has to finish sewing the dress by tomorrow.**

Mi piacciono le toppe che **hai cucito** sulla giacca. **I like the patches you've sewn on your jacket.**

Si è punta con l'ago mentre **cuciva**. **She pricked her finger with the needle while she was sewing.**

Sta **cucendo** uno strappo alla gonna. **She's mending a tear in her skirt.**

Remember that subject pronouns are not used very often in Italian.

cucire

FUTURE

io	**cucirò**
tu	**cucirai**
lui/lei/Lei	**cucirà**
noi	**cuciremo**
voi	**cucirete**
loro	**cuciranno**

CONDITIONAL

io	**cucirei**
tu	**cuciresti**
lui/lei/Lei	**cucirebbe**
noi	**cuciremmo**
voi	**cucireste**
loro	**cucirebbero**

PAST HISTORIC

io	**cucii**
tu	**cucisti**
lui/lei/Lei	**cucì**
noi	**cucimmo**
voi	**cuciste**
loro	**cucirono**

PLUPERFECT

io	**avevo cucito**
tu	**avevi cucito**
lui/lei/Lei	**aveva cucito**
noi	**avevamo cucito**
voi	**avevate cucito**
loro	**avevano cucito**

IMPERATIVE

cuci
cuciamo
cucite

EXAMPLE PHRASES

Domani **cucirò** i bottoni sul vestito. I'll sew the buttons on the dress
tomorrow.

Non so **cucire**. I can't sew.

Italic letters in Italian words show where stress does not follow the usual rules.

cuocere (to cook)

PRESENT

io	**cuocio**
tu	**cuoci**
lui/lei/Lei	**cuoce**
noi	**cuociamo**
voi	**cuocete**
loro	**cuociono**

PRESENT SUBJUNCTIVE

io	**cuocia**
tu	**cuocia**
lui/lei/Lei	**cuocia**
noi	**cuociamo**
voi	**cuociate**
loro	**cuociano**

PERFECT

io	**ho cotto**
tu	**hai cotto**
lui/lei/Lei	**ha cotto**
noi	**abbiamo cotto**
voi	**avete cotto**
loro	**hanno cotto**

IMPERFECT

io	**cuocevo**
tu	**cuocevi**
lui/lei/Lei	**cuoceva**
noi	**cuocevamo**
voi	**cuocevate**
loro	**cuocevano**

GERUND
cuocendo

PAST PARTICIPLE
cotto

EXAMPLE PHRASES

Si è bruciato **cuocendo** la pizza. He burnt himself when he was baking the pizza.

La carne **cuoceva** sulla brace. The meat was cooking on the barbecue.

Mi piace la carne **cotta** sulla piastra. I like meat cooked on the hotplate.

Remember that subject pronouns are not used very often in Italian.

cuocere

FUTURE

io	**cuocerò**
tu	**cuocerai**
lui/lei/Lei	**cuocerà**
noi	**cuoceremo**
voi	**cuocerete**
loro	**cuoceranno**

CONDITIONAL

io	**cuocerei**
tu	**cuoceresti**
lui/lei/Lei	**cuocerebbe**
noi	**cuoceremmo**
voi	**cuocereste**
loro	**cuocerebbero**

PAST HISTORIC

io	**cossi**
tu	**cuocesti**
lui/lei/Lei	**cosse**
noi	**cuocemmo**
voi	**cuoceste**
loro	**cossero**

PLUPERFECT

io	**avevo cotto**
tu	**avevi cotto**
lui/lei/Lei	**aveva cotto**
noi	**avevamo cotto**
voi	**avevate cotto**
loro	**avevano cotto**

IMPERATIVE

cuoci
cuociamo
cuocete

EXAMPLE PHRASES

Stasera, il pesce, lo **cuocerò** alla griglia. This evening I'll grill the fish.

Come lo **cuocerai**? How are you going to cook it?

Avevamo cotto troppo la torta: era immangiabile. We'd left the cake in the oven too long: it was uneatable.

Cuocilo per mezz'ora. Cook it for half an hour.

Italic letters in Italian words show where stress does not follow the usual rules.

dare (to give)

PRESENT

io	**do**
tu	**dai**
lui/lei/Lei	**dà**
noi	**diamo**
voi	**date**
loro	**danno**

PRESENT SUBJUNCTIVE

io	**dia**
tu	**dia**
lui/lei/Lei	**dia**
noi	**diamo**
voi	**diate**
loro	**diano**

PERFECT

io	**ho dato**
tu	**hai dato**
lui/lei/Lei	**ha dato**
noi	**abbiamo dato**
voi	**avete dato**
loro	**hanno dato**

IMPERFECT

io	**davo**
tu	**davi**
lui/lei/Lei	**dava**
noi	**davamo**
voi	**davate**
loro	**davano**

GERUND

dando

PAST PARTICIPLE

dato

EXAMPLE PHRASES

Può **darsi** che sia malata. She may be ill.

La mia finestra **dà** sul giardino. My window looks onto the garden.

Gli **ho dato** un libro. I gave him a book.

Dandoti da fare, potresti ottenere molto di più. If you exerted yourself you could achieve a lot more.

dare

FUTURE

io	**darò**
tu	**darai**
lui/lei/Lei	**darà**
noi	**daremo**
voi	**darete**
loro	**daranno**

CONDITIONAL

io	**darei**
tu	**daresti**
lui/lei/Lei	**darebbe**
noi	**daremmo**
voi	**dareste**
loro	**darebbero**

PAST HISTORIC

io	**diedi** or **detti**
tu	**desti**
lui/lei/Lei	**diede** or **detti**
noi	**demmo**
voi	**deste**
loro	**diedero** or **dettero**

PLUPERFECT

io	**avevo dato**
tu	**avevi dato**
lui/lei/Lei	**aveva dato**
noi	**avevamo dato**
voi	**avevate dato**
loro	**avevano dato**

IMPERATIVE

dai or da'
diamo
date

EXAMPLE PHRASES

Domani sera **daranno** un bel film in TV. There's a good film on TV tomorrow evening.

Quanti anni gli **daresti**? How old would you say he was?

Ci **diede** l'impressione di essere molto infelice. We got the impression he was very unhappy.

Lo ringraziai perché mi aveva **dato** una mano. I thanked him for giving me a hand.

Ricordami di **darti** la lista della spesa. Remind me to give you the shopping list.

Dammelo. Give it to me.

Italic letters in Italian words show where stress does not follow the usual rules.

decidere (to decide)

PRESENT

io	**decido**
tu	**decidi**
lui/lei/Lei	**decide**
noi	**decidiamo**
voi	**decidete**
loro	**decidono**

PRESENT SUBJUNCTIVE

io	**decida**
tu	**decida**
lui/lei/Lei	**decida**
noi	**decidiamo**
voi	**decidiate**
loro	**decidano**

PERFECT

io	**ho deciso**
tu	**hai deciso**
lui/lei/Lei	**ha deciso**
noi	**abbiamo deciso**
voi	**avete deciso**
loro	**hanno deciso**

IMPERFECT

io	**decidevo**
tu	**decidevi**
lui/lei/Lei	**decideva**
noi	**decidevamo**
voi	**decidevate**
loro	**decidevano**

GERUND
decidendo

PAST PARTICIPLE
deciso

EXAMPLE PHRASES

Quand'è che si **decidono** a venirci a trovare? When will they decide to come and see us?

Hai deciso? Have you decided?

Allora ci vai? – Non so, sto ancora **decidendo**. So, are you going? – I don't know, I'm still trying to decide.

Non so **decidermi**. I *can't* decide.

Remember that subject pronouns are not used very often in Italian.

decidere

FUTURE

io	**deciderò**
tu	**deciderai**
lui/lei/Lei	**deciderà**
noi	**decideremo**
voi	**deciderete**
loro	**decideranno**

CONDITIONAL

io	**deciderei**
tu	**decideresti**
lui/lei/Lei	**deciderebbe**
noi	**decideremmo**
voi	**decidereste**
loro	**deciderebbero**

PAST HISTORIC

io	**decisi**
tu	**decidesti**
lui/lei/Lei	**decise**
noi	**decidemmo**
voi	**decideste**
loro	**decisero**

PLUPERFECT

io	**avevo deciso**
tu	**avevi deciso**
lui/lei/Lei	**aveva deciso**
noi	**avevamo deciso**
voi	**avevate deciso**
loro	**avevano deciso**

IMPERATIVE

decidi
decidiamo
decidete

EXAMPLE PHRASES

Deciderai quando sarai sicura. You'll decide when you're sure.

Decidemmo di non andarci. We decided not to go.

Aveva deciso di smettere di fumare, ma non ce l'ha fatta. She'd decided to stop smoking, but she didn't manage to.

Non so scegliere: **decidi** tu al posto mio. I don't know which to choose: you decide for me.

Italic letters in Italian words show where stress does not follow the usual rules.

deludere (to disappoint)

PRESENT

io	deludo
tu	deludi
lui/lei/Lei	delude
noi	deludiamo
voi	deludete
loro	deludono

PRESENT SUBJUNCTIVE

io	deluda
tu	deluda
lui/lei/Lei	deluda
noi	deludiamo
voi	deludiate
loro	deludano

PERFECT

io	ho deluso
tu	hai deluso
lui/lei/Lei	ha deluso
noi	abbiamo deluso
voi	avete deluso
loro	hanno deluso

IMPERFECT

io	deludevo
tu	deludevi
lui/lei/Lei	deludeva
noi	deludevamo
voi	deludevate
loro	deludevano

GERUND

deludendo

PAST PARTICIPLE

deluso

EXAMPLE PHRASES

Spero proprio che tu non mi **deluda**. I really hope you won't disappoint me.

Il suo ultimo film mi **ha deluso**. His last film was disappointing.

Non vorrei **deluderti**, ma l'esame è andato male. I hate to disappoint you, but the exam didn't go well.

Remember that subject pronouns are not used very often in Italian.

deludere

FUTURE

io	**deluderò**
tu	**deluderai**
lui/lei/Lei	**deluderà**
noi	**deluderemo**
voi	**deluderete**
loro	**deluderanno**

CONDITIONAL

io	**deluderei**
tu	**deluderesti**
lui/lei/Lei	**deluderebbe**
noi	**deluderemmo**
voi	**deludereste**
loro	**deluderebbero**

PAST HISTORIC

io	**delusi**
tu	**deludesti**
lui/lei/Lei	**deluse**
noi	**deludemmo**
voi	**deludeste**
loro	**delusero**

PLUPERFECT

io	**avevo deluso**
tu	**avevi deluso**
lui/lei/Lei	**aveva deluso**
noi	**avevamo deluso**
voi	**avevate deluso**
loro	**avevano deluso**

IMPERATIVE

deludi
deludiamo
deludete

EXAMPLE PHRASES

So che vi **deluderò**, ma ormai ho deciso. I know you're going to be disappointed, but I've made up my mind.

Se lo facessero mi **deluderebbero** molto. If they did that I'd be very disappointed in them.

Mi **deluse** molto. It disappointed me very much.

Ci **aveva deluso** e non gli parlammo più. He'd let us down and we didn't speak to him any more.

Italic letters in Italian words show where stress does not follow the usual rules.

dire (to say)

PRESENT		PRESENT SUBJUNCTIVE	
io	**dico**	io	**dica**
tu	**dici**	tu	**dica**
lui/lei/Lei	**dice**	lui/lei/Lei	**dica**
noi	**diciamo**	noi	**diciamo**
voi	**dite**	voi	**diciate**
loro	**dicono**	loro	**dicano**

PERFECT		IMPERFECT	
io	**ho detto**	io	**dicevo**
tu	**hai detto**	tu	**dicevi**
lui/lei/Lei	**ha detto**	lui/lei/Lei	**diceva**
noi	**abbiamo detto**	noi	**dicevamo**
voi	**avete detto**	voi	**dicevate**
loro	**hanno detto**	loro	**dicevano**

GERUND
dicendo

PAST PARTICIPLE
detto

EXAMPLE PHRASES

Come si **dice** "quadro" in inglese? How do you say "quadro" in English?

Ha detto che verrà. He said he'll come.

Era una persona generosa: **diceva** sempre di sì a tutti. She was a generous person: she always said yes to everyone.

Che ne **diresti** di andarcene? Shall we leave?

Che cosa stai **dicendo**? What are you saying?

Remember that subject pronouns are not used very often in Italian.

dire

FUTURE

io	**dirò**
tu	**dirai**
lui/lei/Lei	**dirà**
noi	**diremo**
voi	**direte**
loro	**diranno**

CONDITIONAL

io	**direi**
tu	**diresti**
lui/lei/Lei	**direbbe**
noi	**diremmo**
voi	**direste**
loro	**direbbero**

PAST HISTORIC

io	**dissi**
tu	**dicesti**
lui/lei/Lei	**disse**
noi	**dicemmo**
voi	**diceste**
loro	**dissero**

PLUPERFECT

io	**avevo detto**
tu	**avevi detto**
lui/lei/Lei	**aveva detto**
noi	**avevamo detto**
voi	**avevate detto**
loro	**avevano detto**

IMPERATIVE

di'
diciamo
dite

EXAMPLE PHRASES

Ti **dirò** un segreto. I'll tell you a secret.

Non **disse** una parola. She didn't say a word.

Gli **avevo detto** di andarsene. I'd told him to go away.

Dimmi dov'è. Tell me where it is.

Dovete **dire** la verità. You must tell the truth.

Italic letters in Italian words show where stress does not follow the usual rules.

dirigere (to direct)

PRESENT		PRESENT SUBJUNCTIVE	
io	**dirigo**	io	**diriga**
tu	**dirigi**	tu	**diriga**
lui/lei/Lei	**dirige**	lui/lei/Lei	**diriga**
noi	**dirigiamo**	noi	**dirigiamo**
voi	**dirigete**	voi	**dirigiate**
loro	**dirigono**	loro	**dirigano**

PERFECT		IMPERFECT	
io	**ho diretto**	io	**dirigevo**
tu	**hai diretto**	tu	**dirigevi**
lui/lei/Lei	**ha diretto**	lui/lei/Lei	**dirigeva**
noi	**abbiamo diretto**	noi	**dirigevamo**
voi	**avete diretto**	voi	**dirigevate**
loro	**hanno diretto**	loro	**dirigevano**

GERUND
dirigendo

PAST PARTICIPLE
diretto

EXAMPLE PHRASES

I vigili **dirigono** il traffico. The police are directing the traffic.

Voglio che tu **diriga** il progetto. I want you to manage the project.

Ha diretto l'orchestra con grande abilità. He conducted the orchestra with great skill.

Si **è diretto** verso la porta. He headed for the door.

Prima **dirigeva** un ditta. Before that he managed a company.

dirigere

FUTURE

io	**dirigerò**
tu	**dirigerai**
lui/lei/Lei	**dirigerà**
noi	**dirigeremo**
voi	**dirigerete**
loro	**dirigeranno**

CONDITIONAL

io	**dirigerei**
tu	**dirigeresti**
lui/lei/Lei	**dirigerebbe**
noi	**dirigeremmo**
voi	**dirigereste**
loro	**dirigerebbero**

PAST HISTORIC

io	**diressi**
tu	**dirigesti**
lui/lei/Lei	**diresse**
noi	**dirigemmo**
voi	**dirigeste**
loro	**diressero**

PLUPERFECT

io	**avevo diretto**
tu	**avevi diretto**
lui/lei/Lei	**aveva diretto**
noi	**avevamo diretto**
voi	**avevate diretto**
loro	**avevano diretto**

IMPERATIVE

dirigi
dirigiamo
dirigete

EXAMPLE PHRASES

Chi **dirigerà** i lavori? Who'll be in charge of the work?

Prima dell'incidente **erano diretti** a nord. Before the accident they'd been heading north.

Dirigiamoci verso nord. Let's head north.

Italic letters in Italian words show where stress does not follow the usual rules.

discutere (to discuss)

PRESENT

io	**discuto**
tu	**discuti**
lui/lei/Lei	**discute**
noi	**discutiamo**
voi	**discutete**
loro	**discutono**

PRESENT SUBJUNCTIVE

io	**discuta**
tu	**discuta**
lui/lei/Lei	**discuta**
noi	**discutiamo**
voi	**discutiate**
loro	**discutano**

PERFECT

io	**ho discusso**
tu	**hai discusso**
lui/lei/Lei	**ha discusso**
noi	**abbiamo discusso**
voi	**avete discusso**
loro	**hanno discusso**

IMPERFECT

io	**discutevo**
tu	**discutevi**
lui/lei/Lei	**discuteva**
noi	**discutevamo**
voi	**discutevate**
loro	**discutevano**

GERUND
discutendo

PAST PARTICIPLE
discusso

EXAMPLE PHRASES

Discutono spesso di politica. They often discuss politics.

Ho discusso a lungo con lui. I had a long discussion with him.

C'è stato un periodo in cui **discutevano** sempre. There was a time when they argued constantly.

Il problema non si risolverà solo **discutendo**. Just talking about it won't solve the problem.

Remember that subject pronouns are not used very often in Italian.

discutere

FUTURE

io	discuterò
tu	discuterai
lui/lei/Lei	discuterà
noi	discuteremo
voi	discuterete
loro	discuteranno

CONDITIONAL

io	discuterei
tu	discuteresti
lui/lei/Lei	discuterebbe
noi	discuteremmo
voi	discutereste
loro	discuterebbero

PAST HISTORIC

io	discussi
tu	discutesti
lui/lei/Lei	discusse
noi	discutemmo
voi	discuteste
loro	discussero

PLUPERFECT

io	avevo discusso
tu	avevi discusso
lui/lei/Lei	aveva discusso
noi	avevamo discusso
voi	avevate discusso
loro	avevano discusso

IMPERATIVE

discuti
discutiamo
discutete

EXAMPLE PHRASES

Discuteremo della questione più tardi. We'll discuss the matter later.

Discussero a fondo della possibilità di trasferirsi. They had a detailed discussion about the possibility of moving.

Mi ha ubbidito senza **discutere**. He obeyed me without question.

È inutile che **discutiamo**: ho ragione io. There's no point arguing: I'm right.

distinguere (to see)

PRESENT		PRESENT SUBJUNCTIVE	
io	distinguo	io	distingua
tu	distingui	tu	distingua
lui/lei/Lei	distingue	lui/lei/Lei	distingua
noi	distinguiamo	noi	distinguiamo
voi	distinguete	voi	distinguiate
loro	distinguono	loro	distinguano

PERFECT		IMPERFECT	
io	ho distinto	io	distinguevo
tu	hai distinto	tu	distinguevi
lui/lei/Lei	ha distinto	lui/lei/Lei	distingueva
noi	abbiamo distinto	noi	distinguevamo
voi	avete distinto	voi	distinguevate
loro	hanno distinto	loro	distinguevano

GERUND
distinguendo

PAST PARTICIPLE
distinto

EXAMPLE PHRASES

Non li **distinguo** tra loro. I can't tell the difference between them.

Mi pare che tu non **distingua** bene i colori. I think you have difficulty telling one colour from another.

Non **distinguevo** il numero dell'autobus. I couldn't see the number of the bus.

Si è **distinto** per efficienza. He's exceptionally efficient.

Remember that subject pronouns are not used very often in Italian.

distinguere

FUTURE

io	**distinguerò**
tu	**distinguerai**
lui/lei/Lei	**distinguerà**
noi	**distingueremo**
voi	**distinguerete**
loro	**distingueranno**

CONDITIONAL

io	**distinguerei**
tu	**distingueresti**
lui/lei/Lei	**distinguerebbe**
noi	**distingueremmo**
voi	**distinguereste**
loro	**distinguerebbero**

PAST HISTORIC

io	**distinsi**
tu	**distinguesti**
lui/lei/Lei	**distinse**
noi	**distinguemmo**
voi	**distingueste**
loro	**distinsero**

PLUPERFECT

io	**avevo distinto**
tu	**avevi distinto**
lui/lei/Lei	**aveva distinto**
noi	**avevamo distinto**
voi	**avevate distinto**
loro	**avevano distinto**

IMPERATIVE
distingui
distinguiamo
distinguete

EXAMPLE PHRASES

È una copia perfetta: non **distinguerei** il falso dall'originale. It's a perfect copy: I couldn't tell the fake from the original.

Distinguemmo nella nebbia la sagoma della nave. Through the mist we could see the outline of the ship.

Non sa **distinguere** sogni e realtà. She can't tell the difference between dreams and reality.

Italic letters in Italian words show where stress does not follow the usual rules.

dividere (to divide)

PRESENT		PRESENT SUBJUNCTIVE	
io	**divido**	io	**divida**
tu	**dividi**	tu	**divida**
lui/lei/Lei	**divide**	lui/lei/Lei	**divida**
noi	**dividiamo**	noi	**dividiamo**
voi	**dividete**	voi	**dividiate**
loro	**dividono**	loro	**dividano**

PERFECT		IMPERFECT	
io	**ho diviso**	io	**dividevo**
tu	**hai diviso**	tu	**dividevi**
lui/lei/Lei	**ha diviso**	lui/lei/Lei	**divideva**
noi	**abbiamo diviso**	noi	**dividevamo**
voi	**avete diviso**	voi	**dividevate**
loro	**hanno diviso**	loro	**dividevano**

GERUND
dividendo

PAST PARTICIPLE
diviso

EXAMPLE PHRASES

Il libro si **divide** in tre parti. The book is divided into three parts.

L'**ho diviso** in tre parti. I've divided it into three parts.

Abitavano insieme e **dividevano** le spese. They lived together and shared expenses.

Otto **diviso** quattro fa due. Eight divided by four is two.

Dividendo il lavoro, faremo prima. If we share the work we'll get it done sooner.

Remember that subject pronouns are not used very often in Italian.

dividere

FUTURE

io	**dividerò**
tu	**dividerai**
lui/lei/Lei	**dividerà**
noi	**divideremo**
voi	**dividerete**
loro	**divideranno**

CONDITIONAL

io	**dividerei**
tu	**divideresti**
lui/lei/Lei	**dividerebbe**
noi	**divideremmo**
voi	**dividereste**
loro	**dividerebbero**

PAST HISTORIC

io	**divisi**
tu	**dividesti**
lui/lei/Lei	**divise**
noi	**dividemmo**
voi	**divideste**
loro	**divisero**

PLUPERFECT

io	**avevo diviso**
tu	**avevo diviso**
lui/lei/Lei	**aveva diviso**
noi	**avevamo diviso**
voi	**avevate diviso**
loro	**avevano diviso**

IMPERATIVE

dividi
dividiamo
dividete

EXAMPLE PHRASES

È egoista e non **dividerebbe** mai nulla con nessuno. He's selfish and would never share anything with anyone.

Li **avevano divisi** perché litigavano sempre. They had separated them because they quarrelled all the time.

Dividi la cioccolata con tuo fratello. Share the chocolate with your brother.

Italic letters in Italian words show where stress does not follow the usual rules.

dormire (to sleep)

PRESENT		**PRESENT SUBJUNCTIVE**	
io	**dormo**	io	**dorma**
tu	**dormi**	tu	**dorma**
lui/lei/Lei	**dorme**	lui/lei/Lei	**dorma**
noi	**dormiamo**	noi	**dormiamo**
voi	**dormite**	voi	**dormiate**
loro	**dormono**	loro	**dormano**

PERFECT		**IMPERFECT**	
io	**ho dormito**	io	**dormivo**
tu	**hai dormito**	tu	**dormivi**
lui/lei/Lei	**ha dormito**	lui/lei/Lei	**dormiva**
noi	**abbiamo dormito**	noi	**dormivamo**
voi	**avete dormito**	voi	**dormivate**
loro	**hanno dormito**	loro	**dormivano**

GERUND
dormendo

PAST PARTICIPLE
dormito

EXAMPLE PHRASES

Era così stanco che **dormiva** in piedi. He was so tired he was asleep on his feet.

Dormivo e non ti ho sentita entrare. I was asleep and didn't hear you come in.

Sta **dormendo**. She's sleeping.

Vado a **dormire**. I'm going to bed.

dormire

FUTURE

io	**dormirò**
tu	**dormirai**
lui/lei/Lei	**dormirà**
noi	**dormiremo**
voi	**dormirete**
loro	**dormiranno**

CONDITIONAL

io	**dormirei**
tu	**dormiresti**
lui/lei/Lei	**dormirebbe**
noi	**dormiremmo**
voi	**dormireste**
loro	**dormirebbero**

PAST HISTORIC

io	**dormii**
tu	**dormisti**
lui/lei/Lei	**dormì**
noi	**dormimmo**
voi	**dormiste**
loro	**dormirono**

PLUPERFECT

io	**avevo dormito**
tu	**avevi dormito**
lui/lei/Lei	**aveva dormito**
noi	**avevamo dormito**
voi	**avevate dormito**
loro	**avevano dormito**

IMPERATIVE

dormi
dormiamo
dormite

EXAMPLE PHRASES

Stanotte **dormirò** come un ghiro. I'll sleep like a log tonight.

Se potessi **dormirei** fino a tardi. If I could I'd have a lie-in.

Dormimmo profondamente e ci svegliammo riposati. We slept soundly and woke up refreshed.

Aveva dormito male ed era nervoso. He hadn't slept well and was irritable.

Italic letters in Italian words show where stress does not follow the usual rules.

dovere (to have to)

PRESENT

io	**devo**
tu	**devi**
lui/lei/Lei	**deve**
noi	**dobbiamo**
voi	**dovete**
loro	**devono**

PRESENT SUBJUNCTIVE

io	**debba**
tu	**debba**
lui/lei/Lei	**debba**
noi	**dobbiamo**
voi	**dobbiate**
loro	**debbano**

PERFECT

io	**ho dovuto**
tu	**hai dovuto**
lui/lei/Lei	**ha dovuto**
noi	**abbiamo dovuto**
voi	**avete dovuto**
loro	**hanno dovuto**

IMPERFECT

io	**dovevo**
tu	**dovevi**
lui/lei/Lei	**doveva**
noi	**dovevamo**
voi	**dovevate**
loro	**dovevano**

GERUND

dovendo

PAST PARTICIPLE

dovuto

EXAMPLE PHRASES

Ora **devo** proprio andare. I've really got to go now.

Devi finire i compiti prima di uscire. You must finish your homework before you go out.

Dev'essere tardi. It must be late.

Non è che si **debba** sempre dire la verità. You don't always have to tell the truth.

Gli **dovevo** 30 euro e così l'ho invitato a cena. I owed him 30 euros so I took him out to dinner.

È **dovuto** partire. He had to leave.

Remember that subject pronouns are not used very often in Italian.

dovere

FUTURE

io	**dovrò**
tu	**dovrai**
lui/lei/Lei	**dovrà**
noi	**dovremo**
voi	**dovrete**
loro	**dovranno**

CONDITIONAL

io	**dovrei**
tu	**dovresti**
lui/lei/Lei	**dovrebbe**
noi	**dovremmo**
voi	**dovreste**
loro	**dovrebbero**

PAST HISTORIC

io	**dovetti**
tu	**dovesti**
lui/lei/Lei	**dovette**
noi	**dovemmo**
voi	**doveste**
loro	**dovettero**

PLUPERFECT

io	**avevo dovuto**
tu	**avevi dovuto**
lui/lei/Lei	**aveva dovuto**
noi	**avevamo dovuto**
voi	**avevate dovuto**
loro	**avevano dovuto**

IMPERATIVE

EXAMPLE PHRASES

Per correre la maratona **dovranno** allenarsi molto. They'll have to do a lot of training to run the marathon.

Dovrebbe arrivare alle dieci. He should arrive at ten.

Dovemmo partire all'improvviso. We had to leave unexpectedly.

Dovendo scegliere, preferisco la giacca blu. If I have to choose, I prefer the blue jacket.

Italic letters in Italian words show where stress does not follow the usual rules.

escludere (to exclude)

PRESENT

io	**escludo**
tu	**escludi**
lui/lei/Lei	**esclude**
noi	**escludiamo**
voi	**escludete**
loro	**escludono**

PRESENT SUBJUNCTIVE

io	**escluda**
tu	**escluda**
lui/lei/Lei	**escluda**
noi	**escludiamo**
voi	**escludiate**
loro	**escludano**

PERFECT

io	**ho escluso**
tu	**hai escluso**
lui/lei/Lei	**ha escluso**
noi	**abbiamo escluso**
voi	**avete escluso**
loro	**hanno escluso**

IMPERFECT

io	**escludevo**
tu	**escludevi**
lui/lei/Lei	**escludeva**
noi	**escludevamo**
voi	**escludevate**
loro	**escludevano**

GERUND

escludendo

PAST PARTICIPLE

escluso

EXAMPLE PHRASES

Escludo che possa essere stato lui. I certainly don't think it could have been him.

Una cosa non **esclude** l'altra. The one doesn't rule out the other.

È stato **escluso** dalla gara. He was excluded from the competition.

Non conosceva nessuno e si sentiva **esclusa**. She didn't know anyone and felt excluded.

Escludendo il pesce, mangio di tutto. Apart from fish, I eat everything.

Remember that subject pronouns are not used very often in Italian.

escludere

FUTURE

io	**escluderò**
tu	**escluderai**
lui/lei/Lei	**escluderà**
noi	**escluderemo**
voi	**escluderete**
loro	**escluderanno**

CONDITIONAL

io	**escluderei**
tu	**escluderesti**
lui/lei/Lei	**escluderebbe**
noi	**escluderemmo**
voi	**escludereste**
loro	**escluderebbero**

PAST HISTORIC

io	**esclusi**
tu	**escludesti**
lui/lei/Lei	**escluse**
noi	**escludemmo**
voi	**escludeste**
loro	**esclusero**

PLUPERFECT

io	**avevo escluso**
tu	**avevi escluso**
lui/lei/Lei	**aveva escluso**
noi	**avevamo escluso**
voi	**avevate escluso**
loro	**avevano escluso**

IMPERATIVE

escludi
escludiamo
escludete

EXAMPLE PHRASES

Non **escluderei** questa possibilità. I wouldn't rule out this possibility.

Italic letters in Italian words show where stress does not follow the usual rules.

esigere (to require)

PRESENT

io	**esigo**
tu	**esigi**
lui/lei/Lei	**esige**
noi	**esigiamo**
voi	**esigete**
loro	**esigono**

PRESENT SUBJUNCTIVE

io	**esiga**
tu	**esiga**
lui/lei/Lei	**esiga**
noi	**esigiamo**
voi	**esigiate**
loro	**esigano**

PERFECT

io	–
tu	–
lui/lei/Lei	–
noi	–
voi	–
loro	–

IMPERFECT

io	**esigevo**
tu	**esigevi**
lui/lei/Lei	**esigeva**
noi	**esigevamo**
voi	**esigevate**
loro	**esigevano**

GERUND

esigendo

PAST PARTICIPLE

–

EXAMPLE PHRASES

Il proprietario **esige** il pagamento immediato. The owner is demanding immediate payment.

È un lavoro che **esige** molta concentrazione. It's a job which demands a lot of concentration.

Il capufficio **esigeva** sempre la perfezione. The head clerk always demanded perfection.

esigere

FUTURE

io	**esigerò**
tu	**esigerai**
lui/lei/Lei	**esigerà**
noi	**esigeremo**
voi	**esigerete**
loro	**esigeranno**

CONDITIONAL

io	**esigerei**
tu	**esigeresti**
lui/lei/Lei	**esigerebbe**
noi	**esigeremmo**
voi	**esigereste**
loro	**esigerebbero**

PAST HISTORIC

io	**esigetti**
tu	**esigesti**
lui/lei/Lei	**esigette**
noi	**esigemmo**
voi	**esigeste**
loro	**esigettero**

PLUPERFECT

io	–
tu	–
lui/lei/Lei	–
noi	–
voi	–
loro	–

IMPERATIVE
esigi
esigiamo
esigete

EXAMPLE PHRASES

Esigerò sempre il massimo dagli studenti. I'll always demand the maximum from my students.

Devi **esigere** sempre rispetto dagli altri. You must always demand respect from other people.

Esigemmo una risposta immediata. We demanded an immediate reply.

Italic letters in Italian words show where stress does not follow the usual rules.

esistere (to exist)

	PRESENT		PRESENT SUBJUNCTIVE
io	**esisto**	io	**esista**
tu	**esisti**	tu	**esista**
lui/lei/Lei	**esiste**	lui/lei/Lei	**esista**
noi	**esistiamo**	noi	**esistiamo**
voi	**esistete**	voi	**esistiate**
loro	**esistono**	loro	**esistano**

	PERFECT		IMPERFECT
io	**sono esistito/a**	io	**esistevo**
tu	**sei esistito/a**	tu	**esistevi**
lui/lei/Lei	**è esistito/a**	lui/lei/Lei	**esisteva**
noi	**siamo esistiti/e**	noi	**esistevamo**
voi	**siete esistiti/e**	voi	**esistevate**
loro	**sono esistiti/e**	loro	**esistevano**

GERUND
esistendo

PAST PARTICIPLE
esistito

EXAMPLE PHRASES

Babbo Natale non **esiste**. Father Christmas doesn't exist.

Non **esiste**! No way!

In Italia **esistono** molte tradizioni religiose. There are many religious traditions in Italy.

Non sappiamo se **esista** la vita su altri pianeti. We do not know if life exists on other planets.

Il 221b di Baker Street non **è** mai **esistito**. There never was a 221b Baker Street.

Un tempo qui **esisteva** una grande città. At one time there was a great city here.

Remember that subject pronouns are not used very often in Italian.

esistere

FUTURE

io	esisterò
tu	esisterai
lui/lei/Lei	esisterà
noi	esisteremo
voi	esisterete
loro	esisteranno

CONDITIONAL

io	esisterei
tu	esisteresti
lui/lei/Lei	esisterebbe
noi	esisteremmo
voi	esistereste
loro	esisterebbero

PAST HISTORIC

io	esistei
tu	esistesti
lui/lei/Lei	esistette
noi	esistemmo
voi	esisteste
loro	esistettero

PLUPERFECT

io	ero esistito/a
tu	eri esistito/a
lui/lei/Lei	era esistito/a
noi	eravamo esistiti/e
voi	eravate esistiti/e
loro	erano esistiti/e

IMPERATIVE

esisti
esistiamo
esistite

EXAMPLE PHRASES

Non disperare: **esisterà** pure una soluzione al problema! Don't despair:
  there's sure to be a solution to the problem!

Secondo alcuni **esisterebbe** una quarta dimensione. Some people think
  there's a fourth dimension.

Italic letters in Italian words show where stress does not follow the usual rules.

espellere (to expel)

PRESENT

io	espello
tu	espelli
lui/lei/Lei	espelle
noi	espelliamo
voi	espellete
loro	espellono

PRESENT SUBJUNCTIVE

io	espella
tu	espella
lui/lei/Lei	espella
noi	espelliamo
voi	espelliate
loro	espellano

PERFECT

io	ho espulso
tu	hai espulso
lui/lei/Lei	ha espulso
noi	abbiamo espulso
voi	avete espulso
loro	hanno espulso

IMPERFECT

io	espellevo
tu	espellevi
lui/lei/Lei	espelleva
noi	espellevamo
voi	espellevate
loro	espellevano

GERUND

espellendo

PAST PARTICIPLE

espulso

EXAMPLE PHRASES

Non va a scuola perché l'**hanno espulso**. He doesn't go to school because he's been expelled.

Tutt'e due i calciatori **sono** stati **espulsi**. Both players were sent off.

espellerre

FUTURE

io	**espellerò**
tu	**espellerai**
lui/lei/Lei	**espellerà**
noi	**espelleremo**
voi	**espellerete**
loro	**espelleranno**

CONDITIONAL

io	**espellerei**
tu	**espelleresti**
lui/lei/Lei	**espellerebbe**
noi	**espelleremmo**
voi	**espellereste**
loro	**espellerebbero**

PAST HISTORIC

io	**espulsi**
tu	**espellesti**
lui/lei/Lei	**espulse**
noi	**espellemmo**
voi	**espelleste**
loro	**espulsero**

PLUPERFECT

io	**avevo espulso**
tu	**avevi espulso**
lui/lei/Lei	**aveva espulso**
noi	**avevamo espulso**
voi	**avevate espulso**
loro	**avevano espulso**

IMPERATIVE

espelli
espelliamo
espellete

EXAMPLE PHRASES

Espellerò chi non rispetta la disciplina. I will expel anyone who doesn't obey the rules.

Se farai un altro fallo ti **espelleranno**. If you commit another foul you'll be sent off.

Lo **espulsero** dalla scuola. He was expelled from the school.

Dopo mezz'ora l'arbitro **aveva** già **espulso** due giocatori. After half an hour the referee had already sent two players off.

Italic letters in Italian words show where stress does not follow the usual rules.

esplodere (to explode)

PRESENT

io	esplodo
tu	esplodi
lui/lei/Lei	esplode
noi	esplodiamo
voi	esplodete
loro	esplodono

PRESENT SUBJUNCTIVE

io	esploda
tu	esploda
lui/lei/Lei	esploda
noi	esplodiamo
voi	esplodiate
loro	esplodano

PERFECT

io	sono esploso/a
tu	sei esploso/a
lui/lei/Lei	è esploso/a
noi	siamo esplosi/e
voi	siete esplosi/e
loro	sono esplosi/e

IMPERFECT

io	esplodevo
tu	esplodevi
lui/lei/Lei	esplodeva
noi	esplodevamo
voi	esplodevate
loro	esplodevano

GERUND

esplodendo

PAST PARTICIPLE

esploso

EXAMPLE PHRASES

La nitroglicerina **esplode** facilmente. Nitroglycerin explodes easily.

L'ordigno **è esploso** uccidendo tre persone. The bomb exploded, killing three people.

Tutt'intorno **esplodevano** i colpi di cannone. Guns were firing on all sides.

Remember that subject pronouns are not used very often in Italian.

esplodere

FUTURE

io	**esploderò**
tu	**esploderai**
lui/lei/Lei	**esploderà**
noi	**esploderemo**
voi	**esploderete**
loro	**esploderanno**

CONDITIONAL

io	**esploderei**
tu	**esploderesti**
lui/lei/Lei	**esploderebbe**
noi	**esploderemmo**
voi	**esplodereste**
loro	**esploderebbero**

PAST HISTORIC

io	**esplosi**
tu	**esplodesti**
lui/lei/Lei	**esplose**
noi	**esplodemmo**
voi	**esplodeste**
loro	**esplosero**

PLUPERFECT

io	**ero esploso/a**
tu	**eri esploso/a**
lui/lei/Lei	**era esploso/a**
noi	**eravamo esplosi/e**
voi	**eravate esplosi/e**
loro	**erano esplosi/e**

IMPERATIVE

esplodi
esplodiamo
esplodete

EXAMPLE PHRASES

Cerca di trattenersi, ma prima o poi **esploderà**. He's trying to control himself, but sooner or later he'll explode.

Una bomba **esplose** vicino alla trincea. A bomb exploded near the trench.

Le mina **era esplosa** senza ferire nessuno. The mine exploded without injuring anyone.

Italic letters in Italian words show where stress does not follow the usual rules.

esprimere (to express)

PRESENT

io	**esprimo**
tu	**esprimi**
lui/lei/Lei	**esprime**
noi	**esprimiamo**
voi	**esprimete**
loro	**esprimono**

PRESENT SUBJUNCTIVE

io	**esprima**
tu	**esprima**
lui/lei/Lei	**esprima**
noi	**esprimiamo**
voi	**esprimiate**
loro	**esprimano**

PERFECT

io	**ho espresso**
tu	**hai espresso**
lui/lei/Lei	**ha espresso**
noi	**abbiamo espresso**
voi	**avete espresso**
loro	**hanno espresso**

IMPERFECT

io	**esprimevo**
tu	**esprimevi**
lui/lei/Lei	**esprimeva**
noi	**esprimevamo**
voi	**esprimevate**
loro	**esprimevano**

GERUND

esprimendo

PAST PARTICIPLE

espresso

EXAMPLE PHRASES

Non **esprime** mai la sua opinione. He never expresses his own opinion.

Se non conosco la lingua, mi **esprimo** a gesti. If I don't know the language, I use gestures.

È meglio che tu non **esprima** le tue idee. You'd better not express your ideas.

Abbiamo espresso i nostri dubbi. We expressed our doubts.

esprimere

FUTURE

io	**esprimerò**
tu	**esprimerai**
lui/lei/Lei	**esprimerà**
noi	**esprimeremo**
voi	**esprimerete**
loro	**esprimeranno**

CONDITIONAL

io	**esprimerei**
tu	**esprimeresti**
lui/lei/Lei	**esprimerebbe**
noi	**esprimeremmo**
voi	**esprimereste**
loro	**esprimerebbero**

PAST HISTORIC

io	**espressi**
tu	**esprimesti**
lui/lei/Lei	**espresse**
noi	**esprimemmo**
voi	**esprimeste**
loro	**espressero**

PLUPERFECT

io	**avevo espresso**
tu	**avevi espresso**
lui/lei/Lei	**aveva espresso**
noi	**avevamo espresso**
voi	**avevate espresso**
loro	**avevano espresso**

IMPERATIVE

esprimi
esprimiamo
esprimete

EXAMPLE PHRASES

Il Parlamento si **espresse** a favore della proposta di legge. Parliament
approved the legislation.

Avevano espresso il desiderio di uscire. They had expressed a desire to go out.

Trovo difficile **esprimermi** in inglese. I find it difficult to express myself
in English.

Dai, **esprimi** un desiderio! Go on, make a wish!

Italic letters in Italian words show where stress does not follow the usual rules.

essere (to be)

PRESENT

io	**sono**
tu	**sei**
lui/lei/Lei	**è**
noi	**siamo**
voi	**siete**
loro	**sono**

PRESENT SUBJUNCTIVE

io	**sia**
tu	**sia**
lui/lei/Lei	**sia**
noi	**siamo**
voi	**siate**
loro	**siano**

PERFECT

io	**sono stato/a**
tu	**sei stato/a**
lui/lei/Lei	**è stato/a**
noi	**siamo stati/e**
voi	**siete stati/e**
loro	**sono stati/e**

IMPERFECT

io	**ero**
tu	**eri**
lui/lei/Lei	**era**
noi	**eravamo**
voi	**eravate**
loro	**erano**

GERUND

essendo

PAST PARTICIPLE

stato

EXAMPLE PHRASES

Sono italiana. I'm Italian.

Mario **è** appena partito. Mario has just left.

Siete mai **stati** in Africa? Have you ever been to Africa?

Quando è arrivato **erano** le quattro in punto. When he arrived it was exactly four o'clock.

Essendo così tardi, dubito che verranno più. As it's so late I doubt they'll be coming.

Remember that subject pronouns are not used very often in Italian.

essere

FUTURE

io	**sarò**
tu	**sarai**
lui/lei/Lei	**sarà**
noi	**saremo**
voi	**sarete**
loro	**saranno**

CONDITIONAL

io	**sarei**
tu	**saresti**
lui/lei/Lei	**sarebbe**
noi	**saremmo**
voi	**sareste**
loro	**sarebbero**

PAST HISTORIC

io	**fui**
tu	**fosti**
lui/lei/Lei	**fu**
noi	**fummo**
voi	**foste**
loro	**furono**

PLUPERFECT

io	**ero stato/a**
tu	**eri stato/a**
lui/lei/Lei	**era stato/a**
noi	**eravamo stati/e**
voi	**eravate stati/e**
loro	**erano stati/e**

IMPERATIVE

sii

siamo

siate

EXAMPLE PHRASES

Alla festa ci **saranno** tutti i miei amici. All my friends will be at the party.

Saresti così gentile da aiutarmi? Would you be kind enough to help me?

Quando **fui** pronto, chiusi la valigia e partii. When I was ready I fastened my case and left.

Non **era** mai **stato** così preoccupato in vita sua. He'd never been so worried in his life.

Siate onesti, e ammettete il vostro errore. Be honest and admit your mistake.

Italic letters in Italian words show where stress does not follow the usual rules.

fare (to do, to make)

PRESENT		**PRESENT SUBJUNCTIVE**	
io	**faccio**	io	**faccia**
tu	**fai**	tu	**faccia**
lui/lei/Lei	**fa**	lui/lei/Lei	**faccia**
noi	**facciamo**	noi	**facciamo**
voi	**fate**	voi	**facciate**
loro	**fanno**	loro	**facciano**

PERFECT		**IMPERFECT**	
io	**ho fatto**	io	**facevo**
tu	**hai fatto**	tu	**facevi**
lui/lei/Lei	**ha fatto**	lui/lei/Lei	**faceva**
noi	**abbiamo fatto**	noi	**facevamo**
voi	**avete fatto**	voi	**facevate**
loro	**hanno fatto**	loro	**facevano**

GERUND	**PAST PARTICIPLE**
facendo	fatto

EXAMPLE PHRASES

Due più due **fa** quattro. Two and two makes four.

Fa il medico. He is a doctor.

Fa caldo. It's hot.

Ho fatto un errore. I made a mistake.

Cosa stai **facendo**? What are you doing?

Remember that subject pronouns are not used very often in Italian.

fare

FUTURE

io	**farò**
tu	**farai**
lui/lei/Lei	**farà**
noi	**faremo**
voi	**farete**
loro	**faranno**

CONDITIONAL

io	**farei**
tu	**faresti**
lui/lei/Lei	**farebbe**
noi	**faremmo**
voi	**fareste**
loro	**farebbero**

PAST HISTORIC

io	**feci**
tu	**facesti**
lui/lei/Lei	**fece**
noi	**facemmo**
voi	**faceste**
loro	**fecero**

PLUPERFECT

io	**avevo fatto**
tu	**avevi fatto**
lui/lei/Lei	**aveva fatto**
noi	**avevamo fatto**
voi	**avevate fatto**
loro	**avevano fatto**

IMPERATIVE

fai or **fa'**
facciamo
fate

EXAMPLE PHRASES

Domani si **farà** tagliare i capelli. He's going to get his hair cut tomorrow.

Mi **faresti** un piacere? Would you do me a favour?

Fecero una stupenda vacanza al mare. They had a wonderful holiday at the seaside.

Le **aveva fatto** male la testa tutto il pomeriggio. She'd had a headache all afternoon.

Fammi un favore, ti prego. Please do me a favour.

Italic letters in Italian words show where stress does not follow the usual rules.

fingere (to pretend)

PRESENT

io	**fingo**
tu	**fingi**
lui/lei/Lei	**finge**
noi	**fingiamo**
voi	**fingete**
loro	**fingono**

PRESENT SUBJUNCTIVE

io	**finga**
tu	**finga**
lui/lei/Lei	**finga**
noi	**fingiamo**
voi	**fingiate**
loro	**fingano**

PERFECT

io	**ho finto**
tu	**hai finto**
lui/lei/Lei	**ha finto**
noi	**abbiamo finto**
voi	**avete finto**
loro	**hanno finto**

IMPERFECT

io	**fingevo**
tu	**fingevi**
lui/lei/Lei	**fingeva**
noi	**fingevamo**
voi	**fingevate**
loro	**fingevano**

GERUND
fingendo

PAST PARTICIPLE
finto

EXAMPLE PHRASES

Ha finto di non conoscermi. He pretended he didn't recognize me.

Si **è finto** ubriaco. He pretended he was drunk.

Fingevano sempre di avere capito tutto. They always pretended they'd understood everything.

Non risposi, **fingendo** di non ricordare. I didn't answer, pretending I couldn't remember.

fingere

FUTURE

io	**fingerò**
tu	**fingerai**
lui/lei/Lei	**fingerà**
noi	**fingeremo**
voi	**fingerete**
loro	**fingeranno**

CONDITIONAL

io	**fingerei**
tu	**fingeresti**
lui/lei/Lei	**fingerebbe**
noi	**fingeremmo**
voi	**fingereste**
loro	**fingerebbero**

PAST HISTORIC

io	**finsi**
tu	**fingesti**
lui/lei/Lei	**finse**
noi	**fingemmo**
voi	**fingeste**
loro	**finsero**

PLUPERFECT

io	**avevo finto**
tu	**avevi finto**
lui/lei/Lei	**aveva finto**
noi	**avevamo finto**
voi	**avevate finto**
loro	**avevano finto**

IMPERATIVE

fingi
fingiamo
fingete

EXAMPLE PHRASES

Fingeremo di avere molto da fare. We'll pretend we've got a lot to do.

La spia **finse** di essere un turista. The spy pretended to be a tourist.

Non devi **fingere** sentimenti che non provi. You mustn't pretend you have feelings that you don't have.

Fingiamo di dormire. Let's pretend we're asleep.

Italic letters in Italian words show where stress does not follow the usual rules.

fuggire (to run away)

PRESENT

io	**fuggo**
tu	**fuggi**
lui/lei/Lei	**fugge**
noi	**fuggiamo**
voi	**fuggite**
loro	**fuggono**

PRESENT SUBJUNCTIVE

io	**fugga**
tu	**fugga**
lui/lei/Lei	**fugga**
noi	**fuggiamo**
voi	**fuggiate**
loro	**fuggano**

PERFECT

io	**sono fuggito/a**
tu	**sei fuggito/a**
lui/lei/Lei	**è fuggito/a**
noi	**siamo fuggiti/e**
voi	**siete fuggiti/e**
loro	**sono fuggiti/e**

IMPERFECT

io	**fuggivo**
tu	**fuggivi**
lui/lei/Lei	**fuggiva**
noi	**fuggivamo**
voi	**fuggivate**
loro	**fuggivano**

GERUND

fuggendo

PAST PARTICIPLE

fuggito

EXAMPLE PHRASES

È **fuggita** di casa. She ran away from home.

Non è **fuggendo** che si risolvono i problemi. You won't solve problems by running away from them.

Il ladro stava **fuggendo** su un'auto sportiva. The robber was escaping in a sports car.

fuggire

FUTURE

io	**fuggirò**
tu	**fuggirai**
lui/lei/Lei	**fuggirà**
noi	**fuggiremo**
voi	**fuggirete**
loro	**fuggiranno**

CONDITIONAL

io	**fuggirei**
tu	**fuggiresti**
lui/lei/Lei	**fuggirebbe**
noi	**fuggiremmo**
voi	**fuggireste**
loro	**fuggirebbero**

PAST HISTORIC

io	**fuggii**
tu	**fuggisti**
lui/lei/Lei	**fuggì**
noi	**fuggimmo**
voi	**fuggiste**
loro	**fuggirono**

PLUPERFECT

io	**ero fuggito/a**
tu	**eri fuggito/a**
lui/lei/Lei	**era fuggito/a**
noi	**eravamo fuggiti/e**
voi	**eravate fuggiti/e**
loro	**erano fuggiti/e**

IMPERATIVE

fuggi
fuggiamo
fuggite

EXAMPLE PHRASES

Se non leghi bene il cane, **fuggirà**. If you don't chain up the dog properly he'll run off.

Se ci scopriranno, **fuggiremo**. If they find us we'll run for it.

Fuggirono di prigione. They escaped from prison.

La polizia! **Fuggiamo**! It's the police! Run for it!

Italic letters in Italian words show where stress does not follow the usual rules.

immergere (to immerse)

PRESENT

io	**immergo**
tu	**immergi**
lui/lei/Lei	**immerge**
noi	**immergiamo**
voi	**immergete**
loro	**immergono**

PRESENT SUBJUNCTIVE

io	**immerga**
tu	**immerga**
lui/lei/Lei	**immerga**
noi	**immergiamo**
voi	**immergiate**
loro	**immergano**

PERFECT

io	**ho immerso**
tu	**hai immerso**
lui/lei/Lei	**ha immerso**
noi	**abbiamo immerso**
voi	**avete immerso**
loro	**hanno immerso**

IMPERFECT

io	**immergevo**
tu	**immergevi**
lui/lei/Lei	**immergeva**
noi	**immergevamo**
voi	**immergevate**
loro	**immergevano**

GERUND

immergendo

PAST PARTICIPLE

immerso

EXAMPLE PHRASES

Ha immerso il metallo incandescente nell'acqua. He plunged the red-hot metal into the water.

Non la disturbare: **è immersa** nel lavoro. Don't disturb her: she's deep in her work.

Si **immergevano** nello studio ogni sera. They immersed themselves in their studies every night.

Ha scoperto il relitto **immergendosi** poco lontano. He discovered the wreck when he was diving not far away.

Remember that subject pronouns are not used very often in Italian.

immergere

FUTURE

io	**immergerò**
tu	**immergerai**
lui/lei/Lei	**immergerà**
noi	**immergeremo**
voi	**immergerete**
loro	**immergeranno**

CONDITIONAL

io	**immergerei**
tu	**immergeresti**
lui/lei/Lei	**immergerebbe**
noi	**immergeremmo**
voi	**immergereste**
loro	**immergerebbero**

PAST HISTORIC

io	**immersi**
tu	**immergesti**
lui/lei/Lei	**immerse**
noi	**immergemmo**
voi	**immergeste**
loro	**immersero**

PLUPERFECT

io	**avevo immerso**
tu	**avevi immerso**
lui/lei/Lei	**aveva immerso**
noi	**avevamo immerso**
voi	**avevate immerso**
loro	**avevano immerso**

IMPERATIVE

immergi
immergiamo
immergete

EXAMPLE PHRASES

Ci **immergeremo** nelle acque dell'Adriatico. We'll dive in the waters of the Adriatic.

Il sottomarino si **immerse**. The submarine submerged.

Italic letters in Italian words show where stress does not follow the usual rules.

intendere (to understand)

PRESENT

io	**intendo**
tu	**intendi**
lui/lei/Lei	**intende**
noi	**intendiamo**
voi	**intendete**
loro	**intendono**

PRESENT SUBJUNCTIVE

io	**intenda**
tu	**intenda**
lui/lei/Lei	**intenda**
noi	**intendiamo**
voi	**intendiate**
loro	**intendano**

PERFECT

io	**ho inteso**
tu	**hai inteso**
lui/lei/Lei	**ha inteso**
noi	**abbiamo inteso**
voi	**avete inteso**
loro	**hanno inteso**

IMPERFECT

io	**intendevo**
tu	**intendevi**
lui/lei/Lei	**intendeva**
noi	**intendevamo**
voi	**intendevate**
loro	**intendevano**

GERUND

intendendo

PAST PARTICIPLE

inteso

EXAMPLE PHRASES

Dipende da cosa **intendi** per "giustizia". It depends what you mean by "justice".

Si **intende** di fotografia. She knows about photography.

Non riusciamo a capire che cosa **intendano**. We don't know what they mean.

Siamo sicuri che si **intenda** di automobili? Can we be sure he knows about cars?

Ci **siamo intesi**? Is that clear?

Cosa **intendevi**? What did you mean?

Remember that subject pronouns are not used very often in Italian.

intendere

FUTURE

io	**intenderò**
tu	**intenderai**
lui/lei/Lei	**intenderà**
noi	**intenderemo**
voi	**intenderete**
loro	**intenderanno**

CONDITIONAL

io	**intenderei**
tu	**intenderesti**
lui/lei/Lei	**intenderebbe**
noi	**intenderemmo**
voi	**intendereste**
loro	**intenderebbero**

PAST HISTORIC

io	**intesi**
tu	**intendesti**
lui/lei/Lei	**intese**
noi	**intendemmo**
voi	**intendeste**
loro	**intesero**

PLUPERFECT

io	**avevo inteso**
tu	**avevi inteso**
lui/lei/Lei	**aveva inteso**
noi	**avevamo inteso**
voi	**avevate inteso**
loro	**avevano inteso**

IMPERATIVE

intendi
intendiamo
intendete

EXAMPLE PHRASES

Noi due non ci **intenderemo** mai. We two will never agree.

Intenderesti dire che ho sbagliato? Are you saying I made a mistake?

Italic letters in Italian words show where stress does not follow the usual rules.

invadere (to invade)

PRESENT		PRESENT SUBJUNCTIVE	
io	invado	io	invada
tu	invadi	tu	invada
lui/lei/Lei	invade	lui/lei/Lei	invada
noi	invadiamo	noi	invadiamo
voi	invadete	voi	invadiate
loro	invadono	loro	invadano

PERFECT		IMPERFECT	
io	ho invaso	io	invadevo
tu	hai invaso	tu	invadevi
lui/lei/Lei	ha invaso	lui/lei/Lei	invadeva
noi	abbiamo invaso	noi	invadevamo
voi	avete invaso	voi	invadevate
loro	hanno invaso	loro	invadevano

GERUND
invadendo

PAST PARTICIPLE
invaso

EXAMPLE PHRASES

La folla **invade** la piazza. The crowd is streaming into the square.

I tifosi **hanno invaso** il campo. The fans invaded the pitch.

L'esercito stava **invadendo** la città. The army was taking possession of the city.

invadere

FUTURE

io	**invaderò**
tu	**invaderai**
lui/lei/Lei	**invaderà**
noi	**invaderemo**
voi	**invaderete**
loro	**invaderanno**

CONDITIONAL

io	**invaderei**
tu	**invaderesti**
lui/lei/Lei	**invaderebbe**
noi	**invaderemmo**
voi	**invadereste**
loro	**invaderebbero**

PAST HISTORIC

io	**invasi**
tu	**invadesti**
lui/lei/Lei	**invase**
noi	**invademmo**
voi	**invadeste**
loro	**invasero**

PLUPERFECT

io	**avevo invaso**
tu	**avevi invaso**
lui/lei/Lei	**aveva invaso**
noi	**avevamo invaso**
voi	**avevate invaso**
loro	**avevano invaso**

IMPERATIVE

invadi
invadiamo
invadete

EXAMPLE PHRASES

Senza steccati le pecore **invaderebbero** i campi. Without fences the sheep would overrun the fields.

Il nemico **invase** il Paese. The enemy invaded the country.

invecchiare (to get old)

PRESENT

io	invecchio
tu	invecchi
lui/lei/Lei	invecchia
noi	invecchiamo
voi	invecchiate
loro	invecchiano

PRESENT SUBJUNCTIVE

io	invecchi
tu	invecchi
lui/lei/Lei	invecchi
noi	invecchiamo
voi	invecchiate
loro	invecchino

PERFECT

io	sono invecchiato/a
tu	sei invecchiato/a
lui/lei/Lei	è invecchiato/a
noi	siamo invecchiati/e
voi	siete invecchiati/e
loro	sono invecchiati/e

IMPERFECT

io	invecchiavo
tu	invecchiavi
lui/lei/Lei	invecchiava
noi	invecchiavamo
voi	invecchiavate
loro	invecchiavano

GERUND

invecchiando

PAST PARTICIPLE

invecchiato

EXAMPLE PHRASES

La barba ti **invecchia**. The beard makes you look older.

Tutti **invecchiano** prima o poi. Everyone gets old sooner or later.

Questo vino **è invecchiato** in botti di rovere. This wine is aged in oak casks.

Invecchiava a vista d'occhio. He was visibly ageing.

Il vino migliora **invecchiando**. Wine gets better with age.

Molti hanno paura di **invecchiare**. A lot of people are afraid of getting old.

Remember that subject pronouns are not used very often in Italian.

invecchiare

FUTURE

io	**invecchierò**
tu	**invecchierai**
lui/lei/Lei	**invecchierà**
noi	**invecchieremo**
voi	**invecchierete**
loro	**invecchieranno**

CONDITIONAL

io	**invecchierei**
tu	**invecchieresti**
lui/lei/Lei	**invecchierebbe**
noi	**invecchieremmo**
voi	**invecchiereste**
loro	**invecchierebbero**

PAST HISTORIC

io	**invecchiai**
tu	**invecchiasti**
lui/lei/Lei	**invecchiò**
noi	**invecchiammo**
voi	**invecchiaste**
loro	**invecchiarono**

PLUPERFECT

io	**ero invecchiato/a**
tu	**eri invecchiato/a**
lui/lei/Lei	**era invecchiato/a**
noi	**eravamo invecchiati/e**
voi	**eravate invecchiati/e**
loro	**erano invecchiati/e**

IMPERATIVE

inv**e**cchia
invecchiamo
invecchiate

EXAMPLE PHRASES

Quando la rividi **era** molto **invecchiata**. When I saw her again she'd aged
a lot.

Italic letters in Italian words show where stress does not follow the usual rules.

inviare (to send)

PRESENT

io	**invio**
tu	**invii**
lui/lei/Lei	**invia**
noi	**inviamo**
voi	**inviate**
loro	**inviano**

PRESENT SUBJUNCTIVE

io	**invii**
tu	**invii**
lui/lei/Lei	**invii**
noi	**inviamo**
voi	**inviate**
loro	**iviino**

PERFECT

io	**ho inviato**
tu	**hai inviato**
lui/lei/Lei	**ha inviato**
noi	**abbiamo inviato**
voi	**avete inviato**
loro	**hanno inviato**

IMPERFECT

io	**inviavo**
tu	**inviavi**
lui/lei/Lei	**inviava**
noi	**inviavamo**
voi	**inviavate**
loro	**inviavano**

GERUND

inviando

PAST PARTICIPLE

inviato

EXAMPLE PHRASES

Per prenotare, è necessario che tu **invii** un'email. You have to send an email to book.

Non **ho** ancora **inviato** la domanda di iscrizione. I haven't sent the enrolment form off yet.

Il figlio le **inviava** un sms tutte le sere. Her son texted her every evening.

Potete partecipare **inviando** un'email. You can take part by sending an email.

Remember that subject pronouns are not used very often in Italian.

inviare

FUTURE

io	**invierò**
tu	**invierai**
lui/lei/Lei	**invierà**
noi	**invieremo**
voi	**invierete**
loro	**invieranno**

CONDITIONAL

io	**invierei**
tu	**invieresti**
lui/lei/Lei	**invierebbe**
noi	**invieremmo**
voi	**inviereste**
loro	**invierebbero**

PAST HISTORIC

io	**inviai**
tu	**inviasti**
lui/lei/Lei	**inviò**
noi	**inviammo**
voi	**inviaste**
loro	**inviarono**

PLUPERFECT

io	**avevo inviato**
tu	**avevi inviato**
lui/lei/Lei	**aveva inviato**
noi	**avevamo inviato**
voi	**avevate inviato**
loro	**avevano inviato**

IMPERATIVE

invia
inviamo
inviate

EXAMPLE PHRASES

Vi **invieremo** ulteriori dettagli in seguito. We will send you further
   details later.
Ti **invierei** le informazioni, ma non ho l'indirizzo. I'd send you the information,
   but I haven't got your address.
Quando arrivi, **inviami** un sms. Text me when you arrive.

Italic letters in Italian words show where stress does not follow the usual rules.

lasciare (to leave)

PRESENT

io	*lascio*
tu	**lasci**
lui/lei/Lei	**lascia**
noi	**lasciamo**
voi	**lasciate**
loro	**lasciano**

PRESENT SUBJUNCTIVE

io	**lasci**
tu	**lasci**
lui/lei/Lei	**lasci**
noi	**lasciamo**
voi	**lasciate**
loro	**lascino**

PERFECT

io	**ho lasciato**
tu	**hai lasciato**
lui/lei/Lei	**ha lasciato**
noi	**abbiamo lasciato**
voi	**avete lasciato**
loro	**hanno lasciato**

IMPERFECT

io	**lasciavo**
tu	**lasciavi**
lui/lei/Lei	**lasciava**
noi	**lasciavamo**
voi	**lasciavate**
loro	**lasciavano**

GERUND
lasciando

PAST PARTICIPLE
lasciato

EXAMPLE PHRASES

Mio padre non mi **lascia** uscire fino a tardi. My father doesn't let me stay out late.

È meglio che **lasci** la finestra aperta. You'd better leave the window open.

I miei si **sono lasciati** un anno fa. My parents split up a year ago.

La madre non lo **lasciava** mai solo un minuto. His mother never left him alone for a single minute.

Remember that subject pronouns are not used very often in Italian.

lasciare

FUTURE

io	**lascerò**
tu	**lascerai**
lui/lei/Lei	**lascerà**
noi	**lasceremo**
voi	**lascerete**
loro	**lasceranno**

CONDITIONAL

io	**lascerei**
tu	**lasceresti**
lui/lei/Lei	**lascerebbe**
noi	**lasceremmo**
voi	**lascereste**
loro	**lascerebbero**

PAST HISTORIC

io	**lasciai**
tu	**lasciasti**
lui/lei/Lei	**lasciò**
noi	**lasciammo**
voi	**lasciaste**
loro	**lasciarono**

PLUPERFECT

io	**avevo lasciato**
tu	**avevi lasciato**
lui/lei/Lei	**aveva lasciato**
noi	**avevamo lasciato**
voi	**avevate lasciato**
loro	**avevano lasciato**

IMPERATIVE

lascia
lasciamo
lasciate

EXAMPLE PHRASES

Fa caldo, **lascerò** a casa il maglione. It's hot, so I'll leave my jumper at home.

Il marito la **lasciò** per un'altra. Her husband left her for another woman.

Lascia fare a me. Let me do it.

Lasciamo stare, non vale la pena arrabbiarsi. Let's forget it, it's not worth getting angry about.

Italic letters in Italian words show where stress does not follow the usual rules.

leggere (to read)

PRESENT

io	**leggo**
tu	**leggi**
lui/lei/Lei	**legge**
noi	**leggiamo**
voi	**leggete**
loro	**leggono**

PRESENT SUBJUNCTIVE

io	**legga**
tu	**legga**
lui/lei/Lei	**legga**
noi	**leggiamo**
voi	**leggiate**
loro	**leggano**

PERFECT

io	**ho letto**
tu	**hai letto**
lui/lei/Lei	**ha letto**
noi	**abbiamo letto**
voi	**avete letto**
loro	**hanno letto**

IMPERFECT

io	**leggevo**
tu	**leggevi**
lui/lei/Lei	**leggeva**
noi	**leggevamo**
voi	**leggevate**
loro	**leggevano**

GERUND
leggendo

PAST PARTICIPLE
letto

EXAMPLE PHRASES

Legge il giornale tutti i giorni. She reads the paper every day.

Non **ho** ancora **letto** quel libro. I haven't read that book yet.

Leggevo molto prima di iniziare a lavorare. I read a lot before I started working.

Non li disturbiamo: stanno **leggendo**. Don't let's disturb them, they're reading.

Le piace molto **leggere**. She loves reading.

Remember that subject pronouns are not used very often in Italian.

leggere

FUTURE

io	**leggerò**
tu	**leggerai**
lui/lei/Lei	**leggerà**
noi	**leggeremo**
voi	**leggerete**
loro	**leggeranno**

CONDITIONAL

io	**leggerei**
tu	**leggeresti**
lui/lei/Lei	**leggerebbe**
noi	**leggeremmo**
voi	**leggereste**
loro	**leggerebbero**

PAST HISTORIC

io	**lessi**
tu	**leggesti**
lui/lei/Lei	**lesse**
noi	**leggemmo**
voi	**leggeste**
loro	**lessero**

PLUPERFECT

io	**avevo letto**
tu	**avevi letto**
lui/lei/Lei	**aveva letto**
noi	**avevamo letto**
voi	**avevate letto**
loro	**avevano letto**

IMPERATIVE

leggi
leggiamo
leggete

EXAMPLE PHRASES

Durante le vacanze **leggerò** un romanzo. I'll read a novel during the holidays.
Mi **leggeresti** le istruzioni? Sono senza occhiali. Could you read me the
instructions? I haven't got my glasses.
Leggete a voce alta, per favore. Read aloud please.

Italic letters in Italian words show where stress does not follow the usual rules.

mangiare (to eat)

PRESENT

io	mangio
tu	mangi
lui/lei/Lei	mangia
noi	mangiamo
voi	mangiate
loro	mangiano

PRESENT SUBJUNCTIVE

io	mangi
tu	mangi
lui/lei/Lei	mangi
noi	mangiamo
voi	mangiate
loro	mangino

PERFECT

io	ho mangiato
tu	hai mangiato
lui/lei/Lei	ha mangiato
noi	abbiamo mangiato
voi	avete mangiato
loro	hanno mangiato

IMPERFECT

io	mangiavo
tu	mangiavi
lui/lei/Lei	mangiava
noi	mangiavamo
voi	mangiavate
loro	mangiavano

GERUND

mangiando

PAST PARTICIPLE

mangiato

EXAMPLE PHRASES

Non **mangio** carne. I don't eat meat.

Si **mangia** bene in quel ristorante. The food is good in that restaurant.

Chi **ha mangiato** l'ultima fetta di torta? Who ate the last slice of cake?

Ultimamente sto **mangiando** troppo. I've been eating too much lately.

Remember that subject pronouns are not used very often in Italian.

mangiare

FUTURE

io	**mangerò**
tu	**mangerai**
lui/lei/Lei	**mangerà**
noi	**mangeremo**
voi	**mangerete**
loro	**mangeranno**

CONDITIONAL

io	**mangerei**
tu	**mangeresti**
lui/lei/Lei	**mangerebbe**
noi	**mangeremmo**
voi	**mangereste**
loro	**mangerebbero**

PAST HISTORIC

io	**mangiai**
tu	**mangiasti**
lui/lei/Lei	**mangiò**
noi	**mangiammo**
voi	**mangiaste**
loro	**mangiarono**

PLUPERFECT

io	**avevo mangiato**
tu	**avevi mangiato**
lui/lei/Lei	**aveva mangiato**
noi	**avevamo mangiato**
voi	**avevate mangiato**
loro	**avevano mangiato**

IMPERATIVE

mangia
mangiamo
mangiate

EXAMPLE PHRASES

Domani **mangeremo** pesce. We'll have fish tomorrow.

Mangerei volentieri del gelato. I'd like some ice cream.

Mangiarono troppo e fecero indigestione. They ate too much and got indigestion.

Mangia che la minestra si raffredda. Eat your soup, it's getting cold.

Italic letters in Italian words show where stress does not follow the usual rules.

mettere (to put)

PRESENT

io	**metto**
tu	**metti**
lui/lei/Lei	**mette**
noi	**mettiamo**
voi	**mettete**
loro	**mettono**

PRESENT SUBJUNCTIVE

io	**metta**
tu	**metta**
lui/lei/Lei	**metta**
noi	**mettiamo**
voi	**mettiate**
loro	**mettano**

PERFECT

io	**ho messo**
tu	**hai messo**
lui/lei/Lei	**ha messo**
noi	**abbiamo messo**
voi	**avete messo**
loro	**hanno messo**

IMPERFECT

io	**mettevo**
tu	**mettevi**
lui/lei/Lei	**metteva**
noi	**mettevamo**
voi	**mettevate**
loro	**mettevano**

GERUND

mettendo

PAST PARTICIPLE

messo

EXAMPLE PHRASES

Non **metto** più quelle scarpe. I don't wear those shoes any more.

È meglio che tu **metta** la sveglia. You'd better set the alarm.

Hai messo i bambini a letto? Have you put the children to bed?

Quanto tempo ci **hai messo**? How long did it take you?

Si **metteva** sempre un vecchio maglione blu. She always wore an old blue jumper.

Remember that subject pronouns are not used very often in Italian.

mettere

FUTURE

io	**metterò**
tu	**metterai**
lui/lei/Lei	**metterà**
noi	**metteremo**
voi	**metterete**
loro	**metteranno**

CONDITIONAL

io	**metterei**
tu	**metteresti**
lui/lei/Lei	**metterebbe**
noi	**metteremmo**
voi	**mettereste**
loro	**metterebbero**

PAST HISTORIC

io	**misi**
tu	**mettesti**
lui/lei/Lei	**mise**
noi	**mettemmo**
voi	**metteste**
loro	**misero**

PLUPERFECT

io	**avevo messo**
tu	**avevi messo**
lui/lei/Lei	**aveva messo**
noi	**avevamo messo**
voi	**avevate messo**
loro	**avevano messo**

IMPERATIVE

metti
mettiamo
mettete

EXAMPLE PHRASES

Metterò un annuncio sul giornale. I'll put an advert in the paper.

Quanto ci **metteresti** lavorando giorno e notte? How long would it take you if you worked day and night?

Si **misero** a sedere e aspettarono. They sat down and waited.

Mettiti là e aspetta. Wait there.

Italic letters in Italian words show where stress does not follow the usual rules.

morire (to die)

PRESENT

io	**muoio**
tu	**muori**
lui/lei/Lei	**muore**
noi	**moriamo**
voi	**morite**
loro	**muoiono**

PRESENT SUBJUNCTIVE

io	**muoia**
tu	**muoia**
lui/lei/Lei	**muoia**
noi	**moriamo**
voi	**moriate**
loro	**muoiano**

PERFECT

io	**sono morto/a**
tu	**sei morto/a**
lui/lei/Lei	**è morto/a**
noi	**siamo morti/e**
voi	**siete morti/e**
loro	**sono morti/e**

IMPERFECT

io	**morivo**
tu	**morivi**
lui/lei/Lei	**moriva**
noi	**morivamo**
voi	**morivate**
loro	**morivano**

GERUND

morendo

PAST PARTICIPLE

morto

EXAMPLE PHRASES

Muoio di sete. I'm parched.
Sono morti in un incidente. They were killed in an accident.
Sta **morendo** di fame. She's starving.
Moriva dalla voglia di raccontarle tutto. He was dying to tell her everything.

Remember that subject pronouns are not used very often in Italian.

morire

FUTURE

io	**morirò**
tu	**morirai**
lui/lei/Lei	**morirà**
noi	**moriremo**
voi	**morirete**
loro	**moriranno**

CONDITIONAL

io	**morirei**
tu	**moriresti**
lui/lei/Lei	**morirebbe**
noi	**moriremmo**
voi	**morireste**
loro	**morirebbero**

PAST HISTORIC

io	**morii**
tu	**moristi**
lui/lei/Lei	**morì**
noi	**morimmo**
voi	**moriste**
loro	**morirono**

PLUPERFECT

io	**ero morto/a**
tu	**eri morto/a**
lui/lei/Lei	**era morto/a**
noi	**eravamo morti/e**
voi	**eravate morti/e**
loro	**erano morti/e**

IMPERATIVE

muori
moriamo
morite

EXAMPLE PHRASES

Morirei di paura, ma lo farei. I'd be scared to death, but I'd do it.
Morì nel 1857. He died in 1857.
Il padre **era morto** in un incidente stradale. His father had been killed in
a car crash.

Italic letters in Italian words show where stress does not follow the usual rules.

muovere (to move)

PRESENT

io	**muovo**
tu	**muovi**
lui/lei/Lei	**muove**
noi	**muoviamo**
voi	**muovete**
loro	**muovono**

PRESENT SUBJUNCTIVE

io	**muova**
tu	**muova**
lui/lei/Lei	**muova**
noi	**muoviamo**
voi	**muoviate**
loro	**muovano**

PERFECT

io	**ho mosso**
tu	**hai mosso**
lui/lei/Lei	**ha mosso**
noi	**abbiamo mosso**
voi	**avete mosso**
loro	**hanno mosso**

IMPERFECT

io	**muovevo**
tu	**muovevi**
lui/lei/Lei	**muoveva**
noi	**muovevamo**
voi	**muovevate**
loro	**muovevano**

GERUND

muovendo

PAST PARTICIPLE

mosso

EXAMPLE PHRASES

Non si **muove**. It won't move.

Ho mosso l'alfiere per dare scacco al re. I moved the bishop to check the king.

Ti **sei mosso** e la foto è sfocata. You moved and the photo is out of focus.

Non **muovevo** più la gamba per il dolore. I could no longer move my leg because of the pain.

Il meccanismo si aziona **muovendo** la leva. You work the mechanism by moving the lever.

Remember that subject pronouns are not used very often in Italian.

muovere

FUTURE

io	muoverò
tu	muoverai
lui/lei/Lei	muoverà
noi	muoveremo
voi	muoverete
loro	muoveranno

CONDITIONAL

io	muoverei
tu	muoveresti
lui/lei/Lei	muoverebbe
noi	muoveremmo
voi	muovereste
loro	muoverebbero

PAST HISTORIC

io	mossi
tu	muovesti
lui/lei/Lei	mosse
noi	muovemmo
voi	muoveste
loro	mossero

PLUPERFECT

io	avevo mosso
tu	avevi mosso
lui/lei/Lei	aveva mosso
noi	avevamo mosso
voi	avevate mosso
loro	avevano mosso

IMPERATIVE

muovi
muoviamo
muovete

EXAMPLE PHRASES

Non ti **muovere**! Don't move!

Muoviti, o perdiamo il treno! Hurry up, or we'll miss the train!

Italic letters in Italian words show where stress does not follow the usual rules.

nascere (to be born)

PRESENT

io	**nasco**
tu	**nasci**
lui/lei/Lei	**nasce**
noi	**nasciamo**
voi	**nascete**
loro	**nascono**

PRESENT SUBJUNCTIVE

io	**nasca**
tu	**nasca**
lui/lei/Lei	**nasca**
noi	**nasciamo**
voi	**nasciate**
loro	**nascano**

PERFECT

io	**sono nato/a**
tu	**sei nato/a**
lui/lei/Lei	**è nato/a**
noi	**siamo nati/e**
voi	**siete nati/e**
loro	**sono nati/e**

IMPERFECT

io	**nascevo**
tu	**nascevi**
lui/lei/Lei	**nasceva**
noi	**nascevamo**
voi	**nascevate**
loro	**nascevano**

GERUND

nascendo

PAST PARTICIPLE

nato

EXAMPLE PHRASES

Speriamo che il bambino **nasca** dopo il trasloco. We're hoping the baby will be born after the move.

Sono nata il 28 aprile. I was born on the 28th of April.

È nato nel 1977. He was born in 1977.

nascere

FUTURE

io	**nascerò**
tu	**nascerai**
lui/lei/Lei	**nascerà**
noi	**nasceremo**
voi	**nascerete**
loro	**nasceranno**

CONDITIONAL

io	**nascerei**
tu	**nasceresti**
lui/lei/Lei	**nascerebbe**
noi	**nasceremmo**
voi	**nascereste**
loro	**nascerebbero**

PAST HISTORIC

io	**nacqui**
tu	**nascesti**
lui/lei/Lei	**nacque**
noi	**nascemmo**
voi	**nasceste**
loro	**nacquero**

PLUPERFECT

io	**ero nato/a**
tu	**eri nato/a**
lui/lei/Lei	**era nato/a**
noi	**eravamo nati/e**
voi	**eravate nati/e**
loro	**erano nati/e**

IMPERATIVE

nasci
nasciamo
nascete

EXAMPLE PHRASES

Il bambino **nascerà** tra due settimane. The baby is due in two weeks.

Franz Kafka **nacque** nel 1883. Franz Kafka was born in 1883.

Lasciò molto presto la casa dove **era nato**. Very soon he left the house where he was born.

Italic letters in Italian words show where stress does not follow the usual rules.

nuocere (to harm)

PRESENT

io	**nuoccio**
tu	**nuoci**
lui/lei/Lei	**nuoce**
noi	**nuociamo**
voi	**nuocete**
loro	**nuocciono**

PRESENT SUBJUNCTIVE

io	**nuoccia**
tu	**nuoccia**
lui/lei/Lei	**nuoccia**
noi	**nuociamo**
voi	**nuociate**
loro	**nuocciano**

PERFECT

io	**ho nuociuto**
tu	**hai nuociuto**
lui/lei/Lei	**ha nuociuto**
noi	**abbiamo nuociuto**
voi	**avete nuociuto**
loro	**hanno nuociuto**

IMPERFECT

io	**nuocevo**
tu	**nuocevi**
lui/lei/Lei	**nuoceva**
noi	**nuocevamo**
voi	**nuocevate**
loro	**nuocevano**

GERUND
nuocendo

PAST PARTICIPLE
nuociuto

EXAMPLE PHRASES

Il fumo **nuoce** alla salute. Smoking is bad for your health.

Si pensa che **nuoccia** all'ambiente. It is thought to be bad for the environment.

Le cattive conoscenze **hanno nuociuto** alla sua reputazione. His disreputable associates have damaged his reputation.

Anche se gli **nuoceva**, continuava a bere. Despite the harm it was doing him, he went on drinking.

Remember that subject pronouns are not used very often in Italian.

nuocere

FUTURE

io	**nuocerò**
tu	**nuocerai**
lui/lei/Lei	**nuocerà**
noi	**nuoceremo**
voi	**nuocerete**
loro	**nuoceranno**

CONDITIONAL

io	**nuocerei**
tu	**nuoceresti**
lui/lei/Lei	**nuocerebbe**
noi	**nuoceremmo**
voi	**nuocereste**
loro	**nuocerebbero**

PAST HISTORIC

io	**nocqui**
tu	**nuocesti**
lui/lei/Lei	**nocque**
noi	**nuocemmo**
voi	**nuoceste**
loro	**nocquero**

PLUPERFECT

io	**avevo nuociuto**
tu	**avevi nuociuto**
lui/lei/Lei	**aveva nuociuto**
noi	**avevamo nuociuto**
voi	**avevate nuociuto**
loro	**avevano nuociuto**

IMPERATIVE

nuoci
nuociamo
nuocete

EXAMPLE PHRASES

Un po' di vino non ti **nuocerà**. A drop of wine won't do you any harm.
Una settimana al mare non mi **nuocerebbe**. A week at the seaside would do me no harm.

Italic letters in Italian words show where stress does not follow the usual rules.

offendere (to offend)

PRESENT

io	**offendo**
tu	**offendi**
lui/lei/Lei	**offende**
noi	**offendiamo**
voi	**offendete**
loro	**offendono**

PRESENT SUBJUNCTIVE

io	**offenda**
tu	**offenda**
lui/lei/Lei	**offenda**
noi	**offendiamo**
voi	**offendiate**
loro	**offendano**

PERFECT

io	**ho offeso**
tu	**hai offeso**
lui/lei/Lei	**ha offeso**
noi	**abbiamo offeso**
voi	**avete offeso**
loro	**hanno offeso**

IMPERFECT

io	**offendevo**
tu	**offendevi**
lui/lei/Lei	**offendeva**
noi	**offendevamo**
voi	**offendevate**
loro	**offendevano**

GERUND
offendendo

PAST PARTICIPLE
offeso

EXAMPLE PHRASES

Se non vieni mi **offendo**. I'll be offended if you don't come.

Si è **offeso** per non essere stato invitato. He took offence because they didn't invite him.

Da piccolo si **offendeva** per un nonnulla. When he was a little boy he got upset over the slightest thing.

Cambia tono: mi stai **offendendo**! Don't talk like that: I find it offensive.

Non avevo intenzione di **offenderti**. I didn't mean to insult you.

Remember that subject pronouns are not used very often in Italian.

offendere

FUTURE

io	**offenderò**
tu	**offenderai**
lui/lei/Lei	**offenderà**
noi	**offenderemo**
voi	**offenderete**
loro	**offenderanno**

CONDITIONAL

io	**offenderei**
tu	**offenderesti**
lui/lei/Lei	**offenderebbe**
noi	**offenderemmo**
voi	**offendereste**
loro	**offenderebbero**

PAST HISTORIC

io	**offesi**
tu	**offendesti**
lui/lei/Lei	**offese**
noi	**offendemmo**
voi	**offendeste**
loro	**offesero**

PLUPERFECT

io	**avevo offeso**
tu	**avevi offeso**
lui/lei/Lei	**aveva offeso**
noi	**avevamo offeso**
voi	**avevate offeso**
loro	**avevano offeso**

IMPERATIVE

offendi
offendiamo
offendete

EXAMPLE PHRASES

Dimmi tutto: prometto che non mi **offenderò**. Tell me everything: I promise I won't be offended.

Se glielo dicessi, si **offenderebbe**. If I told him that he'd be offended.

L'**avevamo offeso** e non ci parlava più. We'd offended him and he wouldn't speak to us any more.

Italic letters in Italian words show where stress does not follow the usual rules.

offrire (to offer)

PRESENT

io	**offro**
tu	**offri**
lui/lei/Lei	**offre**
noi	**offriamo**
voi	**offrite**
loro	**offrono**

PRESENT SUBJUNCTIVE

io	**offra**
tu	**offra**
lui/lei/Lei	**offra**
noi	**offriamo**
voi	**offriate**
loro	**offrano**

PERFECT

io	**ho offerto**
tu	**hai offerto**
lui/lei/Lei	**ha offerto**
noi	**abbiamo offerto**
voi	**avete offerto**
loro	**hanno offerto**

IMPERFECT

io	**offrivo**
tu	**offrivi**
lui/lei/Lei	**offriva**
noi	**offrivamo**
voi	**offrivate**
loro	**offrivano**

GERUND

offrendo

PAST PARTICIPLE

offerto

EXAMPLE PHRASES

Offro io, questa volta! I'll pay this time!

Spero si **offrano** di aiutarci. I hope they'll offer to help us.

Mi **ha offerto** un passaggio. He offered me a lift.

Nessuno si **è offerto** volontario. Nobody volunteered.

Offriva sempre il suo aiuto a tutti. She always offered help to everyone.

Remember that subject pronouns are not used very often in Italian.

offrire

FUTURE

io	**offrirò**
tu	**offrirai**
lui/lei/Lei	**offrirà**
noi	**offriremo**
voi	**offrirete**
loro	**offriranno**

CONDITIONAL

io	**offrirei**
tu	**offriresti**
lui/lei/Lei	**offrirebbe**
noi	**offriremmo**
voi	**offrireste**
loro	**offrirebbero**

PAST HISTORIC

io	**offrii**
tu	**offristi**
lui/lei/Lei	**offrì**
noi	**offrimmo**
voi	**offriste**
loro	**offrirono**

PLUPERFECT

io	**avevo offerto**
tu	**avevi offerto**
lui/lei/Lei	**aveva offerto**
noi	**avevamo offerto**
voi	**avevate offerto**
loro	**avevano offerto**

IMPERATIVE

offri
offriamo
offrite

EXAMPLE PHRASES

L'università **offrirà** consulenza e orientamento. The university will provide guidance and advice.

Mi **offriresti** una sigaretta? Could you let me have a cigarette?

Le **offrirono** un lavoro. They offered her a job.

Offri da bere agli amici! Offer our friends a drink!

Italic letters in Italian words show where stress does not follow the usual rules.

pagare (to pay)

PRESENT

io	**pago**
tu	**paghi**
lui/lei/Lei	**paga**
noi	**paghiamo**
voi	**pagate**
loro	**pagano**

PRESENT SUBJUNCTIVE

io	**paghi**
tu	**paghi**
lui/lei/Lei	**paghi**
noi	**paghiamo**
voi	**paghiate**
loro	**paghino**

PERFECT

io	**ho pagato**
tu	**hai pagato**
lui/lei/Lei	**ha pagato**
noi	**abbiamo pagato**
voi	**avete pagato**
loro	**hanno pagato**

IMPERFECT

io	**pagavo**
tu	**pagavi**
lui/lei/Lei	**pagava**
noi	**pagavamo**
voi	**pagavate**
loro	**pagavano**

GERUND

pagando

PAST PARTICIPLE

pagato

EXAMPLE PHRASES

Pago io. I'll pay.

Hai pagato il conto? Have you paid the bill?

Quando uscivamo insieme **pagava** sempre lui. When we went out together he always paid.

Pagando si ottiene tutto. You can get anything if you pay for it.

Avevo finito di **pagare** la macchina il giorno dell'incidente. I'd finished paying for the car on the day of the accident.

Remember that subject pronouns are not used very often in Italian.

pagare

FUTURE

io	**pagherò**
tu	**pagherai**
lui/lei/Lei	**pagherà**
noi	**pagheremo**
voi	**pagherete**
loro	**pagheranno**

CONDITIONAL

io	**pagherei**
tu	**pagheresti**
lui/lei/Lei	**pagherebbe**
noi	**pagheremmo**
voi	**paghereste**
loro	**pagherebbero**

PAST HISTORIC

io	**pagai**
tu	**pagasti**
lui/lei/Lei	**pagò**
noi	**pagammo**
voi	**pagaste**
loro	**pagarono**

PLUPERFECT

io	**avevo pagato**
tu	**avevi pagato**
lui/lei/Lei	**aveva pagato**
noi	**avevamo pagato**
voi	**avevate pagato**
loro	**avevano pagato**

IMPERATIVE

paga
paghiamo
pagate

EXAMPLE PHRASES

La **pagherai**! You'll pay for this!

Pagherei io, ma non accettano carte di credito. I'd pay, but they don't accept credit cards.

Pagò un conto salatissimo. She paid an enormous bill.

Paga tu stavolta! You pay this time!

Italic letters in Italian words show where stress does not follow the usual rules.

parere (to appear)

PRESENT

io	**paio**
tu	**pari**
lui/lei/Lei	**pare**
noi	**pariamo**
voi	**parete**
loro	**paiono**

PRESENT SUBJUNCTIVE

io	**paia**
tu	**paia**
lui/lei/Lei	**paia**
noi	**paiamo**
voi	**paiate**
loro	**paiano**

PERFECT

io	**sono parso/a**
tu	**sei parso/a**
lui/lei/Lei	**è parso/a**
noi	**siamo parsi/e**
voi	**siete parsi/e**
loro	**sono parsi/e**

IMPERFECT

io	**parevo**
tu	**parevi**
lui/lei/Lei	**pareva**
noi	**parevamo**
voi	**parevate**
loro	**parevano**

GERUND
parendo

PAST PARTICIPLE
parso

EXAMPLE PHRASES

Mi **pare** che sia già arrivato. I think he's already here.

Ci **è parso** che foste stanchi. We thought you were tired.

Faceva solo ciò che gli **pareva**. He did just what he liked.

parere

FUTURE		CONDITIONAL	
io	**parrò**	io	**parrei**
tu	**parrai**	tu	**parresti**
lui/lei/Lei	**parrà**	lui/lei/Lei	**parrebbe**
noi	**parremo**	noi	**parremmo**
voi	**parrete**	voi	**parreste**
loro	**parranno**	loro	**parrebbero**

PAST HISTORIC		PLUPERFECT	
io	**parvi**	io	**ero parso/a**
tu	**paresti**	tu	**eri parso/a**
lui/lei/Lei	**parve**	lui/lei/Lei	**era parso/a**
noi	**paremmo**	noi	**eravamo parsi/e**
voi	**pareste**	voi	**eravate parsi/e**
loro	**parvero**	loro	**erano parsi/e**

IMPERATIVE

pari

pariamo

parete

EXAMPLE PHRASES

Mi **parrebbe** di disturbare. I wouldn't want to be a nuisance.

Gli **parve** che non lo volessero con loro. He thought they didn't want him with them.

Quella sera mi **parvero** tutti ubriachi. They all seemed drunk that night.

Mi **era parso** che volessi da bere. I'd thought you wanted something to drink.

Italic letters in Italian words show where stress does not follow the usual rules.

parlare (to speak)

PRESENT		PRESENT SUBJUNCTIVE	
io	parlo	io	parli
tu	parli	tu	parli
lui/lei/Lei	parla	lui/lei/Lei	parli
noi	parliamo	noi	parliamo
voi	parlate	voi	parliate
loro	parlano	loro	parlino

PERFECT		IMPERFECT	
io	ho parlato	io	parlavo
tu	hai parlato	tu	parlavi
lui/lei/Lei	ha parlato	lui/lei/Lei	parlava
noi	abbiamo parlato	noi	parlavamo
voi	avete parlato	voi	parlavate
loro	hanno parlato	loro	parlavano

GERUND
parlando

PAST PARTICIPLE
parlato

EXAMPLE PHRASES

Pronto, chi **parla**? Hello, who's speaking?

Di cosa **parla** quel libro? What is that book about?

Lascia che gli **parli** io. Let me talk to him.

Abbiamo parlato per ore. We talked for hours.

Passammo il pomeriggio **parlando** del più e del meno. We spent the
   afternoon talking about this and that.

Remember that subject pronouns are not used very often in Italian.

parlare

FUTURE

io	**parlerò**
tu	**parlerai**
lui/lei/Lei	**parlerà**
noi	**parleremo**
voi	**parlerete**
loro	**parleranno**

CONDITIONAL

io	**parlerei**
tu	**parleresti**
lui/lei/Lei	**parlerebbe**
noi	**parleremmo**
voi	**parlereste**
loro	**parlerebbero**

PAST HISTORIC

io	**parlai**
tu	**parlasti**
lui/lei/Lei	**parlò**
noi	**parlammo**
voi	**parlaste**
loro	**parlarono**

PLUPERFECT

io	**avevo parlato**
tu	**avevi parlato**
lui/lei/Lei	**aveva parlato**
noi	**avevamo parlato**
voi	**avevate parlato**
loro	**avevano parlato**

IMPERATIVE

parla
parliamo
parlate

EXAMPLE PHRASES

Gli **parlerò** di te. I'll talk to him about you.

Non **parlerei** mai male dei miei amici. I'd never speak ill of my friends.

Mi **avevano** già **parlato** di te. They'd already talked to me about you.

Non **parliamone** più. Let's just forget about it.

pescare (to fish)

PRESENT

io	**pesco**
tu	**peschi**
lui/lei/Lei	**pesca**
noi	**peschiamo**
voi	**pescate**
loro	**pescano**

PRESENT SUBJUNCTIVE

io	**peschi**
tu	**peschi**
lui/lei/Lei	**peschi**
noi	**peschiamo**
voi	**peschiate**
loro	**peschino**

PERFECT

io	**ho pescato**
tu	**hai pescato**
lui/lei/Lei	**ha pescato**
noi	**abbiamo pescato**
voi	**avete pescato**
loro	**hanno pescato**

IMPERFECT

io	**pescavo**
tu	**pescavi**
lui/lei/Lei	**pescava**
noi	**pescavamo**
voi	**pescavate**
loro	**pescavano**

GERUND

pescando

PAST PARTICIPLE

pescato

EXAMPLE PHRASES

Ho pescato un pesce enorme. I caught an enormous fish.

Dove diavolo **hai pescato** quella giacca? Where on earth did you get that jacket?

Ti insegnerò a **pescare**. I'll teach you how to fish.

Remember that subject pronouns are not used very often in Italian.

pescare

FUTURE

io	**pescherò**
tu	**pescherai**
lui/lei/Lei	**pescherà**
noi	**pescheremo**
voi	**pescherete**
loro	**pescheranno**

CONDITIONAL

io	**pescherei**
tu	**pescheresti**
lui/lei/Lei	**pescherebbe**
noi	**pescheremmo**
voi	**peschereste**
loro	**pescherebbero**

PAST HISTORIC

io	**pescai**
tu	**pescasti**
lui/lei/Lei	**pescò**
noi	**pescammo**
voi	**pescaste**
loro	**pescarono**

PLUPERFECT

io	**avevo pescato**
tu	**avevi pescato**
lui/lei/Lei	**aveva pescato**
noi	**avevamo pescato**
voi	**avevate pescato**
loro	**avevano pescato**

IMPERATIVE

pesca
peschiamo
pescate

EXAMPLE PHRASES

Io **pescherò** il pesce e tu lo cucinerai. I'll catch the fish and you can cook it.
Pescammo tutto il giorno. We fished all day.
Avevano pescato molto pesce per la cena. They'd caught a lot of fish for dinner.

Italic letters in Italian words show where stress does not follow the usual rules.

piacere (to be pleasing)

PRESENT		PRESENT SUBJUNCTIVE	
io	**piaccio**	io	**piaccia**
tu	**piaci**	tu	**piaccia**
lui/lei/Lei	**piace**	lui/lei/Lei	**piaccia**
noi	**piacciamo**	noi	**piacciamo**
voi	**piacete**	voi	**piacciate**
loro	**piacciono**	loro	**piacciano**

PERFECT		IMPERFECT	
io	**sono piaciuto/a**	io	**piacevo**
tu	**sei piaciuto/a**	tu	**piacevi**
lui/lei/Lei	**è piaciuto/a**	lui/lei/Lei	**piaceva**
noi	**siamo piaciuti/e**	noi	**piacevamo**
voi	**siete piaciuti/e**	voi	**piacevate**
loro	**sono piaciuti/e**	loro	**piacevano**

GERUND
piacendo

PAST PARTICIPLE
piaciuto

EXAMPLE PHRASES

Questa musica non mi **piace**. I don't like this music.

Spero che il regalo vi **piaccia**. I hope you like the present.

La birra non le **è** mai **piaciuta**. She's never liked beer.

Da piccola non mi **piacevano** i ragni. I didn't like spiders when I was little.

Remember that subject pronouns are not used very often in Italian.

piacere

FUTURE

io	**piacerò**
tu	**piacerai**
lui/lei/Lei	**piacerà**
noi	**piaceremo**
voi	**piacerete**
loro	**piaceranno**

CONDITIONAL

io	**piacerei**
tu	**piaceresti**
lui/lei/Lei	**piacerebbe**
noi	**piaceremmo**
voi	**piacereste**
loro	**piacerebbero**

PAST HISTORIC

io	**piacqui**
tu	**piacesti**
lui/lei/Lei	**piacque**
noi	**piacemmo**
voi	**piaceste**
loro	**piacquero**

PLUPERFECT

io	**ero piaciuto/a**
tu	**eri piaciuto/a**
lui/lei/Lei	**era piaciuto/a**
noi	**eravamo piaciuti/e**
voi	**eravate piaciuti/e**
loro	**erano piaciuti/e**

IMPERATIVE

piaci
piacciamo
piacciate

EXAMPLE PHRASES

La nuova casa ti **piacerà**, vedrai. You'll like the new house, you'll see.

Cosa ti **piacerebbe** fare? What would you like to do?

Mi **piacque** appena la vidi. I liked her as soon as I saw her.

Vi **era piaciuto** il film? Did you like the film?

Italic letters in Italian words show where stress does not follow the usual rules.

piovere (to rain)

PRESENT

io	**piove**
tu	
lui/lei/Lei	
noi	
voi	
loro	

PRESENT SUBJUNCTIVE

io	**piova**
tu	
lui/lei/Lei	
noi	
voi	
loro	

PERFECT

io	**ha** or **è piovuto**
tu	
lui/lei/Lei	
noi	
voi	
loro	

IMPERFECT

io	**pioveva**
tu	
lui/lei/Lei	
noi	
voi	
loro	

GERUND
piovendo

PAST PARTICIPLE
piovuto

EXAMPLE PHRASES

Piove. It's raining.

Speriamo che non **piova**. Let's hope it doesn't rain.

Ha piovuto tutto il giorno. It's rained all day.

Quando sono uscita **pioveva**. When I went out it was raining.

Sta **piovendo**: prendi l'ombrello. It's raining – take your umbrella.

piovere

FUTURE

io	**pioverà**
tu	
lui/lei/Lei	
noi	
voi	
loro	

CONDITIONAL

io	**pioverebbe**
tu	
lui/lei/Lei	
noi	
voi	
loro	

PAST HISTORIC

io	**piovve**
tu	
lui/lei/Lei	
noi	
voi	
loro	

PLUPERFECT

io	**era** or **aveva piovuto**
tu	
lui/lei/Lei	
noi	
voi	
loro	

IMPERATIVE

-

EXAMPLE PHRASES

Guarda che nubi: **pioverà** di certo. Look at those clouds – it's going to rain for sure.

Piovve tutta la notte. It rained all night.

Aveva piovuto e le strade erano bagnate. It had been raining and the roads were wet.

Italic letters in Italian words show where stress does not follow the usual rules.

potere (to be able)

PRESENT		PRESENT SUBJUNCTIVE	
io	**posso**	io	**possa**
tu	**puoi**	tu	**possa**
lui/lei/Lei	**può**	lui/lei/Lei	**possa**
noi	**possiamo**	noi	**possiamo**
voi	**potete**	voi	**possiate**
loro	**possono**	loro	**possano**

PERFECT		IMPERFECT	
io	**ho potuto**	io	**potevo**
tu	**hai potuto**	tu	**potevi**
lui/lei/Lei	**ha potuto**	lui/lei/Lei	**poteva**
noi	**abbiamo potuto**	noi	**potevamo**
voi	**avete potuto**	voi	**potevate**
loro	**hanno potuto**	loro	**potevano**

GERUND
potendo

PAST PARTICIPLE
potuto

EXAMPLE PHRASES

Si **può** visitare il castello tutti i giorni dell'anno. You can visit the castle any day of the year.

Può aver avuto un incidente. She may have had an accident.

Speriamo che voi **possiate** aiutarci. We hope you can help us.

Non è **potuto** venire. He couldn't come.

Non sono venuti perché non **potevano**. They didn't come because they weren't able to.

Potendo, eviterei di partire domani. I'd avoid setting off tomorrow if I could.

Remember that subject pronouns are not used very often in Italian.

potere

FUTURE		CONDITIONAL	
io	**potrò**	io	**potrei**
tu	**potrai**	tu	**potresti**
lui/lei/Lei	**potrà**	lui/lei/Lei	**potrebbe**
noi	**potremo**	noi	**potremmo**
voi	**potrete**	voi	**potreste**
loro	**potranno**	loro	**pot*rebbe*ro**

PAST HISTORIC		PLUPERFECT	
io	**potei**	io	**avevo potuto**
tu	**potesti**	tu	**avevi potuto**
lui/lei/Lei	**pot*é***	lui/lei/Lei	**aveva potuto**
noi	**potemmo**	noi	**avevamo potuto**
voi	**poteste**	voi	**avevate potuto**
loro	**pot*e*rono**	loro	**av*e*vano potuto**

IMPERATIVE

EXAMPLE PHRASES

Non **potrò** venire domani. I won't be able to come tomorrow.

Potresti aprire la finestra? Could you open the window?

Potrebbe *e*ssere vero. It could be true.

Era dispiaciuto perché non **aveva potuto** aiutarci. He was sorry he'd not been able to help us.

Italic letters in Italian words show where stress does not follow the usual rules.

prefiggersi (to set oneself)

PRESENT

io	**mi prefiggo**
tu	**ti prefiggi**
lui/lei/Lei	**si prefigge**
noi	**ci prefiggiamo**
voi	**vi prefiggete**
loro	**si prefiggono**

PRESENT SUBJUNCTIVE

io	**prefigga**
tu	**prefigga**
lui/lei/Lei	**prefigga**
noi	**prefiggiamo**
voi	**prefiggiate**
loro	**prefiggano**

PERFECT

io	**mi sono prefisso/a**
tu	**ti sei prefisso/a**
lui/lei/Lei	**si è prefisso/a**
noi	**ci siamo prefissi/e**
voi	**vi siete prefissi/e**
loro	**si sono prefissi/e**

IMPERFECT

io	**mi prefiggevo**
tu	**ti prefiggevi**
lui/lei/Lei	**si prefiggeva**
noi	**ci prefiggevamo**
voi	**vi prefiggevate**
loro	**si prefiggevano**

GERUND

prefiggendosi

PAST PARTICIPLE

prefisso

EXAMPLE PHRASES

Si **prefiggono** sempre obiettivi irrealizzabili. They always set themselves goals they can't achieve.

Voglio che tu ti **prefigga** un obiettivo. I want you to set yourself a goal.

Mi **prefiggevo** di finire il libro entro domenica. I was aiming to finish the book by Sunday.

Remember that subject pronouns are not used very often in Italian.

prefiggersi

FUTURE

io	**mi prefiggerò**
tu	**ti prefiggerai**
lui/lei/Lei	**si prefiggerà**
noi	**ci prefiggeremo**
voi	**vi prefiggerete**
loro	**si prefiggeranno**

CONDITIONAL

io	**mi prefiggerei**
tu	**ti prefiggeresti**
lui/lei/Lei	**si prefiggerebbe**
noi	**ci prefiggeremmo**
voi	**vi prefiggereste**
loro	**si prefiggerebbero**

PAST HISTORIC

io	**mi prefissi**
tu	**ti prefiggesti**
lui/lei/Lei	**si prefisse**
noi	**ci prefiggemmo**
voi	**vi prefiggeste**
loro	**si prefissero**

PLUPERFECT

io	**ero prefisso/a**
tu	**eri prefisso/a**
lui/lei/Lei	**era prefisso/a**
noi	**eravamo prefissi/e**
voi	**eravate prefissi/e**
loro	**erano prefissi/e**

IMPERATIVE

prefiggiti
prefiggiamoci
prefiggetevi

EXAMPLE PHRASES

Che cosa ti **prefiggerai** per il prossimo anno? What are your aims for next year?

Fossi in te, non mi **prefiggerei** una meta così ambiziosa. If I were you I wouldn't set myself such an ambitious target.

Hai raggiunto i risultati che ti **eri prefisso**? Have you achieved the results you were aiming for?

Questo era lo scopo che mi **ero prefissa**. This was the goal that I had set myself.

Italic letters in Italian words show where stress does not follow the usual rules.

prendere (to take)

PRESENT

io	**prendo**
tu	**prendi**
lui/lei/Lei	**prende**
noi	**prendiamo**
voi	**prendete**
loro	**prendono**

PRESENT SUBJUNCTIVE

io	**prenda**
tu	**prenda**
lui/lei/Lei	**prenda**
noi	**prendiamo**
voi	**prendiate**
loro	**prendano**

PERFECT

io	**ho preso**
tu	**hai preso**
lui/lei/Lei	**ha preso**
noi	**abbiamo preso**
voi	**avete preso**
loro	**hanno preso**

IMPERFECT

io	**prendevo**
tu	**prendevi**
lui/lei/Lei	**prendeva**
noi	**prendevamo**
voi	**prendevate**
loro	**prendevano**

GERUND

prendendo

PAST PARTICIPLE

preso

EXAMPLE PHRASES

Per chi mi **prendi**? Who do you think I am?

Prende qualcosa da bere? Would you like something to drink?

Non so quanto **prenda** per una traduzione. I don't know how much she charges for a translation.

Ho preso un bel voto. I got a good mark.

Remember that subject pronouns are not used very often in Italian.

prendere

FUTURE

io	**prenderò**
tu	**prenderai**
lui/lei/Lei	**prenderà**
noi	**prenderemo**
voi	**prenderete**
loro	**prenderanno**

CONDITIONAL

io	**prenderei**
tu	**prenderesti**
lui/lei/Lei	**prenderebbe**
noi	**prenderemmo**
voi	**prendereste**
loro	**prenderebbero**

PAST HISTORIC

io	**presi**
tu	**prendesti**
lui/lei/Lei	**prese**
noi	**prendemmo**
voi	**prendeste**
loro	**presero**

PLUPERFECT

io	**avevo preso**
tu	**avevi preso**
lui/lei/Lei	**aveva preso**
noi	**avevamo preso**
voi	**avevate preso**
loro	**avevano preso**

IMPERATIVE

prendi
prendiamo
prendete

EXAMPLE PHRASES

Copriti o **prenderai** l'influenza. Cover yourself up or you'll get flu.

Quanto **prenderemo** per quel lavoro? How much will we get for that job?

Prenderei volentieri un caffè. I'd love a coffee.

Quella volta **prendemmo** una bella paura. That time we got a real fright.

Aveva preso un grosso pesce e lo cucinò. He'd caught a big fish so he cooked it.

Prendi quella borsa. Take that bag.

Italic letters in Italian words show where stress does not follow the usual rules.

prevedere (to foresee)

PRESENT

io	**prevedo**
tu	**prevedi**
lui/lei/Lei	**prevede**
noi	**prevediamo**
voi	**prevedete**
loro	**prevedono**

PRESENT SUBJUNCTIVE

io	**preveda**
tu	**preveda**
lui/lei/Lei	**preveda**
noi	**prevediamo**
voi	**prevediate**
loro	**prevedano**

PERFECT

io	**ho previsto**
tu	**hai previsto**
lui/lei/Lei	**ha previsto**
noi	**abbiamo previsto**
voi	**avete previsto**
loro	**hanno previsto**

IMPERFECT

io	**prevedevo**
tu	**prevedevi**
lui/lei/Lei	**prevedeva**
noi	**prevedevamo**
voi	**prevedevate**
loro	**prevedevano**

GERUND

prevedendo

PAST PARTICIPLE

previsto

EXAMPLE PHRASES

Si **prevede** maltempo per il fine settimana. Bad weather is forecast for the weekend.

Come **previsto**, arriveremo in orario. As we planned, we'll get there on time.

È **previsto** per martedì. It's planned for Tuesday.

Prevedevamo che arrivaste più tardi. We thought the plan was for you to arrive later.

Non possiamo **prevedere** cosa succederà. We can't foresee what will happen.

Remember that subject pronouns are not used very often in Italian.

prevedere

FUTURE

io	**prevederò**
tu	**prevederai**
lui/lei/Lei	**prevederà**
noi	**prevederemo**
voi	**prevederete**
loro	**prevederanno**

CONDITIONAL

io	**prevederei**
tu	**prevederesti**
lui/lei/Lei	**prevederebbe**
noi	**prevederemmo**
voi	**prevedereste**
loro	**prevederebbero**

PAST HISTORIC

io	**previdi**
tu	**prevedesti**
lui/lei/Lei	**previde**
noi	**prevedemmo**
voi	**prevedeste**
loro	**previdero**

PLUPERFECT

io	**avevo previsto**
tu	**avevi previsto**
lui/lei/Lei	**aveva previsto**
noi	**avevamo previsto**
voi	**avevate previsto**
loro	**avevano previsto**

IMPERATIVE

prevedi
prevediamo
prevedete

EXAMPLE PHRASES

Il mago **previde** il nostro incontro. The clairvoyant foresaw that we'd meet.

Non **avevano previsto** questi cambiamenti. They hadn't foreseen these changes.

È un ansioso che vuole **prevedere** tutto. He's a worrier who wants to plan everything ahead.

Italic letters in Italian words show where stress does not follow the usual rules.

procedere (to move along)

PRESENT

io	**procedo**
tu	**procedi**
lui/lei/Lei	**procede**
noi	**procediamo**
voi	**procedete**
loro	**procedono**

PRESENT SUBJUNCTIVE

io	**proceda**
tu	**proceda**
lui/lei/Lei	**proceda**
noi	**procediamo**
voi	**procediate**
loro	**procedano**

PERFECT

io	**sono proceduto/a**
tu	**sei proceduto/a**
lui/lei/Lei	**è proceduto/a**
noi	**siamo proceduti/e**
voi	**siete proceduti/e**
loro	**sono proceduti/e**

IMPERFECT

io	**procedevo**
tu	**procedevi**
lui/lei/Lei	**procedeva**
noi	**procedevamo**
voi	**procedevate**
loro	**procedevano**

GERUND

procedendo

PAST PARTICIPLE

proceduto

EXAMPLE PHRASES

Come **procede** il lavoro? How's the work getting on?

Gli affari **procedono** bene. Business is going well.

Voglio che tutto **proceda** senza intoppi. I want everything to go ahead without any hitches.

I miei studi **procedevano** con lentezza. My studies were making slow progress.

Il traffico sta **procedendo** lentamente. The traffic is moving slowly.

Remember that subject pronouns are not used very often in Italian.

procedere

FUTURE

io	procederò
tu	procederai
lui/lei/Lei	procederà
noi	procederemo
voi	procederete
loro	procederanno

CONDITIONAL

io	procederei
tu	procederesti
lui/lei/Lei	procederebbe
noi	procederemmo
voi	procedereste
loro	procederebbero

PAST HISTORIC

io	procedetti
tu	procedesti
lui/lei/Lei	procedette
noi	procedemmo
voi	procedeste
loro	procedettero

PLUPERFECT

io	ero proceduto/a
tu	eri proceduto/a
lui/lei/Lei	era proceduto/a
noi	eravamo proceduti/e
voi	eravate proceduti/e
loro	erano proceduti/e

IMPERATIVE

procedi
procediamo
procedete

EXAMPLE PHRASES

Procedettero lungo il corridoio. They moved along the corridor.

La strada è ghiacciata, **procedete** con cautela. The road is icy, drive
   with caution.

Italic letters in Italian words show where stress does not follow the usual rules.

produrre (to produce)

PRESENT

io	**produco**
tu	**produci**
lui/lei/Lei	**produce**
noi	**produciamo**
voi	**producete**
loro	**producono**

PRESENT SUBJUNCTIVE

io	**produca**
tu	**produca**
lui/lei/Lei	**produca**
noi	**produciamo**
voi	**produciate**
loro	**producano**

PERFECT

io	**ho prodotto**
tu	**hai prodotto**
lui/lei/Lei	**ha prodotto**
noi	**abbiamo prodotto**
voi	**avete prodotto**
loro	**hanno prodotto**

IMPERFECT

io	**producevo**
tu	**producevi**
lui/lei/Lei	**produceva**
noi	**producevamo**
voi	**producevate**
loro	**producevano**

GERUND

producendo

PAST PARTICIPLE

prodotto

EXAMPLE PHRASES

La ditta **produce** scarpe. The company produces shoes.

Questa soluzione non **ha prodotto** buoni risultati. This solution did not produce good results.

Questi macchinari **sono prodotti** in Giappone. This machinery is produced in Japan.

L'Italia **produceva** molto grano. Italy used to produce a lot of wheat.

Si sono arricchiti **producendo** maglie. They got rich by manufacturing knitwear.

Remember that subject pronouns are not used very often in Italian.

produrre

FUTURE

io	**produrrò**
tu	**produrrai**
lui/lei/Lei	**produrrà**
noi	**produrremo**
voi	**produrrete**
loro	**produrranno**

CONDITIONAL

io	**produrrei**
tu	**produrresti**
lui/lei/Lei	**produrrebbe**
noi	**produrremmo**
voi	**produrreste**
loro	**produrrebbero**

PAST HISTORIC

io	**produssi**
tu	**producesti**
lui/lei/Lei	**produsse**
noi	**producemmo**
voi	**produceste**
loro	**produssero**

PLUPERFECT

io	**avevo prodotto**
tu	**avevi prodotto**
lui/lei/Lei	**aveva prodotto**
noi	**avevamo prodotto**
voi	**avevate prodotto**
loro	**avevano prodotto**

IMPERATIVE

produci
produciamo
producete

EXAMPLE PHRASES

Se lavorerai sodo, **produrrai** di più. If you work hard you'll produce more.

Avevamo prodotto articoli di grande successo. We'd manufactured very successful products.

proporre (to suggest)

PRESENT

io	**propongo**
tu	**proponi**
lui/lei/Lei	**propone**
noi	**proponiamo**
voi	**proponete**
loro	**propongono**

PRESENT SUBJUNCTIVE

io	**proponga**
tu	**proponga**
lui/lei/Lei	**proponga**
noi	**proponiamo**
voi	**proponiate**
loro	**propongano**

PERFECT

io	**ho proposto**
tu	**hai proposto**
lui/lei/Lei	**ha proposto**
noi	**abbiamo proposto**
voi	**avete proposto**
loro	**hanno proposto**

IMPERFECT

io	**proponevo**
tu	**proponevi**
lui/lei/Lei	**proponeva**
noi	**proponevamo**
voi	**proponevate**
loro	**proponevano**

GERUND

proponendo

PAST PARTICIPLE

proposto

EXAMPLE PHRASES

Che cosa **propone** lo chef? What does the chef recommend?

Ho proposto di andare al cinema. I suggested going to the cinema.

Maria **proponeva** una pizza, ma non ne ho voglia. Maria suggested a pizza, but I don't feel like one.

Remember that subject pronouns are not used very often in Italian.

proporre

FUTURE

io	**proporrò**
tu	**proporrai**
lui/lei/Lei	**proporrà**
noi	**proporremo**
voi	**proporrete**
loro	**proporranno**

CONDITIONAL

io	**proporrei**
tu	**proporresti**
lui/lei/Lei	**proporrebbe**
noi	**proporremmo**
voi	**proporreste**
loro	**proporrebbero**

PAST HISTORIC

io	**proposi**
tu	**proponesti**
lui/lei/Lei	**propose**
noi	**proponemmo**
voi	**proponeste**
loro	**proposero**

PLUPERFECT

io	**avevo proposto**
tu	**avevi proposto**
lui/lei/Lei	**aveva proposto**
noi	**avevamo proposto**
voi	**avevate proposto**
loro	**avevano proposto**

IMPERATIVE

proponi
proponiamo
proponete

EXAMPLE PHRASES

Non **proporrei** mai una cosa del genere. I'd never suggest something like that.

Propose un brindisi alla salute dell'invitato. He proposed a toast to the guest.

Avevano proposto di fermarci, ma continuammo. They'd suggested we should stop, but we continued.

Forza, **proponete** qualcosa di nuovo per stasera. Go on, suggest something new for this evening.

Italic letters in Italian words show where stress does not follow the usual rules.

raggiungere (to reach)

PRESENT

io	**raggiungo**
tu	**raggiungi**
lui/lei/Lei	**raggiunge**
noi	**raggiungiamo**
voi	**raggiungete**
loro	**raggiungono**

PRESENT SUBJUNCTIVE

io	**raggiunga**
tu	**raggiunga**
lui/lei/Lei	**raggiunga**
noi	**raggiungiamo**
voi	**raggiungiate**
loro	**raggiungano**

PERFECT

io	**ho raggiunto**
tu	**hai raggiunto**
lui/lei/Lei	**ha raggiunto**
noi	**abbiamo raggiunto**
voi	**avete raggiunto**
loro	**hanno raggiunto**

IMPERFECT

io	**raggiungevo**
tu	**raggiungevi**
lui/lei/Lei	**raggiungeva**
noi	**raggiungevamo**
voi	**raggiungevate**
loro	**raggiungevano**

GERUND

raggiungendo

PAST PARTICIPLE

raggiunto

EXAMPLE PHRASES

La temperatura può **raggiungere** i quaranta gradi. The temperature can reach forty degrees.

Vi **raggiungo** più tardi. I'll join you later.

Non **ho** ancora **raggiunto** il mio scopo. I haven't yet achieved my aim.

raggiungere

FUTURE

io	raggiungerò
tu	raggiungerai
lui/lei/Lei	raggiungerà
noi	raggiungeremo
voi	raggiungerete
loro	raggiungeranno

CONDITIONAL

io	raggiungerei
tu	raggiungeresti
lui/lei/Lei	raggiungerebbe
noi	raggiungeremmo
voi	raggiungereste
loro	raggiungerebbero

PAST HISTORIC

io	raggiunsi
tu	raggiungesti
lui/lei/Lei	raggiunse
noi	raggiungemmo
voi	raggiungeste
loro	raggiunsero

PLUPERFECT

io	avevo raggiunto
tu	avevi raggiunto
lui/lei/Lei	aveva raggiunto
noi	avevamo raggiunto
voi	avevate raggiunto
loro	avevano raggiunto

IMPERATIVE

raggiungi
raggiungiamo
raggiungete

EXAMPLE PHRASES

Vi **raggiungeremo** in albergo. We'll meet you in the hotel.

Ci rincorsero e ci **raggiunsero**. They ran after us and caught us up.

Il fiume **aveva raggiunto** il livello di guardia. The river had reached the high-water mark.

I tuoi amici ti aspettano: **raggiungili**. Your friends are waiting for you: go and join them.

Italic letters in Italian words show where stress does not follow the usual rules.

rendere (to make)

PRESENT

io	**rendo**
tu	**rendi**
lui/lei/Lei	**rende**
noi	**rendiamo**
voi	**rendete**
loro	**rendono**

PRESENT SUBJUNCTIVE

io	**renda**
tu	**renda**
lui/lei/Lei	**renda**
noi	**rendiamo**
voi	**rendiate**
loro	**rendano**

PERFECT

io	**ho reso**
tu	**hai reso**
lui/lei/Lei	**ha reso**
noi	**abbiamo reso**
voi	**avete reso**
loro	**hanno reso**

IMPERFECT

io	**rendevo**
tu	**rendevi**
lui/lei/Lei	**rendeva**
noi	**rendevamo**
voi	**rendevate**
loro	**rendevano**

GERUND

rendendo

PAST PARTICIPLE

reso

EXAMPLE PHRASES

Forse non ti **rendi** conto di quanto sia pericoloso. Maybe you don't realize how dangerous it is.

Scusa, non mi **ero reso** conto di averti offeso. I'm sorry, I didn't realize I'd upset you.

Non si è mai **resa** conto dei suoi limiti. She's never recognized her limitations.

Potresti **rendermi** la penna? Could you give me back my pen?

Remember that subject pronouns are not used very often in Italian.

rendere

FUTURE

io	**renderò**
tu	**renderai**
lui/lei/Lei	**renderà**
noi	**renderemo**
voi	**renderete**
loro	**renderanno**

CONDITIONAL

io	**renderei**
tu	**renderesti**
lui/lei/Lei	**renderebbe**
noi	**renderemmo**
voi	**rendereste**
loro	**renderebbero**

PAST HISTORIC

io	**resi**
tu	**rendesti**
lui/lei/Lei	**rese**
noi	**rendemmo**
voi	**rendeste**
loro	**resero**

PLUPERFECT

io	**avevo reso**
tu	**avevi reso**
lui/lei/Lei	**aveva reso**
noi	**avevamo reso**
voi	**avevate reso**
loro	**avevano reso**

IMPERATIVE

rendi
rendiamo
rendete

EXAMPLE PHRASES

Questa crema **renderà** i capelli luminosi. This cream will make your hair shiny.

Un po' di diplom*a*zia **renderebbe** tutto più facile. A bit of diplomacy would make everything easier.

Il ladro **rese** la refurtiva. The burglar returned the stolen goods.

Fai qualcosa! **Rend*i*ti** *u*tile! Do something! Make yourself useful!

Italic letters in Italian words show where stress does not follow the usual rules.

restare (to stay)

PRESENT

io	**resto**
tu	**resti**
lui/lei/Lei	**resta**
noi	**restiamo**
voi	**restate**
loro	**restano**

PRESENT SUBJUNCTIVE

io	**resti**
tu	**resti**
lui/lei/Lei	**resti**
noi	**restiamo**
voi	**restaste**
loro	**restino**

PERFECT

io	**sono restato/a**
tu	**sei restato/a**
lui/lei/Lei	**è restato/a**
noi	**siamo restati/e**
voi	**siete restati/e**
loro	**sono restati/e**

IMPERFECT

io	**restavo**
tu	**restavi**
lui/lei/Lei	**restava**
noi	**restavamo**
voi	**restavate**
loro	**restavano**

GERUND
restando

PAST PARTICIPLE
restato

EXAMPLE PHRASES

Ne **restano** solo due. There are only two left.

Sono restato a casa tutto il giorno. I stayed at home all day.

Restava solo da pulire la cucina. The only thing left to do was cleaning the kitchen.

restare

FUTURE

io	**resterò**
tu	**resterai**
lui/lei/Lei	**resterà**
noi	**resteremo**
voi	**resterete**
loro	**resteranno**

CONDITIONAL

io	**resterei**
tu	**resteresti**
lui/lei/Lei	**resterebbe**
noi	**resteremmo**
voi	**restereste**
loro	**resterebbero**

PAST HISTORIC

io	**restai**
tu	**restasti**
lui/lei/Lei	**restò**
noi	**restammo**
voi	**restaste**
loro	**restarono**

PLUPERFECT

io	**ero restato/a**
tu	**eri restato/a**
lui/lei/Lei	**era restato/a**
noi	**eravamo restati/e**
voi	**eravate restati/e**
loro	**erano restati/e**

IMPERATIVE

resta
restiamo
restate

EXAMPLE PHRASES

Resterò in Italia per tutta l'estate. I'll stay in Italy for the whole summer.

Resterei, ma ho ha fare. I'd stay, but I've got things to do.

Mi **restarono** solo cinquanta sterline. I only had fity pounds left.

Era restato da solo tutta la sera. He'd been alone all evening.

Dai, **resta** ancora un po'. Go on, stay a bit longer.

Italic letters in Italian words show where stress does not follow the usual rules.

ridere (to laugh)

PRESENT
io	**rido**
tu	**ridi**
lui/lei/Lei	**ride**
noi	**ridiamo**
voi	**ridete**
loro	**ridono**

PRESENT SUBJUNCTIVE
io	**rida**
tu	**rida**
lui/lei/Lei	**rida**
noi	**ridiamo**
voi	**ridiate**
loro	**ridano**

PERFECT
io	**ho riso**
tu	**hai riso**
lui/lei/Lei	**ha riso**
noi	**abbiamo riso**
voi	**avete riso**
loro	**hanno riso**

IMPERFECT
io	**ridevo**
tu	**ridevi**
lui/lei/Lei	**rideva**
noi	**ridevamo**
voi	**ridevate**
loro	**ridevano**

GERUND
ridendo

PAST PARTICIPLE
riso

EXAMPLE PHRASES
Perché **ridi**? Why are you laughing?

Abbiamo riso per tutto lo spettacolo. We laughed all through the show.

State **ridendo** di me? Are you laughing at me?

Tutti sono scoppiati a **ridere**. They all burst out laughing.

Non c'è niente da **ridere**. It's not funny.

ridere

FUTURE

io	**riderò**
tu	**riderai**
lui/lei/Lei	**riderà**
noi	**rideremo**
voi	**riderete**
loro	**rideranno**

CONDITIONAL

io	**riderei**
tu	**rideresti**
lui/lei/Lei	**riderebbe**
noi	**rideremmo**
voi	**ridereste**
loro	**riderebbero**

PAST HISTORIC

io	**risi**
tu	**ridesti**
lui/lei/Lei	**rise**
noi	**ridemmo**
voi	**rideste**
loro	**risero**

PLUPERFECT

io	**avevo riso**
tu	**avevi riso**
lui/lei/Lei	**aveva riso**
noi	**avevamo riso**
voi	**avevate riso**
loro	**avevano riso**

IMPERATIVE

ridi
ridiamo
ridete

EXAMPLE PHRASES

Rideresti meno se sapessi la verità. You wouldn't laugh so much if you knew the truth.

Non **avevo** mai **riso** tanto in vita mia. I'd never laughed so much in all my life.

Italic letters in Italian words show where stress does not follow the usual rules.

riempire (to fill)

PRESENT

io	**riempio**
tu	**riempi**
lui/lei/Lei	**riempie**
noi	**riempiamo**
voi	**riempite**
loro	**riempiono**

PRESENT SUBJUNCTIVE

io	**riempia**
tu	**riempia**
lui/lei/Lei	**riempia**
noi	**riempiamo**
voi	**riempiate**
loro	**riempiano**

PERFECT

io	**ho riempito**
tu	**hai riempito**
lui/lei/Lei	**ha riempito**
noi	**abbiamo riempito**
voi	**avete riempito**
loro	**hanno riempito**

IMPERFECT

io	**riempivo**
tu	**riempivi**
lui/lei/Lei	**riempiva**
noi	**riempivamo**
voi	**riempivate**
loro	**riempivano**

GERUND

riempiendo

PAST PARTICIPLE

riempito

EXAMPLE PHRASES

Vedervi ci **riempie** di gioia. It's always a joy to see you.

È meglio che tu **riempia** la borraccia prima di partire. You'd better fill your water bottle before you set off.

Tieni, **ho riempito** il termos di caffè, va bene? Here, I've filled the flask with coffee, okay?

riempire

FUTURE

io	**riempirò**
tu	**riempirai**
lui/lei/Lei	**riempirà**
noi	**riempiremo**
voi	**riempirete**
loro	**riempiranno**

CONDITIONAL

io	**riempirei**
tu	**riempiresti**
lui/lei/Lei	**riempirebbe**
noi	**riempiremmo**
voi	**riempireste**
loro	**riempirebbero**

PAST HISTORIC

io	**riempii**
tu	**riempisti**
lui/lei/Lei	**riempì**
noi	**riempimmo**
voi	**riempiste**
loro	**riempirono**

PLUPERFECT

io	**avevo riempito**
tu	**avevi riempito**
lui/lei/Lei	**aveva riempito**
noi	**avevamo riempito**
voi	**avevate riempito**
loro	**avevano riempito**

IMPERATIVE

riempi
riempiamo
riempite

EXAMPLE PHRASES

Riempiremo tutte le bottiglie col vino del nonno. We're going to fill all the bottles with granddad's wine.

Mi **riempì** la testa di sciocchezze. She filled my head with nonsense.

Riempi il modulo, per favore. Fill in the form, please.

Italic letters in Italian words show where stress does not follow the usual rules.

riflettere (to think)

PRESENT

io	**rifletto**
tu	**rifletti**
lui/lei/Lei	**riflette**
noi	**riflettiamo**
voi	**riflettete**
loro	**riflettono**

PRESENT SUBJUNCTIVE

io	**rifletta**
tu	**rifletta**
lui/lei/Lei	**rifletta**
noi	**riflettiamo**
voi	**riflettiate**
loro	**riflettano**

PERFECT

io	**ho riflettuto**
tu	**hai riflettuto**
lui/lei/Lei	**ha riflettuto**
noi	**abbiamo riflettuto**
voi	**avete riflettuto**
loro	**hanno riflettuto**

IMPERFECT

io	**riflettevo**
tu	**riflettevi**
lui/lei/Lei	**rifletteva**
noi	**riflettevamo**
voi	**riflettevate**
loro	**riflettevano**

GERUND

riflettendo

PAST PARTICIPLE

riflettuto

EXAMPLE PHRASES

È una persona cauta: **riflette** molto prima di agire. He's a cautious person:
   he thinks a lot before he does anything.

Ci **ho riflettuto** su e ho deciso di accettare. I've thought about it and have
   decided to accept.

Guardavo la TV mentre **riflettevo** sul da farsi. I watched TV while I thought
   about what should be done.

Riflettendo un po', troveremo la soluzione. If we think a bit we'll find a solution.

Agisce senza **riflettere**. He does things without thinking.

Remember that subject pronouns are not used very often in Italian.

riflettere

FUTURE

io	**rifletterò**
tu	**rifletterai**
lui/lei/Lei	**rifletterà**
noi	**rifletteremo**
voi	**rifletterete**
loro	**rifletteranno**

CONDITIONAL

io	**rifletterei**
tu	**rifletteresti**
lui/lei/Lei	**rifletterebbe**
noi	**rifletteremmo**
voi	**riflettereste**
loro	**rifletterebbero**

PAST HISTORIC

io	**riflettei**
tu	**riflettesti**
lui/lei/Lei	**rifletté**
noi	**riflettemmo**
voi	**rifletteste**
loro	**rifletterono**

PLUPERFECT

io	**avevo riflettuto**
tu	**avevi riflettuto**
lui/lei/Lei	**aveva riflettuto**
noi	**avevamo riflettuto**
voi	**avevate riflettuto**
loro	**avevano riflettuto**

IMPERATIVE

rifletti
riflettiamo
riflettete

EXAMPLE PHRASES

Io **rifletterei** un po' prima di fare una simile scelta. I'd think a bit before I made a choice like that.

Rifletti prima di parlare! Think before you speak!

Italic letters in Italian words show where stress does not follow the usual rules.

rimanere (to stay)

PRESENT

io	**rimango**
tu	**rimani**
lui/lei/Lei	**rimane**
noi	**rimaniamo**
voi	**rimanete**
loro	**rimangono**

PRESENT SUBJUNCTIVE

io	**rimanga**
tu	**rimanga**
lui/lei/Lei	**rimanga**
noi	**rimaniamo**
voi	**rimaniate**
loro	**rimangano**

PERFECT

io	**sono rimasto/a**
tu	**sei rimasto/a**
lui/lei/Lei	**è rimasto/a**
noi	**siamo rimasti/e**
voi	**siete rimasti/e**
loro	**sono rimasti/e**

IMPERFECT

io	**rimanevo**
tu	**rimanevi**
lui/lei/Lei	**rimaneva**
noi	**rimanevamo**
voi	**rimanevate**
loro	**rimanevano**

GERUND
rimanendo

PAST PARTICIPLE
rimasto

EXAMPLE PHRASES

Temo che **rimanga** poco tempo. I'm afraid she won't stay long.

Sono rimasto a casa tutto il giorno. I stayed at home all day.

Rimanevano sempre indietro. They were always behind.

Mi piacerebbe **rimanere** qualche altro giorno. I'd like to stay a few more days.

Remember that subject pronouns are not used very often in Italian.

rimanere

FUTURE

io	**rimarrò**
tu	**rimarrai**
lui/lei/Lei	**rimarrà**
noi	**rimarremo**
voi	**rimarrete**
loro	**rimarranno**

CONDITIONAL

io	**rimarrei**
tu	**rimarresti**
lui/lei/Lei	**rimarrebbe**
noi	**rimarremmo**
voi	**rimarreste**
loro	**rimarrebbero**

PAST HISTORIC

io	**rimasi**
tu	**rimanesti**
lui/lei/Lei	**rimase**
noi	**rimanemmo**
voi	**rimaneste**
loro	**rimasero**

PLUPERFECT

io	**ero rimasto/a**
tu	**eri rimasto/a**
lui/lei/Lei	**era rimasto/a**
noi	**eravamo rimasti/e**
voi	**eravate rimasti/e**
loro	**erano rimasti/e**

IMPERATIVE

rimani
rimaniamo
rimanete

EXAMPLE PHRASES

Rimarrete senza parole. You'll be speechless.

Ci **rimarrebbero** molto male. They'd be very hurt.

Ne **rimase** solo uno. There was only one left.

Eravamo rimasti senza pane, così andai a comprarlo. We had no bread left, so I went to get some.

Italic letters in Italian words show where stress does not follow the usual rules.

risolvere (to solve)

PRESENT

io	**risolvo**
tu	**risolvi**
lui/lei/Lei	**risolve**
noi	**risolviamo**
voi	**risolvete**
loro	**risolvono**

PRESENT SUBJUNCTIVE

io	**risolva**
tu	**risolva**
lui/lei/Lei	**risolva**
noi	**risolviamo**
voi	**risolviate**
loro	**risolvano**

PERFECT

io	**ho risolto**
tu	**hai risolto**
lui/lei/Lei	**ha risolto**
noi	**abbiamo risolto**
voi	**avete risolto**
loro	**hanno risolto**

IMPERFECT

io	**risolvevo**
tu	**risolvevi**
lui/lei/Lei	**risolveva**
noi	**risolvevamo**
voi	**risolvevate**
loro	**risolvevano**

GERUND

risolvendo

PAST PARTICIPLE

risolto

EXAMPLE PHRASES

Così non **risolvi** nulla. You won't solve the problems that way.

Ho risolto l'indovinello! I've worked out the riddle!

risolvere

FUTURE

io	**risolverò**
tu	**risolverai**
lui/lei/Lei	**risolverà**
noi	**risolveremo**
voi	**risolverete**
loro	**risolveranno**

CONDITIONAL

io	**risolverei**
tu	**risolveresti**
lui/lei/Lei	**risolverebbe**
noi	**risolveremmo**
voi	**risolvereste**
loro	**risolverebbero**

PAST HISTORIC

io	**risolsi**
tu	**risolvesti**
lui/lei/Lei	**risolse**
noi	**risolvemmo**
voi	**risolveste**
loro	**risolsero**

PLUPERFECT

io	**avevo risolto**
tu	**avevi risolto**
lui/lei/Lei	**aveva risolto**
noi	**avevamo risolto**
voi	**avevate risolto**
loro	**avevano risolto**

IMPERATIVE

risolvi
risolviamo
risolvete

EXAMPLE PHRASES

Solo se ti calmerai **risolverai** i tuoi problemi. You'll only solve your problems if you calm down.

Una tua parola **risolverebbe** molte questioni. If you said something it would resolve many issues.

Il suo intervento **risolse** la controversia. His intervention settled the dispute.

Aveva risolto un'equazione difficilissima. He'd worked out a very difficult equation.

Italic letters in Italian words show where stress does not follow the usual rules.

rispondere (to answer)

PRESENT

io	**rispondo**
tu	**rispondi**
lui/lei/Lei	**risponde**
noi	**rispondiamo**
voi	**rispondete**
loro	**rispondono**

PRESENT SUBJUNCTIVE

io	**risponda**
tu	**risponda**
lui/lei/Lei	**risponda**
noi	**rispondiamo**
voi	**rispondiate**
loro	**rispondano**

PERFECT

io	**ho risposto**
tu	**hai risposto**
lui/lei/Lei	**ha risposto**
noi	**abbiamo risposto**
voi	**avete risposto**
loro	**hanno risposto**

IMPERFECT

io	**rispondevo**
tu	**rispondevi**
lui/lei/Lei	**rispondeva**
noi	**rispondevamo**
voi	**rispondevate**
loro	**rispondevano**

GERUND
rispondendo

PAST PARTICIPLE
risposto

EXAMPLE PHRASES

Cosa vuoi che ti **risponda**? What do you want me to say?

Ho telefonato ma non **ha risposto** nessuno. I phoned, but nobody answered.

Rispondeva sempre di sì a tutti. She always said yes to everyone.

Remember that subject pronouns are not used very often in Italian.

rispondere

FUTURE

io	**risponderò**
tu	**risponderai**
lui/lei/Lei	**risponderà**
noi	**risponderemo**
voi	**risponderete**
loro	**risponderanno**

CONDITIONAL

io	**risponderei**
tu	**risponderesti**
lui/lei/Lei	**risponderebbe**
noi	**risponderemmo**
voi	**rispondereste**
loro	**risponderebbero**

PAST HISTORIC

io	**risposi**
tu	**rispondesti**
lui/lei/Lei	**rispose**
noi	**rispondemmo**
voi	**rispondeste**
loro	**risposero**

PLUPERFECT

io	**avevo risposto**
tu	**avevi risposto**
lui/lei/Lei	**aveva risposto**
noi	**avevamo risposto**
voi	**avevate risposto**
loro	**avevano risposto**

IMPERATIVE

rispondi
rispondiamo
rispondete

EXAMPLE PHRASES

Risponderai di tutti i tuoi crimini. You will answer for all your crimes.

Cosa **rispondereste** a una domanda simile? How would you answer a question like that?

Rispose di no. He said no.

Avevate risposto alle sue lettere? Had you replied to her letters?

Rispondi alla mia domanda. Answer my question.

Italic letters in Italian words show where stress does not follow the usual rules.

rivolgere (to turn)

PRESENT

io	**rivolgo**
tu	**rivolgi**
lui/lei/Lei	**rivolge**
noi	**rivolgiamo**
voi	**rivolgete**
loro	**rivolgono**

PRESENT SUBJUNCTIVE

io	**rivolga**
tu	**rivolga**
lui/lei/Lei	**rivolga**
noi	**rivolgiamo**
voi	**rivolgiate**
loro	**rivolgano**

PERFECT

io	**ho rivolto**
tu	**hai rivolto**
lui/lei/Lei	**ha rivolto**
noi	**abbiamo rivolto**
voi	**avete rivolto**
loro	**hanno rivolto**

IMPERFECT

io	**rivolgevo**
tu	**rivolgevi**
lui/lei/Lei	**rivolgeva**
noi	**rivolgevamo**
voi	**rivolgevate**
loro	**rivolgevano**

GERUND

rivolgendo

PAST PARTICIPLE

rivolto

EXAMPLE PHRASES

Sono due giorni che non mi **rivolge** la parola. She hasn't spoken to me for two days.

È meglio che si **rivolga** all'impiegato laggiù. You'd better go and ask the man over there.

Si **è rivolta** a me per un consiglio. She came to me for advice.

Remember that subject pronouns are not used very often in Italian.

rivolgere

FUTURE

io	**rivolgerò**
tu	**rivolgerai**
lui/lei/Lei	**rivolgerà**
noi	**rivolgeremo**
voi	**rivolgerete**
loro	**rivolgeranno**

CONDITIONAL

io	**rivolgerei**
tu	**rivolgeresti**
lui/lei/Lei	**rivolgerebbe**
noi	**rivolgeremmo**
voi	**rivolgereste**
loro	**rivolgerebbero**

PAST HISTORIC

io	**rivolsi**
tu	**rivolgesti**
lui/lei/Lei	**rivolse**
noi	**rivolgemmo**
voi	**rivolgeste**
loro	**rivolsero**

PLUPERFECT

io	**avevo rivolto**
tu	**avevi rivolto**
lui/lei/Lei	**aveva rivolto**
noi	**avevamo rivolto**
voi	**avevate rivolto**
loro	**avevano rivolto**

IMPERATIVE

rivolgi
rivolgiamo
rivolgete

EXAMPLE PHRASES

Ci **rivolgeremo** alle autorità. We'll go to the authorities

In caso di problemi, ci **rivolgevamo** a lui. If there was a problem we went to him.

Non mi **rivolgerei** mai a te per avere aiuto. I'd never come to you for help.

Si **rivolse** a me in tono aggressivo. She spoke to me aggressively.

Rivolgetevi all'ufficio informazioni. Go to the information office.

Non so a chi **rivolgermi**. I don't know who to go to.

Italic letters in Italian words show where stress does not follow the usual rules.

rompere (to break)

PRESENT

io	**rompo**
tu	**rompi**
lui/lei/Lei	**rompe**
noi	**rompiamo**
voi	**rompete**
loro	**rompono**

PRESENT SUBJUNCTIVE

io	**rompa**
tu	**rompa**
lui/lei/Lei	**rompa**
noi	**rompiamo**
voi	**rompiate**
loro	**rompano**

PERFECT

io	**ho rotto**
tu	**hai rotto**
lui/lei/Lei	**ha rotto**
noi	**abbiamo rotto**
voi	**avete rotto**
loro	**hanno rotto**

IMPERFECT

io	**rompevo**
tu	**rompevi**
lui/lei/Lei	**rompeva**
noi	**rompevamo**
voi	**rompevate**
loro	**rompevano**

GERUND
rompendo

PAST PARTICIPLE
rotto

EXAMPLE PHRASES

Uffa quanto **rompi**! What a pain you are!

Ho rotto un bicchiere! I've broken a glass!

Il piatto si **è rotto**. The plate broke.

Da piccolo **rompeva** tutto quello che toccava. When he was little he broke everything he touched.

rompere

FUTURE

io	romperò
tu	romperai
lui/lei/Lei	romperà
noi	romperemo
voi	romperete
loro	romperanno

CONDITIONAL

io	romperei
tu	romperesti
lui/lei/Lei	romperebbe
noi	romperemmo
voi	rompereste
loro	romperebbero

PAST HISTORIC

io	ruppi
tu	rompesti
lui/lei/Lei	ruppe
noi	rompemmo
voi	rompeste
loro	ruppero

PLUPERFECT

io	avevo rotto
tu	avevi rotto
lui/lei/Lei	aveva rotto
noi	avevamo rotto
voi	avevate rotto
loro	avevano rotto

IMPERATIVE

rompi
rompiamo
rompete

EXAMPLE PHRASES

Rischia troppo: si **romperà** una gamba. She takes too many risks: she'll break her leg.

La corda si **romperebbe** se tirassi troppo. The rope would break if I pulled too hard.

La macchina si **ruppe** sull'autostrada. The car broke down on the motorway.

Italic letters in Italian words show where stress does not follow the usual rules.

salire (to go up)

PRESENT

io	**salgo**
tu	**sali**
lui/lei/Lei	**sale**
noi	**saliamo**
voi	**salite**
loro	**salgono**

PRESENT SUBJUNCTIVE

io	**salga**
tu	**salga**
lui/lei/Lei	**salga**
noi	**saliamo**
voi	**saliate**
loro	**salgano**

PERFECT

io	**sono salito/a**
tu	**sei salito/a**
lui/lei/Lei	**è salito/a**
noi	**siamo saliti/e**
voi	**siete saliti/e**
loro	**sono saliti/e**

IMPERFECT

io	**salivo**
tu	**salivi**
lui/lei/Lei	**saliva**
noi	**salivamo**
voi	**salivate**
loro	**salivano**

GERUND

salendo

PAST PARTICIPLE

salito

EXAMPLE PHRASES

Sali tu o scendo io? Are you coming up or shall I come down?

Non voglio che i tuoi amici **salgano** in casa. I don't want your friends to come into the house.

I prezzi **sono saliti**. Prices have gone up.

Mentre **saliva** verso la cima, si sentì senza forze. As she climbed up to the summit she felt weak.

Remember that subject pronouns are not used very often in Italian.

salire

FUTURE

io	**salirò**
tu	**salirai**
lui/lei/Lei	**salirà**
noi	**saliremo**
voi	**salirete**
loro	**saliranno**

CONDITIONAL

io	**salirei**
tu	**saliresti**
lui/lei/Lei	**salirebbe**
noi	**saliremmo**
voi	**salireste**
loro	**salirebbero**

PAST HISTORIC

io	**salii**
tu	**salisti**
lui/lei/Lei	**salì**
noi	**salimmo**
voi	**saliste**
loro	**salirono**

PLUPERFECT

io	**ero salito/a**
tu	**eri salito/a**
lui/lei/Lei	**era salito/a**
noi	**eravamo saliti/e**
voi	**eravate saliti/e**
loro	**erano saliti/e**

IMPERATIVE

sali

saliamo

salite

EXAMPLE PHRASES

Dopo cena **salirai** in camera tua. After dinner you'll go up to your room.

Non **salirei** mai su un aereo. I'd never go on a plane.

Salì sull'albero per raccogliere le ciliegie. She climbed up the tree to pick the cherries.

Sali in macchina e partiamo. Get in the car and we'll be off.

Italic letters in Italian words show where stress does not follow the usual rules.

sapere (to know)

PRESENT

io	**so**
tu	**sai**
lui/lei/Lei	**sa**
noi	**sappiamo**
voi	**sapete**
loro	**sanno**

PRESENT SUBJUNCTIVE

io	**sappia**
tu	**sappia**
lui/lei/Lei	**sappia**
noi	**sappiamo**
voi	**sappiate**
loro	**sappiano**

PERFECT

io	**ho saputo**
tu	**hai saputo**
lui/lei/Lei	**ha saputo**
noi	**abbiamo saputo**
voi	**avete saputo**
loro	**hanno saputo**

IMPERFECT

io	**sapevo**
tu	**sapevi**
lui/lei/Lei	**sapeva**
noi	**sapevamo**
voi	**sapevate**
loro	**sapevano**

GERUND

sapendo

PAST PARTICIPLE

saputo

EXAMPLE PHRASES

Sai dove abita? Do you know where he lives?

Non ne **so** nulla. I don't know anything about it.

Sa di fragola. It tastes of strawberries.

Sa di pesce. It smells of fish.

Non **abbiamo** più **saputo** nulla di lui. We didn't hear anything more about him.

Non **sapeva** andare in bicicletta. He couldn't ride a bike.

Remember that subject pronouns are not used very often in Italian.

sapere

FUTURE

io	**saprò**
tu	**saprai**
lui/lei/Lei	**saprà**
noi	**sapremo**
voi	**saprete**
loro	**sapranno**

CONDITIONAL

io	**saprei**
tu	**sapresti**
lui/lei/Lei	**saprebbe**
noi	**sapremmo**
voi	**sapreste**
loro	**saprebbero**

PAST HISTORIC

io	**seppi**
tu	**sapesti**
lui/lei/Lei	**seppe**
noi	**sapemmo**
voi	**sapeste**
loro	**seppero**

PLUPERFECT

io	**avevo saputo**
tu	**avevi saputo**
lui/lei/Lei	**aveva saputo**
noi	**avevamo saputo**
voi	**avevate saputo**
loro	**avevano saputo**

IMPERATIVE

sappi
sappiamo
sappiate

EXAMPLE PHRASES

Come **saprete**, abbiamo deciso di traslocare. As you know, we've decided to move.

Sapreste indicarmi la strada per la stazione? Could you tell me the way to the station?

Solo dopo molti anni **sapemmo** che era emigrato. Only after many years did we hear that he'd emigrated.

Sappi che non sono disposto a perdonarti. I want you to know that I'm not prepared to forgive you.

Italic letters in Italian words show where stress does not follow the usual rules.

sbagliare (to make a mistake)

PRESENT		PRESENT SUBJUNCTIVE	
io	sbaglio	io	sbagli
tu	sbagli	tu	sbagli
lui/lei/Lei	sbaglia	lui/lei/Lei	sbagli
noi	sbagliamo	noi	sbagliamo
voi	sbagliate	voi	sbagliate
loro	sbagliano	loro	sbaglino

PERFECT		IMPERFECT	
io	ho sbagliato	io	sbagliavo
tu	hai sbagliato	tu	sbagliavi
lui/lei/Lei	ha sbagliato	lui/lei/Lei	sbagliava
noi	abbiamo sbagliato	noi	sbagliavamo
voi	avete sbagliato	voi	sbagliavate
loro	hanno sbagliato	loro	sbagliavano

GERUND
sbagliando

PAST PARTICIPLE
sbagliato

EXAMPLE PHRASES

Mi dispiace, **avete sbagliato**. I'm sorry, you've made a mistake.

Scusi, **ho sbagliato** numero. Sorry, I've got the wrong number.

Pensavo fosse lei, ma mi **sono sbagliato**. I thought it was her, but I was wrong.

Ci eravamo persi e **sbagliavamo** sempre strada. We were lost and kept taking the wrong road.

Sbagliando s'impara. You learn by your mistakes.

Remember that subject pronouns are not used very often in Italian.

sbagliare

FUTURE

io	**sbaglierò**
tu	**sbaglierai**
lui/lei/Lei	**sbaglierà**
noi	**sbaglieremo**
voi	**sbaglierete**
loro	**sbaglieranno**

CONDITIONAL

io	**sbaglierei**
tu	**sbaglieresti**
lui/lei/Lei	**sbaglierebbe**
noi	**sbaglieremmo**
voi	**sbagliereste**
loro	**sbaglierebbero**

PAST HISTORIC

io	**sbagliai**
tu	**sbagliasti**
lui/lei/Lei	**sbagliò**
noi	**sbagliammo**
voi	**sbagliaste**
loro	**sbagliarono**

PLUPERFECT

io	**avevo sbagliato**
tu	**avevi sbagliato**
lui/lei/Lei	**aveva sbagliato**
noi	**avevamo sbagliato**
voi	**avevate sbagliato**
loro	**avevano sbagliato**

IMPERATIVE

sbaglia
sbagliamo
sbagliate

EXAMPLE PHRASES

Mi **sbaglierò**, ma per me questa è la risposta giusta. I may be mistaken,
but I think this is the right answer.

Sbaglieresti, se pensassi che non mi importa. You'd be wrong if you thought
I didn't care.

Aveva sbagliato e non voleva ammetterlo. He'd been wrong but didn't want
to admit it.

Italic letters in Italian words show where stress does not follow the usual rules.

scegliere (to choose)

PRESENT		PRESENT SUBJUNCTIVE	
io	scelgo	io	scelga
tu	scegli	tu	scelga
lui/lei/Lei	sceglie	lui/lei/Lei	scelga
noi	scegliamo	noi	scegliamo
voi	scegliete	voi	scegliate
loro	scelgono	loro	scelgano

PERFECT		IMPERFECT	
io	ho scelto	io	sceglievo
tu	hai scelto	tu	sceglievi
lui/lei/Lei	ha scelto	lui/lei/Lei	sceglieva
noi	abbiamo scelto	noi	sceglievamo
voi	avete scelto	voi	sceglievate
loro	hanno scelto	loro	sceglievano

GERUND	PAST PARTICIPLE
scegliendo	scelto

EXAMPLE PHRASES

Chi **sceglie** il vino? Who's going to choose the wine?

Hai scelto il regalo per lei? Have you chosen her present?

Sceglievano sempre il vino più costoso. They always chose the most expensive wine.

Stavo **scegliendo** le pesche più mature. I was choosing the ripest peaches.

Remember that subject pronouns are not used very often in Italian.

scegliere

FUTURE

io	**sceglierò**
tu	**sceglierai**
lui/lei/Lei	**sceglierà**
noi	**sceglieremo**
voi	**sceglierete**
loro	**sceglieranno**

CONDITIONAL

io	**sceglierei**
tu	**sceglieresti**
lui/lei/Lei	**sceglierebbe**
noi	**sceglieremmo**
voi	**scegliereste**
loro	**sceglierebbero**

PAST HISTORIC

io	**scelsi**
tu	**scegliesti**
lui/lei/Lei	**scelse**
noi	**scegliemmo**
voi	**sceglieste**
loro	**scelsero**

PLUPERFECT

io	**avevo scelto**
tu	**avevi scelto**
lui/lei/Lei	**aveva scelto**
noi	**avevamo scelto**
voi	**avevate scelto**
loro	**avevano scelto**

IMPERATIVE

scegli
scegliamo
scegliete

EXAMPLE PHRASES

Non sa ancora quale abito **sceglierà**. She hasn't decided yet which dress she'll choose.

Il cappello che **aveva scelto** con tanta cura ora non le piace più. She no longer likes the hat she'd chosen with such care.

Scegli la pizza che vuoi. Choose which pizza you want.

Italic letters in Italian words show where stress does not follow the usual rules.

scendere (to go down)

PRESENT

io	**scendo**
tu	**scendi**
lui/lei/Lei	**scende**
noi	**scendiamo**
voi	**scendete**
loro	**scendono**

PRESENT SUBJUNCTIVE

io	**scenda**
tu	**scenda**
lui/lei/Lei	**scenda**
noi	**scendiamo**
voi	**scendiate**
loro	**scendano**

PERFECT

io	**sono sceso/a**
tu	**sei sceso/a**
lui/lei/Lei	**è sceso/a**
noi	**siamo scesi/e**
voi	**siete scesi/e**
loro	**sono scesi/e**

IMPERFECT

io	**scendevo**
tu	**scendevi**
lui/lei/Lei	**scendeva**
noi	**scendevamo**
voi	**scendevate**
loro	**scendevano**

GERUND

scendendo

PAST PARTICIPLE

sceso

EXAMPLE PHRASES

Sali tu o **scendo** io? Are you coming up or shall I come down?

Scendo subito! I'm coming!

La temperatura **è scesa** di due gradi. The temperature fell by two degrees.

Scendevo le scale quando sono inciampata. I tripped coming down the stairs.

Si è storto una caviglia **scendendo** dalla macchina. He twisted his ankle getting out of the car.

Remember that subject pronouns are not used very often in Italian.

scendere

FUTURE

io	**scenderò**
tu	**scenderai**
lui/lei/Lei	**scenderà**
noi	**scenderemo**
voi	**scenderete**
loro	**scenderanno**

CONDITIONAL

io	**scenderei**
tu	**scenderesti**
lui/lei/Lei	**scenderebbe**
noi	**scenderemmo**
voi	**scendereste**
loro	**scenderebbero**

PAST HISTORIC

io	**scesi**
tu	**scendesti**
lui/lei/Lei	**scese**
noi	**scendemmo**
voi	**scendeste**
loro	**scesero**

PLUPERFECT

io	**ero sceso/a**
tu	**eri sceso/a**
lui/lei/Lei	**era sceso/a**
noi	**eravamo scesi/e**
voi	**eravate scesi/e**
loro	**erano scesi/e**

IMPERATIVE

scendi
scendiamo
scendete

EXAMPLE PHRASES

Dopo le feste i prezzi **scenderanno**. After the holidays prices will come down.

Sono arrivati. **Scendi** ad aprire la porta. They're here. Go down and open the door.

Italic letters in Italian words show where stress does not follow the usual rules.

sciare (to ski)

PRESENT

io	scio
tu	scii
lui/lei/Lei	scia
noi	sciamo
voi	sciate
loro	sciano

PRESENT SUBJUNCTIVE

io	scii
tu	scii
lui/lei/Lei	scii
noi	sciamo
voi	sciate
loro	sciino

PERFECT

io	ho sciato
tu	hai sciato
lui/lei/Lei	ha sciato
noi	abbiamo sciato
voi	avete sciato
loro	hanno sciato

IMPERFECT

io	sciavo
tu	sciavi
lui/lei/Lei	sciava
noi	sciavamo
voi	sciavate
loro	sciavano

GERUND

sciando

PAST PARTICIPLE

sciato

EXAMPLE PHRASES

Scia come un campione. He skis like a champion.

Sai **sciare**? Can you ski?

Abbiamo sciato tutto il giorno. We skied all day.

Si è rotto la gamba **sciando**. He broke his leg when he was skiing.

sciare

FUTURE

io	**scierò**
tu	**scierai**
lui/lei/Lei	**scierà**
noi	**scieremo**
voi	**scierete**
loro	**scieranno**

CONDITIONAL

io	**scierei**
tu	**scieresti**
lui/lei/Lei	**scierebbe**
noi	**scieremmo**
voi	**sciereste**
loro	**scierebbero**

PAST HISTORIC

io	**sciai**
tu	**sciasti**
lui/lei/Lei	**sciò**
noi	**sciammo**
voi	**sciaste**
loro	**sciarono**

PLUPERFECT

io	**avevo sciato**
tu	**avevi sciato**
lui/lei/Lei	**aveva sciato**
noi	**avevamo sciato**
voi	**avevate sciato**
loro	**avevano sciato**

IMPERATIVE

scia
sciamo
sciate

EXAMPLE PHRASES

Se seguirai i miei consigli **scierai** meglio. If you follow my advice you'll ski better.

Adoro la montagna: **scierei** sempre. I love the mountains: I'd like to spend all my time skiing.

Sciò molto bene e vinse la gara. She skied very well and won the competition.

Avevamo sciato a lungo ed eravamo stanchi. We'd been skiing for a long time and were tired.

Italic letters in Italian words show where stress does not follow the usual rules.

sciogliere (to melt)

PRESENT

io	**sciolgo**
tu	**sciogli**
lui/lei/Lei	**scioglie**
noi	**sciogliamo**
voi	**sciogliete**
loro	**sciolgono**

PRESENT SUBJUNCTIVE

io	**sciolga**
tu	**sciolga**
lui/lei/Lei	**sciolga**
noi	**sciogliamo**
voi	**sciogliate**
loro	**sciolgano**

PERFECT

io	**ho sciolto**
tu	**hai sciolto**
lui/lei/Lei	**ha sciolto**
noi	**abbiamo sciolto**
voi	**avete sciolto**
loro	**hanno sciolto**

IMPERFECT

io	**scioglievo**
tu	**scioglievi**
lui/lei/Lei	**scioglieva**
noi	**scioglievamo**
voi	**scioglievate**
loro	**scioglievano**

GERUND
sciogliendo

PAST PARTICIPLE
sciolto

EXAMPLE PHRASES

Nell'acqua il sale si **scioglie**. Salt dissolves in water.

Fai attenzione che i nodi non si **sciolgano**. Be careful that the knots don't come undone.

Il sole **ha sciolto** la neve. The sun has melted the snow.

La neve si **è sciolta** al sole. The snow melted in the sun.

Remember that subject pronouns are not used very often in Italian.

sciogliere

FUTURE

io	**scioglierò**
tu	**scioglierai**
lui/lei/Lei	**scioglierà**
noi	**scioglieremo**
voi	**scioglierete**
loro	**scioglieranno**

CONDITIONAL

io	**scioglierei**
tu	**scioglieresti**
lui/lei/Lei	**scioglierebbe**
noi	**scioglieremmo**
voi	**sciogliereste**
loro	**scioglierebbero**

PAST HISTORIC

io	**sciolsi**
tu	**sciogliesti**
lui/lei/Lei	**sciolse**
noi	**sciogliemmo**
voi	**scioglieste**
loro	**sciolsero**

PLUPERFECT

io	**avevo sciolto**
tu	**avevi sciolto**
lui/lei/Lei	**aveva sciolto**
noi	**avevamo sciolto**
voi	**avevate sciolto**
loro	**avevano sciolto**

IMPERATIVE

sciogli
sciogliamo
sciogliete

EXAMPLE PHRASES

Si **sciolse** i capelli. She undid her hair.
Sciogli la barca che salpiamo! Untie the boat so we can move off.
Facevamo esercizi per **sciogliere** i muscoli. We did exercises to loosen up our muscles.

sconfiggere (to defeat)

PRESENT

io	**sconfiggo**
tu	**sconfiggi**
lui/lei/Lei	**sconfigge**
noi	**sconfiggiamo**
voi	**sconfiggete**
loro	**sconfiggono**

PRESENT SUBJUNCTIVE

io	**sconfigga**
tu	**sconfigga**
lui/lei/Lei	**sconfigga**
noi	**sconfiggiamo**
voi	**sconfiggiate**
loro	**sconfiggano**

PERFECT

io	**ho sconfitto**
tu	**hai sconfitto**
lui/lei/Lei	**ha sconfitto**
noi	**abbiamo sconfitto**
voi	**avete sconfitto**
loro	**hanno sconfitto**

IMPERFECT

io	**sconfiggevo**
tu	**sconfiggevi**
lui/lei/Lei	**sconfiggeva**
noi	**sconfiggevamo**
voi	**sconfiggevate**
loro	**sconfiggevano**

GERUND
sconfiggendo

PAST PARTICIPLE
sconfitto

EXAMPLE PHRASES

Hanno finalmente **sconfitto** la malattia. They have at last conquered the disease.

Li **hanno sconfitti** uno a zero. They beat them one nil.

La mia squadra è stata **sconfitta**. My team was beaten.

sconfiggere

FUTURE

io	sconfiggerò
tu	sconfiggerai
lui/lei/Lei	sconfiggerà
noi	sconfiggeremo
voi	sconfiggerete
loro	sconfiggeranno

CONDITIONAL

io	sconfiggerei
tu	sconfiggeresti
lui/lei/Lei	sconfiggerebbe
noi	sconfiggeremmo
voi	sconfiggereste
loro	sconfiggerebbero

PAST HISTORIC

io	sconfissi
tu	sconfiggesti
lui/lei/Lei	sconfisse
noi	sconfiggemmo
voi	sconfiggeste
loro	sconfissero

PLUPERFECT

io	avevo sconfitto
tu	avevi sconfitto
lui/lei/Lei	aveva sconfitto
noi	avevamo sconfitto
voi	avevate sconfitto
loro	avevano sconfitto

IMPERATIVE

sconfiggi
sconfiggiamo
sconfiggete

EXAMPLE PHRASES

Quel candidato **sconfiggerà** certamente tutti gli altri. This candidate is sure to defeat all the others.

Se fossi in forma non mi **sconfiggeresti** mai. If I was fit you'd never beat me.

L'esercito **sconfisse** i nemici. The army defeated the enemy.

Era triste perché lo **avevano sconfitto**. He was unhappy because they'd beaten him.

Attacchiamo e **sconfiggiamoli**! Let's attack and defeat them!

Italic letters in Italian words show where stress does not follow the usual rules.

scrivere (to write)

PRESENT		**PRESENT SUBJUNCTIVE**	
io	**scrivo**	io	**scriva**
tu	**scrivi**	tu	**scriva**
lui/lei/Lei	**scrive**	lui/lei/Lei	**scriva**
noi	**scriviamo**	noi	**scriviamo**
voi	**scrivete**	voi	**scriviate**
loro	**scrivono**	loro	**scrivano**

PERFECT		**IMPERFECT**	
io	**ho scritto**	io	**scrivevo**
tu	**hai scritto**	tu	**scrivevi**
lui/lei/Lei	**ha scritto**	lui/lei/Lei	**scriveva**
noi	**abbiamo scritto**	noi	**scrivevamo**
voi	**avete scritto**	voi	**scrivevate**
loro	**hanno scritto**	loro	**scrivevano**

GERUND	**PAST PARTICIPLE**
scrivendo	scritto

EXAMPLE PHRASES

Scrivo sempre cartoline a tutti i miei amici. I always write postcards to all my friends.

Come si **scrive**? How do you spell it?

Ho scritto una lettera a Luca. I wrote Luca a letter.

A Natale ci **scrivevano** sempre. They always wrote to us at Christmas.

Non so **scrivere** a macchina. I can't type.

Sta **scrivendo** la tesi di laurea. She's writing her thesis.

Remember that subject pronouns are not used very often in Italian.

scrivere

FUTURE

io	**scriverò**
tu	**scriverai**
lui/lei/Lei	**scriverà**
noi	**scriveremo**
voi	**scriverete**
loro	**scriveranno**

CONDITIONAL

io	**scriverei**
tu	**scriveresti**
lui/lei/Lei	**scriverebbe**
noi	**scriveremmo**
voi	**scrivereste**
loro	**scriverebbero**

PAST HISTORIC

io	**scrissi**
tu	**scrivesti**
lui/lei/Lei	**scrisse**
noi	**scrivemmo**
voi	**scriveste**
loro	**scrissero**

PLUPERFECT

io	**avevo scritto**
tu	**avevi scritto**
lui/lei/Lei	**aveva scritto**
noi	**avevamo scritto**
voi	**avevate scritto**
loro	**avevano scritto**

IMPERATIVE

scrivi
scriviamo
scrivete

EXAMPLE PHRASES

Avevo scritto un appunto ma l'ho perso. I'd written a note but lost it.
Scrivimi presto. Write to me soon.

Italic letters in Italian words show where stress does not follow the usual rules.

scuotere (to shake)

PRESENT

io	**scuoto**
tu	**scuoti**
lui/lei/Lei	**scuote**
noi	**scuotiamo**
voi	**scuotete**
loro	**scuotono**

PRESENT SUBJUNCTIVE

io	**scuota**
tu	**scuota**
lui/lei/Lei	**scuota**
noi	**scuotiamo**
voi	**scuotiate**
loro	**scuotano**

PERFECT

io	**ho scosso**
tu	**hai scosso**
lui/lei/Lei	**ha scosso**
noi	**abbiamo scosso**
voi	**avete scosso**
loro	**hanno scosso**

IMPERFECT

io	**scuotevo**
tu	**scuotevi**
lui/lei/Lei	**scuoteva**
noi	**scuotevamo**
voi	**scuotevate**
loro	**scuotevano**

GERUND

scuotendo

PAST PARTICIPLE

scosso

EXAMPLE PHRASES

È sul terrazzo che **scuote** i tappeti. She's on the balcony shaking the rugs.

Ha scosso la testa. He shook his head.

Scuoteva la scatola per capire cosa conteneva. He shook the box to see what was in it.

Stava **scuotendo** la borsa per farne uscire il contenuto. She was shaking the contents out of the bag.

Se ne andò **scuotendo** la testa senza parlare. She went off, shaking her head but saying nothing.

Remember that subject pronouns are not used very often in Italian.

scuotere

FUTURE

io	**scuoterò**
tu	**scuoterai**
lui/lei/Lei	**scuoterà**
noi	**scuoteremo**
voi	**scuoterete**
loro	**scuoteranno**

CONDITIONAL

io	**scuoterei**
tu	**scuoteresti**
lui/lei/Lei	**scuoterebbe**
noi	**scuoteremmo**
voi	**scuotereste**
loro	**scuoterebbero**

PAST HISTORIC

io	**scossi**
tu	**scuotesti**
lui/lei/Lei	**scosse**
noi	**scuotemmo**
voi	**scuoteste**
loro	**scossero**

PLUPERFECT

io	**avevo scosso**
tu	**avevi scosso**
lui/lei/Lei	**aveva scosso**
noi	**avevamo scosso**
voi	**avevate scosso**
loro	**avevano scosso**

IMPERATIVE

scuoti
scuotiamo
scuotete

EXAMPLE PHRASES

Quel rumore mi **scosse** i nervi. That noise drove me mad.

Italic letters in Italian words show where stress does not follow the usual rules.

sedere (to sit)

PRESENT		PRESENT SUBJUNCTIVE	
io	**siedo**	io	**sieda**
tu	**siedi**	tu	**sieda**
lui/lei/Lei	**siede**	lui/lei/Lei	**sieda**
noi	**sediamo**	noi	**sediamo**
voi	**sedete**	voi	**sediate**
loro	**siedono**	loro	**siedano**

PERFECT		IMPERFECT	
io	**sono seduto/a**	io	**sedevo**
tu	**sei seduto/a**	tu	**sedevi**
lui/lei/Lei	**è seduto/a**	lui/lei/Lei	**sedeva**
noi	**siamo seduti/e**	noi	**sedevamo**
voi	**siete seduti/e**	voi	**sedevate**
loro	**sono seduti/e**	loro	**sedevano**

GERUND
sedendo

PAST PARTICIPLE
seduto

EXAMPLE PHRASES

Si **siede** sempre in ultima fila. She always sits in the back row.

Prego, si **sieda** qui accanto. Please sit here beside me.

Si **è seduto** per terra. He sat on the floor.

Sono stato **seduto** tutto il giorno. I've been sitting down all day.

Sedevano in silenzio e leggevano. They were sitting in silence reading.

sedere

FUTURE

io	**sederò**
tu	**sederai**
lui/lei/Lei	**sederà**
noi	**sederemo**
voi	**sederete**
loro	**sederanno**

CONDITIONAL

io	**sederei**
tu	**sederesti**
lui/lei/Lei	**sederebbe**
noi	**sederemmo**
voi	**sedereste**
loro	**sederebbero**

PAST HISTORIC

io	**sedetti**
tu	**sedesti**
lui/lei/Lei	**sedette**
noi	**sedemmo**
voi	**sedeste**
loro	**sedettero**

PLUPERFECT

io	**ero seduto/a**
tu	**eri seduto/a**
lui/lei/Lei	**era seduto/a**
noi	**eravamo seduti/e**
voi	**eravate seduti/e**
loro	**erano seduti/e**

IMPERATIVE

siedi
sediamo
sedete

EXAMPLE PHRASES

Si **sedettero** a tavola e iniziarono la cena. They sat down at the table and started dinner.

Era seduta accanto a me. She was sitting beside me.

Siediti qui! Sit here!

soddisfare (to satisfy)

PRESENT		PRESENT SUBJUNCTIVE	
io	**soddisfo**	io	**soddisfi**
tu	**soddisfi**	tu	**soddisfi**
lui/lei/Lei	**soddisfa**	lui/lei/Lei	**soddisfi**
noi	**soddisfiamo**	noi	**soddisfiamo**
voi	**soddisfate**	voi	**soddisfiate**
loro	**soddisfano**	loro	**soddisfino**

PERFECT		IMPERFECT	
io	**ho soddisfatto**	io	**soddisfacevo**
tu	**hai soddisfatto**	tu	**soddisfacevi**
lui/lei/Lei	**ha soddisfatto**	lui/lei/Lei	**soddisfaceva**
noi	**abbiamo soddisfatto**	noi	**soddisfacevamo**
voi	**avete soddisfatto**	voi	**soddisfacevate**
loro	**hanno soddisfatto**	loro	**soddisfacevano**

GERUND	PAST PARTICIPLE
soddisfacendo	soddisfatto

EXAMPLE PHRASES

Il mio lavoro non mi **soddisfa**. My job doesn't satisfy me.

Soddisfaceva ogni desiderio della moglie. He satisfied his wife's every wish.

soddisfare

FUTURE

io	**soddisferò**
tu	**soddisferai**
lui/lei/Lei	**soddisferà**
noi	**soddisferemo**
voi	**soddisferete**
loro	**soddisferanno**

CONDITIONAL

io	**soddisferei**
tu	**soddisferesti**
lui/lei/Lei	**soddisferebbe**
noi	**soddisferemmo**
voi	**soddisfereste**
loro	**soddisferebbero**

PAST HISTORIC

io	**soddisfeci**
tu	**soddisfacesti**
lui/lei/Lei	**soddisfece**
noi	**soddisfacemmo**
voi	**soddisfaceste**
loro	**soddisfecero**

PLUPERFECT

io	**avevo soddisfatto**
tu	**avevi soddisfatto**
lui/lei/Lei	**aveva soddisfatto**
noi	**avevamo soddisfatto**
voi	**avevate soddisfatto**
loro	**avevano soddisfatto**

IMPERATIVE

soddisfa
soddisfiamo
soddisfate

EXAMPLE PHRASES

Questo libro **soddisferà** i lettori più esigenti. This book will please the most demanding readers.

Questa soluzione non ci **soddisferebbe**. We wouldn't be satisfied by this solution.

La sua scelta non li **aveva soddisfatti**. They hadn't been pleased with her choice.

Italic letters in Italian words show where stress does not follow the usual rules.

sognare (to dream)

PRESENT		PRESENT SUBJUNCTIVE	
io	**sogno**	io	**sogni**
tu	**sogni**	tu	**sogni**
lui/lei/Lei	**sogna**	lui/lei/Lei	**sogni**
noi	**sogniamo**	noi	**sogniamo**
voi	**sognate**	voi	**sogniate**
loro	**sognano**	loro	**sognino**

PERFECT		IMPERFECT	
io	**ho sognato**	io	**sognavo**
tu	**hai sognato**	tu	**sognavi**
lui/lei/Lei	**ha sognato**	lui/lei/Lei	**sognava**
noi	**abbiamo sognato**	noi	**sognavamo**
voi	**avete sognato**	voi	**sognavate**
loro	**hanno sognato**	loro	**sognavano**

GERUND

sognando

PAST PARTICIPLE

sognato

EXAMPLE PHRASES

Stanotte ti **ho sognato**. I dreamt about you last night.

Tutte le notti **sognavo** la stessa cosa. I had the same dream every night.

Stavo **sognando** ad occhi aperti. I was daydreaming.

sognare

FUTURE

io	**sognerò**
tu	**sognerai**
lui/lei/Lei	**sognerà**
noi	**sogneremo**
voi	**sognerete**
loro	**sogneranno**

CONDITIONAL

io	**sognerei**
tu	**sogneresti**
lui/lei/Lei	**sognerebbe**
noi	**sogneremmo**
voi	**sognereste**
loro	**sognerebbero**

PAST HISTORIC

io	**sognai**
tu	**sognasti**
lui/lei/Lei	**sognò**
noi	**sognammo**
voi	**sognaste**
loro	**sognarono**

PLUPERFECT

io	**avevo sognato**
tu	**avevi sognato**
lui/lei/Lei	**aveva sognato**
noi	**avevamo sognato**
voi	**avevate sognato**
loro	**avevano sognato**

IMPERATIVE

sogna
sogniamo
sognate

EXAMPLE PHRASES

Non ci **sogneremmo** mai di chiedere una cosa simile. We'd never dream
   of asking for something like that.
Sognai di essere sulla luna. I dreamt I was on the moon.
Avevo sempre **sognato** una casa così. I'd always dreamt of a house like that.
Smetti di **sognare** e sii realista. Stop dreaming and be realistic.
Ve lo **sognate**! You can forget it!

Italic letters in Italian words show where stress does not follow the usual rules.

sparire (to disappear)

PRESENT

io	**sparisco**
tu	**sparisci**
lui/lei/Lei	**sparisce**
noi	**spariamo**
voi	**sparite**
loro	**spariscono**

PRESENT SUBJUNCTIVE

io	**sparisca**
tu	**sparisca**
lui/lei/Lei	**sparisca**
noi	**spariamo**
voi	**spariate**
loro	**spariscano**

PERFECT

io	**sono sparito/a**
tu	**sei sparito/a**
lui/lei/Lei	**è sparito/a**
noi	**siamo spariti/e**
voi	**siete spariti/e**
loro	**sono spariti/e**

IMPERFECT

io	**sparivo**
tu	**sparivi**
lui/lei/Lei	**spariva**
noi	**sparivamo**
voi	**sparivate**
loro	**sparivano**

GERUND

sparendo

PAST PARTICIPLE

sparito

EXAMPLE PHRASES

Sparisce ogni volta che c'è bisogno di lui. He disappears whenever he's needed.

La nave **è sparita** all'orizzonte. The ship disappeared over the horizon.

Dov'**è sparita** la mia penna? Where has my pen gone?

sparire

FUTURE

io	**sparirò**
tu	**spariai**
lui/lei/Lei	**sparirà**
noi	**spariremo**
voi	**sparirete**
loro	**spariranno**

CONDITIONAL

io	**sparirei**
tu	**spariresti**
lui/lei/Lei	**sparirebbe**
noi	**spariremmo**
voi	**sparireste**
loro	**sparir*e*bbero**

PAST HISTORIC

io	**sparii**
tu	**sparisti**
lui/lei/Lei	**sparì**
noi	**sparimmo**
voi	**spariste**
loro	**spar*i*rono**

PLUPERFECT

io	**ero sparito/a**
tu	**eri sparito/a**
lui/lei/Lei	**era sparito/a**
noi	**eravamo spariti/e**
voi	**eravate spariti/e**
loro	**erano spariti/e**

IMPERATIVE

sparisci
spariamo
sparite

EXAMPLE PHRASES

Spariranno dopo cena, come al solito. They'll go off after dinner, as usual.
Sparì senza salutare nessuno. He went off without saying goodbye
  to anyone.
Erano spariti senza lasciare traccia. They had disappeared without trace.
Sparisci e non farti più vedere! Be off and don't show your face around
  here again!

Italic letters in Italian words show where stress does not follow the usual rules.

spegnere (to put out)

PRESENT

io	**spengo**
tu	**spegni**
lui/lei/Lei	**spegne**
noi	**spegniamo**
voi	**spegnete**
loro	**spengono**

PRESENT SUBJUNCTIVE

io	**spenga**
tu	**spenga**
lui/lei/Lei	**spenga**
noi	**spegniamo**
voi	**spegniate**
loro	**spengano**

PERFECT

io	**ho spento**
tu	**hai spento**
lui/lei/Lei	**ha spento**
noi	**abbiamo spento**
voi	**avete spento**
loro	**hanno spento**

IMPERFECT

io	**spegnevo**
tu	**spegnevi**
lui/lei/Lei	**spegneva**
noi	**spegnevamo**
voi	**spegnevate**
loro	**spegnevano**

GERUND
spegnendo

PAST PARTICIPLE
spento

EXAMPLE PHRASES

L'ultimo **spenga** la luce e chiuda la porta. Will the last person turn off the light and shut the door.

Hai spento la sigaretta? Have you put your cigarette out?

La luce si **è spenta** all'improvviso. The light went off suddenly.

La candela si stava **spegnendo** lentamente. The candle was slowly going out.

Remember that subject pronouns are not used very often in Italian.

spegnere

FUTURE

io	**spegnerò**
tu	**spegnerai**
lui/lei/Lei	**spegnerà**
noi	**spegneremo**
voi	**spegnerete**
loro	**spegneranno**

CONDITIONAL

io	**spegnerei**
tu	**spegneresti**
lui/lei/Lei	**spegnerebbe**
noi	**spegneremmo**
voi	**spegnereste**
loro	**spegnerebbero**

PAST HISTORIC

io	**spensi**
tu	**spegnesti**
lui/lei/Lei	**spense**
noi	**spegnemmo**
voi	**spegneste**
loro	**spensero**

PLUPERFECT

io	**avevo spento**
tu	**avevi spento**
lui/lei/Lei	**aveva spento**
noi	**avevamo spento**
voi	**avevate spento**
loro	**avevano spento**

IMPERATIVE

spegni
spegniamo
spegnete

EXAMPLE PHRASES

Senza ossigeno il fuoco si **spegnerebbe**. Without oxygen the fire would go out.

Il motore si **spense** al semaforo. The engine stalled at the traffic lights.

Spegnete le luci che guardiamo il film. Turn off the lights and we'll watch the film.

Italic letters in Italian words show where stress does not follow the usual rules.

spendere (to spend)

PRESENT

io	spendo
tu	spendi
lui/lei/Lei	spende
noi	spendiamo
voi	spendete
loro	spendono

PRESENT SUBJUNCTIVE

io	spenda
tu	spenda
lui/lei/Lei	spenda
noi	spendiamo
voi	spendiate
loro	spendano

PERFECT

io	ho speso
tu	hai speso
lui/lei/Lei	ha speso
noi	abbiamo speso
voi	avete speso
loro	hanno speso

IMPERFECT

io	spendevo
tu	spendevi
lui/lei/Lei	spendeva
noi	spendevamo
voi	spendevate
loro	spendevano

GERUND

spendendo

PAST PARTICIPLE

speso

EXAMPLE PHRASES

Si mangia bene e si **spende** poco. The food's good and it doesn't cost much.

Quanto **hai speso**? How much did you spend?

Spendeva tutto quello che guadagnava. He spent all he earned.

Ultimamente stiamo **spendendo** troppo. We've been spending too much lately.

spendere

FUTURE

io	**spenderò**
tu	**spenderai**
lui/lei/Lei	**spenderà**
noi	**spenderemo**
voi	**spenderete**
loro	**spenderanno**

CONDITIONAL

io	**spenderei**
tu	**spenderesti**
lui/lei/Lei	**spenderebbe**
noi	**spenderemmo**
voi	**spendereste**
loro	**spenderebbero**

PAST HISTORIC

io	**spesi**
tu	**spendesti**
lui/lei/Lei	**spese**
noi	**spendemmo**
voi	**spendeste**
loro	**spesero**

PLUPERFECT

io	**avevo speso**
tu	**avevi speso**
lui/lei/Lei	**aveva speso**
noi	**avevamo speso**
voi	**avevate speso**
loro	**avevano speso**

IMPERATIVE

spendi
spendiamo
spendete

EXAMPLE PHRASES

Lì **spenderete** poco e starete bene. You won't have to pay much there, and you'll be comfortable.

Non **spenderei** mai una cifra simile. I'd never spend as much as that.

Entrò nel negozio e **spese** tutto ciò che aveva. She went into the shop and spent all she had.

Aveva speso tutto al gioco e si è indebitato. He'd spent all his money gambling and was in debt.

Italic letters in Italian words show where stress does not follow the usual rules.

sporgersi (to lean out)

PRESENT

io	**mi sporgo**
tu	**ti sporgi**
lui/lei/Lei	**si sporge**
noi	**ci sporgiamo**
voi	**vi sporgete**
loro	**si sporgono**

PRESENT SUBJUNCTIVE

io	**mi sporga**
tu	**ti sporga**
lui/lei/Lei	**si sporga**
noi	**ci sporgiamo**
voi	**vi sporgiate**
loro	**si sporgano**

PERFECT

io	**mi sono sporto/a**
tu	**ti sei sporto/a**
lui/lei/Lei	**si è sporto/a**
noi	**ci siamo sporti/e**
voi	**vi siete sporti/e**
loro	**si sono sporti/e**

IMPERFECT

io	**mi sporgevo**
tu	**ti sporgevi**
lui/lei/Lei	**si sporgeva**
noi	**ci sporgevamo**
voi	**vi sporgevate**
loro	**si sporgevano**

GERUND
sporgendosi

PAST PARTICIPLE
sporto

EXAMPLE PHRASES

Sporgendoti, vedrai meglio. If you lean out you'll see better.

sporgersi

FUTURE

io	**mi sporgerò**
tu	**ti sporgerai**
lui/lei/Lei	**si sporgerà**
noi	**ci sporgeremo**
voi	**vi sporgerete**
loro	**si sporgeranno**

CONDITIONAL

io	**mi sporgerei**
tu	**ti sporgeresti**
lui/lei/Lei	**si sporgerebbe**
noi	**ci sporgeremmo**
voi	**vi sporgereste**
loro	**si sporgerebbero**

PAST HISTORIC

io	**mi sporsi**
tu	**ti sporgesti**
lui/lei/Lei	**si sporse**
noi	**ci sporgemmo**
voi	**vi sporgeste**
loro	**si sporsero**

PLUPERFECT

io	**mi ero sporto/a**
tu	**ti eri sporto/a**
lui/lei/Lei	**si era sporto/a**
noi	**ci eravamo sporti/e**
voi	**vi eravate sporti/e**
loro	**si erano sporti/e**

IMPERATIVE

sporgiti
sporgiamoci
sporgetevi

EXAMPLE PHRASES

Si **sporsero** per guardare la sfilata. They leaned out to watch the parade.
Si **era sporto** per salutare. He'd leant out to say hello.
Non **sporgerti** dal finestrino. Don't lean out of the window.

Italic letters in Italian words show where stress does not follow the usual rules.

stare (to be)

PRESENT

io	**sto**
tu	**stai**
lui/lei/Lei	**sta**
noi	**stiamo**
voi	**state**
loro	**stanno**

PRESENT SUBJUNCTIVE

io	**stia**
tu	**stia**
lui/lei/Lei	**stia**
noi	**stiamo**
voi	**stiate**
loro	**stiano**

PERFECT

io	**sono stato/a**
tu	**sei stato/a**
lui/lei/Lei	**è stato/a**
noi	**siamo stati/e**
voi	**siete stati/e**
loro	**sono stati/e**

IMPERFECT

io	**stavo**
tu	**stavi**
lui/lei/Lei	**stava**
noi	**stavamo**
voi	**stavate**
loro	**stavano**

GERUND

stando

PAST PARTICIPLE

stato

EXAMPLE PHRASES

Come **stai**? How are you?

Sta a te decidere. It's up to you to decide.

Sei mai **stato** in Francia? Have you ever been to France?

Stavo per uscire quando ha squillato il telefono. I was about to go out when the phone rang.

Stavo andando a casa. I was going home.

Stando così le cose, non voglio aiutarti. In this situation I don't want to help you.

Remember that subject pronouns are not used very often in Italian.

stare

FUTURE

io	**starò**
tu	**starai**
lui/lei/Lei	**starà**
noi	**staremo**
voi	**starete**
loro	**staranno**

CONDITIONAL

io	**starei**
tu	**staresti**
lui/lei/Lei	**starebbe**
noi	**staremmo**
voi	**stareste**
loro	**starebbero**

PAST HISTORIC

io	**stetti**
tu	**stesti**
lui/lei/Lei	**stette**
noi	**stemmo**
voi	**steste**
loro	**stettero**

PLUPERFECT

io	**ero stato/a**
tu	**eri stato/a**
lui/lei/Lei	**era stato/a**
noi	**eravamo stati/e**
voi	**eravate stati/e**
loro	**erano stati/e**

IMPERATIVE

stai
stiamo
state

EXAMPLE PHRASES

A Londra **starò** da amici. I'll be staying with friends in London.
Ci **stareste** a fare uno scherzo a Monica? Do you want to play a trick
   on Monica?
Era stata zitta tutta la sera. She'd been silent all evening.
Stai ancora un po'! Stay a bit longer!

Italic letters in Italian words show where stress does not follow the usual rules.

storcere (to twist)

PRESENT

io	**storco**
tu	**storci**
lui/lei/Lei	**storce**
noi	**storciamo**
voi	**storcete**
loro	**storcono**

PRESENT SUBJUNCTIVE

io	**storca**
tu	**storca**
lui/lei/Lei	**storca**
noi	**storciamo**
voi	**storciate**
loro	**storcano**

PERFECT

io	**ho storto**
tu	**hai storto**
lui/lei/Lei	**ha storto**
noi	**abbiamo storto**
voi	**avete storto**
loro	**hanno storto**

IMPERFECT

io	**storcevo**
tu	**storcevi**
lui/lei/Lei	**storceva**
noi	**storcevamo**
voi	**storcevate**
loro	**storcevano**

GERUND

storcendo

PAST PARTICIPLE

storto

EXAMPLE PHRASES

Storce sempre il naso se c'è da lavorare. He always turns up his nose if there's any work to be done.

È inutile che tu **storca** il naso. There's no point turning up your nose.

Le **ha storto** un braccio. He twisted her arm.

Mi **sono storto** una caviglia. I've twisted my ankle.

Remember that subject pronouns are not used very often in Italian.

storcere

FUTURE

io	**storcerò**
tu	**storcerai**
lui/lei/Lei	**storcerà**
noi	**storceremo**
voi	**storcerete**
loro	**storceranno**

CONDITIONAL

io	**storcerei**
tu	**storceresti**
lui/lei/Lei	**storcerebbe**
noi	**storceremmo**
voi	**storcereste**
loro	**storcerebbero**

PAST HISTORIC

io	**storsi**
tu	**storcesti**
lui/lei/Lei	**storse**
noi	**storcemmo**
voi	**storceste**
loro	**storsero**

PLUPERFECT

io	**avevo storto**
tu	**avevi storto**
lui/lei/Lei	**aveva storto**
noi	**avevamo storto**
voi	**avevate storto**
loro	**avevano storto**

IMPERATIVE

storci
storciamo
storcete

EXAMPLE PHRASES

Non **storceresti** il naso se fossi meno schizzinoso. You wouldn't turn up your nose if you weren't so fussy.

Guardò il cibo e **storse** il naso. He looked at the food and turned up his nose.

Italic letters in Italian words show where stress does not follow the usual rules.

stringere (to tighten)

PRESENT		PRESENT SUBJUNCTIVE	
io	**stringo**	io	**stringa**
tu	**stringi**	tu	**stringa**
lui/lei/Lei	**stringe**	lui/lei/Lei	**stringa**
noi	**stringiamo**	noi	**stringiamo**
voi	**stringete**	voi	**stringiate**
loro	**stringono**	loro	**stringano**

PERFECT		IMPERFECT	
io	**ho stretto**	io	**stringevo**
tu	**hai stretto**	tu	**stringevi**
lui/lei/Lei	**ha stretto**	lui/lei/Lei	**stringeva**
noi	**abbiamo stretto**	noi	**stringevamo**
voi	**avete stretto**	voi	**stringevate**
loro	**hanno stretto**	loro	**stringevano**

GERUND	PAST PARTICIPLE
stringendo	stretto

EXAMPLE PHRASES

La gonna è larga: bisogna che la **stringa**. The skirt is too loose: I'll have to take it in.

Ho stretto la cintura perché sono dimagrita. I've tightened my belt because I've lost weight.

Ci **siamo stretti** la mano. We shook hands.

Le scarpe **stringevano** e ho dovuto cambiarle. The shoes were too tight so I had to change them.

Remember that subject pronouns are not used very often in Italian.

stringere

FUTURE

io	**stringerò**
tu	**stringerai**
lui/lei/Lei	**stringerà**
noi	**stringeremo**
voi	**stringerete**
loro	**stringeranno**

CONDITIONAL

io	**stringerei**
tu	**stringeresti**
lui/lei/Lei	**stringerebbe**
noi	**stringeremmo**
voi	**stringereste**
loro	**stringerebbero**

PAST HISTORIC

io	**strinsi**
tu	**stringesti**
lui/lei/Lei	**strinse**
noi	**stringemmo**
voi	**stringeste**
loro	**strinsero**

PLUPERFECT

io	**avevo stretto**
tu	**avevi stretto**
lui/lei/Lei	**aveva stretto**
noi	**avevamo stretto**
voi	**avevate stretto**
loro	**avevano stretto**

IMPERATIVE

stringi
stringiamo
stringete

EXAMPLE PHRASES

Se ci **stringeremo** ci staremo tutti. If we squeeze up we'll all get in.

Stringiamo i denti e continuiamo. Let's grit our teeth and carry on.

Italic letters in Italian words show where stress does not follow the usual rules.

succedere (to happen)

PRESENT

io	–
tu	–
lui/lei/Lei	**succede**
noi	–
voi	–
loro	**succedono**

PRESENT SUBJUNCTIVE

io	–
tu	–
lui/lei/Lei	**succeda**
noi	–
voi	–
loro	**succedano**

PERFECT

io	–
tu	–
lui/lei/Lei	**è successo/a**
noi	–
voi	–
loro	**sono successi/e**

IMPERFECT

io	–
tu	–
lui/lei/Lei	**succedeva**
noi	–
voi	–
loro	**succedevano**

GERUND

succedendo

PAST PARTICIPLE

successo

EXAMPLE PHRASES

Sono cose che **succedono**. These things happen.

Non capisco cosa **succeda**. I don't know what might be happening.

Cos'**è successo**? What happened?

Dev'essergli **successo** qualcosa. Something must have happened to him.

succedere

FUTURE

io	–
tu	–
lui/lei/Lei	**succederà**
noi	–
voi	–
loro	**succederanno**

CONDITIONAL

io	–
tu	–
lui/lei/Lei	**succederebbe**
noi	–
voi	–
loro	**succederebbero**

PAST HISTORIC

io	–
tu	–
lui/lei/Lei	**successe**
noi	–
voi	–
loro	**successero**

PLUPERFECT

io	–
tu	–
lui/lei/Lei	**era successo/a**
noi	–
voi	–
loro	**erano successi/e**

IMPERATIVE

–

EXAMPLE PHRASES

Ho paura di ciò che **succederà**. I'm afraid of what will happen.

Cosa **succederebbe** se lui tornasse? What would happen if he came back?

Dalla sua partenza erano **successe** molte cose. A lot of things happened as a consequence of his departure.

Successe il finimondo. All hell broke loose.

Italic letters in Italian words show where stress does not follow the usual rules.

tacere (to be quiet)

PRESENT

io	**taccio**
tu	**taci**
lui/lei/Lei	**tace**
noi	**tacciamo**
voi	**tacete**
loro	**tacciono**

PRESENT SUBJUNCTIVE

io	**taccia**
tu	**taccia**
lui/lei/Lei	**taccia**
noi	**tacciamo**
voi	**tacciate**
loro	**tacciano**

PERFECT

io	**ho taciuto**
tu	**hai taciuto**
lui/lei/Lei	**ha taciuto**
noi	**abbiamo taciuto**
voi	**avete taciuto**
loro	**hanno taciuto**

IMPERFECT

io	**tacevo**
tu	**tacevi**
lui/lei/Lei	**taceva**
noi	**tacevamo**
voi	**tacevate**
loro	**tacevano**

GERUND

tacendo

PAST PARTICIPLE

taciuto

EXAMPLE PHRASES

È meglio che **tacciate**. It's best if you say nothing.

Tacevano e si guardavano. They said nothing and looked at each other.

Pur **tacendo**, gli fece capire che sbagliava. Even though she didn't say anything, she made him realize he was wrong.

tacere

FUTURE

io	**tacerò**
tu	**tacerai**
lui/lei/Lei	**tacerà**
noi	**taceremo**
voi	**tacerete**
loro	**taceranno**

CONDITIONAL

io	**tacerei**
tu	**taceresti**
lui/lei/Lei	**tacerebbe**
noi	**taceremmo**
voi	**tacereste**
loro	**tacerebbero**

PAST HISTORIC

io	**tacqui**
tu	**tacesti**
lui/lei/Lei	**tacque**
noi	**tacemmo**
voi	**taceste**
loro	**tacquero**

PLUPERFECT

io	**avevo taciuto**
tu	**avevi taciuto**
lui/lei/Lei	**aveva taciuto**
noi	**avevamo taciuto**
voi	**avevate taciuto**
loro	**avevano taciuto**

IMPERATIVE

taci
tacciamo
tacete

EXAMPLE PHRASES

Improvvisamente **tacque** e sorrise. He suddenly stopped talking and smiled.

Avevo taciuto a lungo prima di parlare. I'd been silent a long time before
I spoke.

Taci! Be quiet!

Italic letters in Italian words show where stress does not follow the usual rules.

tenere (to hold)

PRESENT

io	**tengo**
tu	**tieni**
lui/lei/Lei	**tiene**
noi	**teniamo**
voi	**tenete**
loro	**tengono**

PRESENT SUBJUNCTIVE

io	**tenga**
tu	**tenga**
lui/lei/Lei	**tenga**
noi	**teniamo**
voi	**teniate**
loro	**tengano**

PERFECT

io	**ho tenuto**
tu	**hai tenuto**
lui/lei/Lei	**ha tenuto**
noi	**abbiamo tenuto**
voi	**avete tenuto**
loro	**hanno tenuto**

IMPERFECT

io	**tenevo**
tu	**tenevi**
lui/lei/Lei	**teneva**
noi	**tenevamo**
voi	**tenevate**
loro	**tenevano**

GERUND

tenendo

PAST PARTICIPLE

tenuto

EXAMPLE PHRASES

Tiene la racchetta con la sinistra. He holds the racket with his left hand.

La mamma **tiene** in braccio il bambino. The mother is holding the baby.

Ecco il conto, **tenga** pure il resto. Here's the money, keep the change.

Si **tenevano** per mano. They were holding hands.

tenere

FUTURE

io	**terrò**
tu	**terrai**
lui/lei/Lei	**terrà**
noi	**terremo**
voi	**terrete**
loro	**terranno**

CONDITIONAL

io	**terrei**
tu	**terresti**
lui/lei/Lei	**terrebbe**
noi	**terremmo**
voi	**terreste**
loro	**terrebbero**

PAST HISTORIC

io	**tenni**
tu	**tenesti**
lui/lei/Lei	**tenne**
noi	**tenemmo**
voi	**teneste**
loro	**tennero**

PLUPERFECT

io	**avevo tenuto**
tu	**avevi tenuto**
lui/lei/Lei	**aveva tenuto**
noi	**avevamo tenuto**
voi	**avevate tenuto**
loro	**avevano tenuto**

IMPERATIVE

tieni
teniamo
tenete

EXAMPLE PHRASES

Se non ti serve, lo **terrò** io. If you don't need it I'll keep it.

Mi **terresti** il posto? Torno subito. Could you keep my place for me? I'll be right back.

Ci dettero un parte dei soldi e **tennero** il resto per sé. They gave us some of the money and kept the rest for themselves.

Tieni, questo è per te. Here, this is for you.

Tieniti pronta per le cinque. Be ready by five.

Tieniti forte! Hold on tight!

Italic letters in Italian words show where stress does not follow the usual rules.

togliere (to take off)

PRESENT

io	**tolgo**
tu	**togli**
lui/lei/Lei	**toglie**
noi	**togliamo**
voi	**togliete**
loro	**tolgono**

PRESENT SUBJUNCTIVE

io	**tolga**
tu	**tolga**
lui/lei/Lei	**tolga**
noi	**togliamo**
voi	**togliate**
loro	**tolgano**

PERFECT

io	**ho tolto**
tu	**hai tolto**
lui/lei/Lei	**ha tolto**
noi	**abbiamo tolto**
voi	**avete tolto**
loro	**hanno tolto**

IMPERFECT

io	**toglievo**
tu	**toglievi**
lui/lei/Lei	**toglieva**
noi	**toglievamo**
voi	**toglievate**
loro	**toglievano**

GERUND

togliendo

PAST PARTICIPLE

tolto

EXAMPLE PHRASES

Avevo caldo e mi **sono tolto** la giacca. I was hot and took my jacket off.

Ho tolto il poster dalla parete. I took the poster off the wall.

Stavo **togliendo** i vestiti dall'armadio quando mi hanno chiamato. I was taking clothes out of the cupboard when they phoned me.

Remember that subject pronouns are not used very often in Italian.

togliere

FUTURE

io	**toglierò**
tu	**toglierai**
lui/lei/Lei	**toglierà**
noi	**toglieremo**
voi	**toglierete**
loro	**toglieranno**

CONDITIONAL

io	**toglierei**
tu	**toglieresti**
lui/lei/Lei	**toglierebbe**
noi	**toglieremmo**
voi	**togliereste**
loro	**toglierebbero**

PAST HISTORIC

io	**tolsi**
tu	**togliesti**
lui/lei/Lei	**tolse**
noi	**togliemmo**
voi	**toglieste**
loro	**tolsero**

PLUPERFECT

io	**avevo tolto**
tu	**avevi tolto**
lui/lei/Lei	**aveva tolto**
noi	**avevamo tolto**
voi	**avevate tolto**
loro	**avevano tolto**

IMPERATIVE

togli
togliamo
togliete

EXAMPLE PHRASES

Mi **toglieranno** due denti. I'm going to have two teeth out.

Lo riconobbi solo quando si **tolse** il cappello. I only recognized him when he took his hat off.

Togliti il cappotto. Take off your coat.

Italic letters in Italian words show where stress does not follow the usual rules.

trarre (to draw)

PRESENT

io	**traggo**
tu	**trai**
lui/lei/Lei	**trae**
noi	**traiamo**
voi	**traete**
loro	**traggono**

PRESENT SUBJUNCTIVE

io	**tragga**
tu	**tragga**
lui/lei/Lei	**tragga**
noi	**traiamo**
voi	**traiate**
loro	**traggano**

PERFECT

io	**ho tratto**
tu	**hai tratto**
lui/lei/Lei	**ha tratto**
noi	**abbiamo tratto**
voi	**avete tratto**
loro	**hanno tratto**

IMPERFECT

io	**traevo**
tu	**traevi**
lui/lei/Lei	**traeva**
noi	**traevamo**
voi	**traevate**
loro	**traevano**

GERUND
traendo

PAST PARTICIPLE
tratto

EXAMPLE PHRASES

Il suo modo di fare **trae** in inganno. His manner is misleading.

Sono stati **tratti** in salvo dai vigili del fuoco. They were rescued by the firemen.

un film **tratto** da un romanzo di A. Christie. A film based on a novel by A. Christie.

Dalla ricerca **hanno tratto** conclusioni interessanti. They've drawn some interesting conclusions from the research.

Traeva tutti in inganno con la sua falsa modestia. She deceived everyone with her false modesty.

Remember that subject pronouns are not used very often in Italian.

trarre

FUTURE

io	**trarrò**
tu	**trarrai**
lui/lei/Lei	**trarrà**
noi	**trarremo**
voi	**trarrete**
loro	**trarranno**

CONDITIONAL

io	**trarrei**
tu	**trarresti**
lui/lei/Lei	**trerrebbe**
noi	**trarremmo**
voi	**trerreste**
loro	**trarrebbero**

PAST HISTORIC

io	**trassi**
tu	**traesti**
lui/lei/Lei	**trasse**
noi	**traemmo**
voi	**traeste**
loro	**trassero**

PLUPERFECT

io	**avevo tratto**
tu	**avevi tratto**
lui/lei/Lei	**aveva tratto**
noi	**avevamo tratto**
voi	**avevate tratto**
loro	**avevano tratto**

IMPERATIVE

trai
traiamo
traete

EXAMPLE PHRASES

Non **trarrei** delle conclusioni così affrettate. I wouldn't draw such hasty conclusions.

Trassero in salvo l'alpinista ferito. They rescued the injured climber.

uscire (to go out)

PRESENT

io	**esco**
tu	**esci**
lui/lei/Lei	**esce**
noi	**usciamo**
voi	**uscite**
loro	**escono**

PRESENT SUBJUNCTIVE

io	**esca**
tu	**esca**
lui/lei/Lei	**esca**
noi	**usciamo**
voi	**usciate**
loro	**escano**

PERFECT

io	**sono uscito/a**
tu	**sei uscito/a**
lui/lei/Lei	**è uscito/a**
noi	**siamo usciti/e**
voi	**siete usciti/e**
loro	**sono usciti/e**

IMPERFECT

io	**uscivo**
tu	**uscivi**
lui/lei/Lei	**usciva**
noi	**uscivamo**
voi	**uscivate**
loro	**uscivano**

GERUND
uscendo

PAST PARTICIPLE
uscito

EXAMPLE PHRASES

La rivista **esce** di lunedì. The magazine comes out on Mondays.

I suoi non sono contenti che **esca** tutte le sere. Her parents aren't happy with the fact she goes out every evening.

È uscita a comprare il giornale. She's gone out to buy a newspaper.

Li ho incontrati **uscendo**. I met them as I was going out.

L'ho incontrata che **usciva** dalla farmacia. I met her coming out of the chemist's.

Remember that subject pronouns are not used very often in Italian.

uscire

FUTURE

io	**uscirò**
tu	**uscirai**
lui/lei/Lei	**uscirà**
noi	**usciremo**
voi	**uscirete**
loro	**usciranno**

CONDITIONAL

io	**uscirei**
tu	**usciresti**
lui/lei/Lei	**uscirebbe**
noi	**usciremmo**
voi	**uscireste**
loro	**uscirebbero**

PAST HISTORIC

io	**uscii**
tu	**uscisti**
lui/lei/Lei	**uscì**
noi	**uscimmo**
voi	**usciste**
loro	**uscirono**

PLUPERFECT

io	**ero uscito/a**
tu	**eri uscito/a**
lui/lei/Lei	**era uscito/a**
noi	**eravamo usciti/e**
voi	**eravate usciti/e**
loro	**erano usciti/e**

IMPERATIVE

esci
usciamo
uscite

EXAMPLE PHRASES

Uscirà dall'ospedale domani. He's coming out of hospital tomorrow.
Usciresti con me stasera? Would you go out with me this evening?
La macchina **uscì** di strada. The car came off the road.
Quando siamo arrivati **era** appena **uscita**. When we arrived she'd just left.
Uscite di qui immediatamente! Get out of here this minute!

Italic letters in Italian words show where stress does not follow the usual rules.

valere (to be worth)

PRESENT

io	**valgo**
tu	**vali**
lui/lei/Lei	**vale**
noi	**valiamo**
voi	**valete**
loro	**valgono**

PRESENT SUBJUNCTIVE

io	**valga**
tu	**valga**
lui/lei/Lei	**valga**
noi	**valiamo**
voi	**valiate**
loro	**valgano**

PERFECT

io	**sono valso/a**
tu	**sei valso/a**
lui/lei/Lei	**è valso/a**
noi	**siamo valsi/e**
voi	**siete valsi/e**
loro	**sono valsi/e**

IMPERFECT

io	**valevo**
tu	**valevi**
lui/lei/Lei	**valeva**
noi	**valevamo**
voi	**valevate**
loro	**valevano**

GERUND

valendo

PAST PARTICIPLE

valso

EXAMPLE PHRASES

L'auto **vale** tremila euro.The car is worth three thousand euros.

Non ne **vale** la pena. It's not worth it.

È stato difficile, ma ne **è valsa** la pena. It was difficult, but it was worth it.

Non **valeva** la pena arrabbiarsi tanto. It wasn't worth getting so angry.

Valendo poco, questa moto è difficile da vendere. Since it's worth so little, this bike is difficult to sell.

valere

FUTURE

io	**varrò**
tu	**varrai**
lui/lei/Lei	**varrà**
noi	**varremo**
voi	**varrete**
loro	**varranno**

CONDITIONAL

io	**varrei**
tu	**varresti**
lui/lei/Lei	**varrebbe**
noi	**varremmo**
voi	**varreste**
loro	**varrebbero**

PAST HISTORIC

io	**valsi**
tu	**valesti**
lui/lei/Lei	**valse**
noi	**valemmo**
voi	**valeste**
loro	**.valsero**

PLUPERFECT

io	**ero valso/a**
tu	**eri valso/a**
lui/lei/Lei	**era valso/a**
noi	**eravamo valsi/e**
voi	**eravate valsi/e**
loro	**erano valsi/e**

IMPERATIVE

vali
valiamo
valete

EXAMPLE PHRASES

Senza il giardino la casa non **varrebbe** niente. Without the garden the house wouldn't be worth anything.

Italic letters in Italian words show where stress does not follow the usual rules.

vedere (to see)

PRESENT

io	**vedo**
tu	**vedi**
lui/lei/Lei	**vede**
noi	**vediamo**
voi	**vedete**
loro	**vedono**

PRESENT SUBJUNCTIVE

io	**veda**
tu	**veda**
lui/lei/Lei	**veda**
noi	**vediamo**
voi	**vediate**
loro	**vedano**

PERFECT

io	**ho visto**
tu	**hai visto**
lui/lei/Lei	**ha visto**
noi	**abbiamo visto**
voi	**avete visto**
loro	**hanno visto**

IMPERFECT

io	**vedevo**
tu	**vedevi**
lui/lei/Lei	**vedeva**
noi	**vedevamo**
voi	**vedevate**
loro	**vedevano**

GERUND
vedendo

PAST PARTICIPLE
visto

EXAMPLE PHRASES

Non ci **vedo** senza occhiali. I can't see without my glasses.

Ci **vediamo** domani! See you tomorrow!

Non **vedevo** l'ora di conoscerla. I couldn't wait to meet her.

Avete visto Marco? Have you seen Marco?

Non **vedendovi** arrivare, ce ne siamo andati. As we didn't see you arriving,
   we went away.

Remember that subject pronouns are not used very often in Italian.

vedere

FUTURE

io	**vedrò**
tu	**vedrai**
lui/lei/Lei	**vedrà**
noi	**vedremo**
voi	**vedrete**
loro	**vedranno**

CONDITIONAL

io	**vedrei**
tu	**vedresti**
lui/lei/Lei	**vedrebbe**
noi	**vedremmo**
voi	**vedreste**
loro	**vedrebbero**

PAST HISTORIC

io	**vidi**
tu	**vedesti**
lui/lei/Lei	**vide**
noi	**vedemmo**
voi	**vedeste**
loro	**videro**

PLUPERFECT

io	**avevo visto**
tu	**avevi visto**
lui/lei/Lei	**aveva visto**
noi	**avevamo visto**
voi	**avevate visto**
loro	**avevano visto**

IMPERATIVE

vedi
vediamo
vedete

EXAMPLE PHRASES

Stasera **vedremo** un film in TV. We're going to watch a film on TV this evening.

Finalmente **vedemmo** una nave all'orizzonte. At last we saw a ship on the horizon.

Non **avevo** mai **visto** una cosa simile. I'd never seen such a thing.

Vediamo un po' il tuo tema. Let's have a look at your essay.

Italic letters in Italian words show where stress does not follow the usual rules.

venire (to come)

PRESENT

io	**vengo**
tu	**vieni**
lui/lei/Lei	**viene**
noi	**veniamo**
voi	**venite**
loro	**vengono**

PRESENT SUBJUNCTIVE

io	**venga**
tu	**venga**
lui/lei/Lei	**venga**
noi	**veniamo**
voi	**veniate**
loro	**vengano**

PERFECT

io	**sono venuto/a**
tu	**sei venuto/a**
lui/lei/Lei	**è venuto/a**
noi	**siamo venuti/e**
voi	**siete venuti/e**
loro	**sono venuti/e**

IMPERFECT

io	**venivo**
tu	**venivi**
lui/lei/Lei	**veniva**
noi	**venivamo**
voi	**venivate**
loro	**venivano**

GERUND

venendo

PAST PARTICIPLE

venuto

EXAMPLE PHRASES

Da dove **vieni**? Where do you come from?

Quanto **viene**? How much is it?

È venuto in macchina. He came by car.

Era depressa e le **veniva** sempre da piangere. She was depressed and always felt like crying.

La casa sta **venendo** bene. The house is taking shape.

Remember that subject pronouns are not used very often in Italian.

venire

FUTURE

io	**verrò**
tu	**verrai**
lui/lei/Lei	**verrà**
noi	**verremo**
voi	**verrete**
loro	**verranno**

CONDITIONAL

io	**verrei**
tu	**verresti**
lui/lei/Lei	**verrebbe**
noi	**verremmo**
voi	**verreste**
loro	**verrebbero**

PAST HISTORIC

io	**venni**
tu	**venisti**
lui/lei/Lei	**venne**
noi	**venimmo**
voi	**veniste**
loro	**vennero**

PLUPERFECT

io	**ero venuto/a**
tu	**eri venuto/a**
lui/lei/Lei	**era venuto/a**
noi	**eravamo venuti/e**
voi	**eravate venuti/e**
loro	**erano venuti/e**

IMPERATIVE

vieni
veniamo
venite

EXAMPLE PHRASES

A forza di bere gli **verrà** il mal di testa. He'll get a headache if he drinks like that.

Verresti a cena da me domani? Would you come to dinner tomorrow?

Mi **venne** un'idea. I had an idea.

Erano venuti per parlare con te, ma non c'eri. They'd come to talk to you, but you weren't there.

Vieni a trovarci. Come and see us!

Italic letters in Italian words show where stress does not follow the usual rules.

vincere (to defeat)

PRESENT

io	**vinco**
tu	**vinci**
lui/lei/Lei	**vince**
noi	**vinciamo**
voi	**vincete**
loro	**vincono**

PRESENT SUBJUNCTIVE

io	**vinca**
tu	**vinca**
lui/lei/Lei	**vinca**
noi	**vinciamo**
voi	**vinciate**
loro	**vincano**

PERFECT

io	**ho vinto**
tu	**hai vinto**
lui/lei/Lei	**ha vinto**
noi	**abbiamo vinto**
voi	**avete vinto**
loro	**hanno vinto**

IMPERFECT

io	**vincevo**
tu	**vincevi**
lui/lei/Lei	**vinceva**
noi	**vincevamo**
voi	**vincevate**
loro	**vincevano**

GERUND

vincendo

PAST PARTICIPLE

vinto

EXAMPLE PHRASES

Quando giochiamo **vince** sempre lui. When we play he always wins.

Che **vinca** il migliore! May the best man win!

Ieri **abbiamo vinto** la partita. We won the match yesterday.

Vincendo l'incontro, si sono aggiudicati il campionato. By winning the match they won the championship.

vincere

FUTURE

io	**vincerò**
tu	**vincerai**
lui/lei/Lei	**vincerà**
noi	**vinceremo**
voi	**vincerete**
loro	**vinceranno**

CONDITIONAL

io	**vincerei**
tu	**vinceresti**
lui/lei/Lei	**vincerebbe**
noi	**vinceremmo**
voi	**vincereste**
loro	**vincerebbero**

PAST HISTORIC

io	**vinsi**
tu	**vincesti**
lui/lei/Lei	**vinse**
noi	**vincemmo**
voi	**vinceste**
loro	**vinsero**

PLUPERFECT

io	**avevo vinto**
tu	**avevi vinto**
lui/lei/Lei	**aveva vinto**
noi	**avevamo vinto**
voi	**avevate vinto**
loro	**avevano vinto**

IMPERATIVE

vinci
vinciamo
vincete

EXAMPLE PHRASES

Stavolta **vincerò** io. I'm going to win this time.

Non **vincerebbero** mai senza di lui in squadra. They'd never win without him in the team.

Vinsero la lotteria e cambiarono vita. They won the lottery and changed their lives.

Italic letters in Italian words show where stress does not follow the usual rules.

vivere (to live)

PRESENT

io	**vivo**
tu	**vivi**
lui/lei/Lei	**vive**
noi	**viviamo**
voi	**vivete**
loro	**vivono**

PRESENT SUBJUNCTIVE

io	**viva**
tu	**viva**
lui/lei/Lei	**viva**
noi	**viviamo**
voi	**viviate**
loro	**vivano**

PERFECT

io	**ho vissuto**
tu	**hai vissuto**
lui/lei/Lei	**ha vissuto**
noi	**abbiamo vissuto**
voi	**avete vissuto**
loro	**hanno vissuto**

IMPERFECT

io	**vivevo**
tu	**vivevi**
lui/lei/Lei	**viveva**
noi	**vivevamo**
voi	**vivevate**
loro	**vivevano**

GERUND
vivendo

PAST PARTICIPLE
vissuto

EXAMPLE PHRASES

Vivevano in una piccola casa di periferia. They lived in a small house in the suburbs.

Vivendo in città si respira molto smog. If you live in a city you breathe a lot of smog.

vivere

FUTURE

io	**vivrò**
tu	**vivrai**
lui/lei/Lei	**vivrà**
noi	**vivremo**
voi	**vivrete**
loro	**vivranno**

CONDITIONAL

io	**vivrei**
tu	**vivresti**
lui/lei/Lei	**vivrebbe**
noi	**vivremmo**
voi	**vivreste**
loro	**vivrebbero**

PAST HISTORIC

io	**vissi**
tu	**vivesti**
lui/lei/Lei	**visse**
noi	**vivemmo**
voi	**viveste**
loro	**vissero**

PLUPERFECT

io	**avevo vissuto**
tu	**avevi vissuto**
lui/lei/Lei	**aveva vissuto**
noi	**avevamo vissuto**
voi	**avevate vissuto**
loro	**avevano vissuto**

IMPERATIVE

vivi
viviamo
vivete

EXAMPLE PHRASES

Non **vivrei** mai in un Paese caldo. I'd never live in a hot country.
Vivemmo un'esperienza indimenticabile. We had an unforgettable experience.
Non **avevo** mai **vissuto** prima in un condominio. I'd never lived in
   a condominium before.
Vivi la tua vita giorno per giorno. Live your life day by day.

Italic letters in Italian words show where stress does not follow the usual rules.

volere (to want)

PRESENT

io	**voglio**
tu	**vuoi**
lui/lei/Lei	**vuole**
noi	**vogliamo**
voi	**volete**
loro	**vogliono**

PRESENT SUBJUNCTIVE

io	**voglia**
tu	**voglia**
lui/lei/Lei	**voglia**
noi	**vogliamo**
voi	**vogliate**
loro	**vogliano**

PERFECT

io	**ho voluto**
tu	**hai voluto**
lui/lei/Lei	**ha voluto**
noi	**abbiamo voluto**
voi	**avete voluto**
loro	**hanno voluto**

IMPERFECT

io	**volevo**
tu	**volevi**
lui/lei/Lei	**voleva**
noi	**volevamo**
voi	**volevate**
loro	**volevano**

GERUND
volendo

PAST PARTICIPLE
voluto

EXAMPLE PHRASES

Voglio comprare una macchina nuova. I want to buy a new car.

Devo pagare subito o posso pagare domani? – Come **vuole**. Do I have to pay now or can I pay tomorrow? – As you prefer.

La campanella **voleva** dire che la lezione era finita. The bell meant the lesson was finished.

Anche **volendo** non posso invitarti: la festa è sua. I'd like to, but I can't invite you: it's his party.

volere

FUTURE

io	**vorrò**
tu	**vorrai**
lui/lei/Lei	**vorrà**
noi	**vorremo**
voi	**vorrete**
loro	**vorranno**

CONDITIONAL

io	**vorrei**
tu	**vorresti**
lui/lei/Lei	**vorrebbe**
noi	**vorremmo**
voi	**vorreste**
loro	**vorrebbero**

PAST HISTORIC

io	**volli**
tu	**volesti**
lui/lei/Lei	**volle**
noi	**volemmo**
voi	**voleste**
loro	**vollero**

PLUPERFECT

io	**avevo voluto**
tu	**avevi voluto**
lui/lei/Lei	**aveva voluto**
noi	**avevamo voluto**
voi	**avevate voluto**
loro	**avevano voluto**

IMPERATIVE

–

EXAMPLE PHRASES

Quanto ci **vorrà** prima che finiate? How long will it take you to finish?

Per fare il dolce ci **vorrà** molto burro. To make this dessert you'll need a lot of butter.

Mi chiedo che cosa **vorrà** dire tutto ciò. I wonder what it all will mean.

Che cosa **vorresti** che faccia? What would you like me to do?

Volle pagare lui a tutti i costi. He wanted to pay at all costs.

Il figlio **aveva voluto** la macchina come regalo di laurea. Their son had wanted a car as a graduation present.

Italic letters in Italian words show where stress does not follow the usual rules.

How to use the Verb Index

The verbs in bold are the model verbs which you will find in the verb tables. All the other verbs follow one of these patterns, so the number next to each verb indicates which pattern fits this particular verb. For example, **divertire** (to amuse) follows the same pattern as **dire** (to say), which is number 66 in the verb tables.

All the verbs are in alphabetical order. Superior numbers (^{1}, ^{2} etc) refer you to notes on page 247. These notes explain any differences between the verbs and their model.

With the exception of reflexive verbs which *always* take **essere**, all verbs have the same auxiliary (**essere** or **avere**) as their model verbs. There are a few exceptions which are indicated by superior numbers ^{1} to ^{4}. An asterisk (*) means that the verb takes **avere** when it is used with a direct object, and **essere** when it isn't.

*For more information on verbs that take either **avere** or **essere**, see pages 43–47.*

Notes

[1] Auxiliary = **avere**.
[2] Auxiliary = *essere*.
[3] Auxiliary = either *essere* or **avere**.
[4] Past participle of this verb is rare.